Introduction to Structural Equation Modelling using SPSS and AMOS

Introduction to Structural Equation Modelling using SPSS and AMOS

Niels J. Blunch

Los Angeles • London • New Delhi • Singapore

First published 2008

Reprinted 2008

SAGE Publications Ltd
1 Oliver's Yard
55 City Road
London EC1Y 1SP

SAGE Publications Inc.
2455 Teller Road
Thousand Oaks, California 91320

SAGE Publications India Pvt Ltd
B 1/I 1 Mohan Cooperative Industrial Area
Mathura Road, New Delhi 110 044
India

SAGE Publications Asia-Pacific Pte Ltd
33 Pekin Street #02-01
Far East Square
Singapore 048763

Library of Congress Control Number: 2007935947

British Library Cataloguing in Publication data

A catalogue record for this book is available from
the British Library

ISBN 978-1-4129-4556-1
ISBN 978-1-4129-4557-8 (pbk)

Typeset by CEPHA Imaging Pvt. Ltd., Bangalore, India
Printed in Great Britain by The Cromwell Press Ltd, Trowbridge, Wiltshire
Printed on paper from sustainable resources

Contents

Preface

This book contains what I consider to be the essentials for a non-mathematical introductory course in structural equation modelling (SEM) for the social and behavioral sciences.

It builds on material that I have used during the years in a compulsory course in behavioral science methods for first year graduate students at Aarhus School of Business (Denmark).

The book should be well suited for introductory courses in SEM for last year undergraduate or first year graduate students who have had an introductory course in statistics up to and including multiple regression. The book contains an appendix on statistical prerequisites that could be used as a refresher. The appendix could be read as an introduction to the text or consulted when necessary during reading.

The examples in the book are real life examples taken from a wide range of disciplines—including psychology, political science, marketing and health—and the same goes for the exercises downloadable from the books homepage: they build on real data. The companion web page for this title, along with exercises, is available at: www.sagepub.co.uk/blunch.

A book on SEM could either illustrate the programming aspects by showing examples of how models are programmed in the various computer programs available (e.g. LISREL, EQS, AMOS, Mplus, Mx Graph)—or one could concentrate on one and only one computer program and use it all through the book.

I have chosen the last-mentioned method using SPSS and AMOS as the workhorses: SPSS is a statistics program used at most universities and it should be well-known to many students in the social and behavioral sciences. AMOS is now sold as an add-on to SPSS and it is very easy to use as it was originally developed with a view to its use in the classroom.

The book is divided into two sections, of which the first (containing three chapters) lays the basis for structural equation modelling. Among the subjects covered here are scale construction and the concepts of reliability and validity along the lines of classical test theory (Chapter 2) and component analysis and exploratory factor analysis (Chapter 3).

Then, in the second part AMOS is introduced and the reader is taken through five chapters, from the simplest SEM model, consisting of only manifest variables to more complicated ones involving latent variables, models that build on several samples from different populations and problems like incomplete and in other ways problematic data.

I would like to thank my two reviewers professor Dale R. Fuqua of Oklahoma State University (US) and research associate Elizabeth Ackerly of Lancaster University (UK) for helpful comments and suggestions. The same thanks go to professor Joachim Scholderer from Aarhus School of Business (Denmark), who has done careful reading of the first three chapters at an early stage of the project, and professor Carsten Stig Poulsen from Aalborg University (Denmark) who, despite a busy life, found time to work his way through the complete manuscript in its (nearly) final form.

I would also like to thank the many persons who have allowed me to use their data for examples and exercises—without them it would have been impossible to write the book. They are too many to mention here, but credits are given where the data are introduced.

Last—but not least—my thanks go to my wife Anne-Marie for her loving support during the long writing process.

Niels J. Blunch
02.11.07

Section I

Exploring your Data

1

Introduction

As is the case with all scientific analysis, the techniques for analyzing causal structures based on non-experimental data presented in this book are based on models of the phenomena being studied. Therefore this first chapter begins with an intuitive introduction to *structural equation models* (SEM) by showing a few examples of such models.

Then I discuss two problems differentiating the social and behavioral sciences from the natural sciences. The first problem is that the ideal way of doing causal research, namely experimentation, is, more often than not, impossible to implement in the social and behavioral sciences. This being the case we face a series of problems of a practical as well as a philosophical nature. Another problem differentiating the social and behavioral sciences from the natural sciences is the vague nature of the concepts we are studying (intelligence, preference, social status, attitude, literacy and the like) for which no generally accepted measuring instruments exist.

You will also meet a short introduction to the matrices found in the output from AMOS (Analysis of Moment Structures)—the computer program used in this book.

I will not go deeply into the mathematical and statistical calculations, which are the basis for SEM-estimation, but a brief intuitive explanation of the principles is presented. A short outline of the history of SEM follows and an overview of the rest of the book ends the chapter.

A companion website with exercises is available at: www.sagepub.co. uk/blunch.

1. Theory and Model

This is a book about drawing conclusions based on non-experimental data about causal relationships (although, as pointed out below, the word 'causal' must be used with care in SEM) between non-measurable concepts—and about using

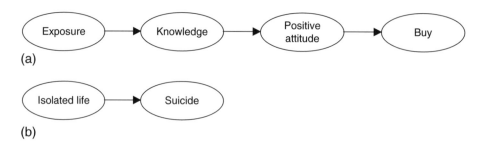

(a)

(b)

Figure 1.1   The hierarchy-of-effects model (a) and Durkheim's suicide model (b)

the computer program AMOS (Analysis of Moment Structures) to facilitate the analysis.

The first step is to form a graphical depiction—*a model*—showing how the various concepts fit together. An example of such a model is the well-known hierarchy-of-effects model depicting the various stages through which a receiver of an advertising message is supposed to move from awareness to (hopefully!) the final purchase (e.g. Lavidge and Steiner, 1961). See Figure 1.1a.

Another example is the pioneering French sociologist and philosopher Emile Durkheim's theory that living an isolated life increases the probability of suicide (Durkheim, 1897). This theory can be depicted as in Figure 1.1b.

We see that a scientific theory may be depicted in a graphical model in which the hypothesized causal connections among the concepts of the theory are shown as arrows.

In order to verify such a model (or theory) two conditions must be met:

1. We must make clear what we mean with the various concepts making up the model: The concepts must be defined *conceptually*.
2. We must construct instruments to measure the concepts: The concepts must be defined *operationally*.

Example 1

Taking Durkheim's theory as a point of departure, the concepts 'isolated life' and 'suicide' must be defined conceptually and operationally. Now, the definition of 'isolated life' seems to be the more problematic of the two. What is an 'isolated life'? Are there several forms of isolation? This latter question should probably be answered in the affirmative: You can be physically isolated because you spend a large part of your time alone or you can be psychologically isolated even if you are together with several people—just as you are not necessarily psychologically alone if you are only surrounded by few or no people.

You can also look at the various situations in which you are 'isolated' and e.g. distinguish between work and leisure.

In this way we can tentatively split our concept 'isolated life' into four dimensions, as shown in Table 1.1.

Table 1.1 Four dimensions of the concept 'isolated life'

	Physical isolation	*Psychological isolation*
At leisure	1	2
At work	3	4

Other/more dimensions could of course be mentioned—depending on the problem at hand—but these will do as an illustration.

Now, the question is: Are all four dimensions relevant for the present problem or only some of them? The relevant dimensions are now included in the model as shown in Figure 1.2a, and the next step is to define conceptually the four dimensions now making up the independent variables.

A characteristic of the four independent variables in the model in Figure 1.2a is that they are not directly measurable by a generally accepted measuring instrument, a characteristic they share with many of the concepts from the social and behavioral sciences: satisfaction; preference; intelligence; life style; social class and literacy; just to mention a few. Such non-measurable variables are called *latent variables*.

As latent variables cannot be measured directly, they are measured by *indicators*, usually questions in a questionnaire or some sort of test—these are the so-called *manifest variables*. If we add such indicators the model becomes 1.2b.

In accordance with general tradition, latent variables are depicted as circles or ellipses and manifest variables as squares or rectangles.

The model includes ten additional latent variables.

The nine ε-variables indicate that factors other than the latent variable affect the result of a measurement—ε (*error*) is the combined effect of all such 'disturbing' effects. In other words: ε is the measurement error of the indicator in question. The δ (*disturbance*) is the combined effect of all factors having an effect on the dependent variable, but not being explicitly included in the model.

As can be seen the model contains the hypothesized causal effects of the four 'isolation-variables' on suicide as well as the connections between the latent (non-measurable) variables and their manifest (measurable) indicators.

The model thus consists of two parts:

1. The *structural model* describing the causal connections among the latent variables. Mapping of these connections is the main purpose of the analysis.
2. The *measurement model* describing the connections between the latent variables and their manifest indicators. When—as is the case with suicide—a variable has only one indicator, the variance of the error is often taken to be 0.00, meaning that the measurement is without error—and the latent variable is in reality manifest.

While the arrows connecting the latent variables depict (possible) causal effects, the arrows connecting a latent variable with its manifest variables should be interpreted as follows.

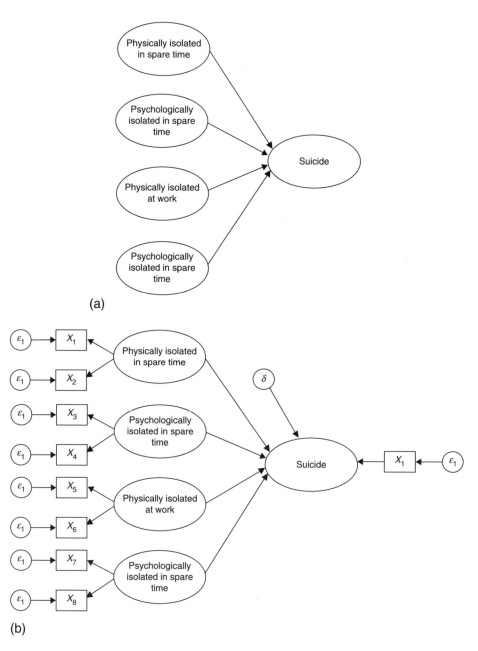

Figure 1.2 (a) The four dimensions of the concept 'isolated life,' (b) The final model with latent and manifest variables

If a latent variable were measurable on a continuous scale—which of course is not the case as a latent variable is not measurable on *any* scale—variations in a person's (or whatever the analytical unit may be) position on this scale would be mirrored in variations in its manifest variables. This is the reason why the arrows point *from* the latent variable *towards* its manifest indicators and not the other way round.

To sum up: A theory is a number of hypothesized connections among conceptually defined variables. These variables are usually latent, i.e. they are not directly measurable and must be operationalized in a series of manifest variables.

These manifest variables and their interrelations are all we have at our disposal to uncover the causal structure among the latent variables.

Let us have a look at an empirical example before we go deeper into the many problems of using structural equation modelling for causal analysis.

Example 2

106 salesmen in a large company were interviewed in order to map the factors influencing their performance (Bagozzi, 1976; Aaker and Bagozzi, 1979). One of the models used is shown in Figure 1.3.

The figures can be interpreted as standardized regression coefficients—so-called *Beta Coefficients* (see Appendix A), and the coefficients of the δ and ε terms are fixed at '1' in accordance with traditional regression analysis (see Appendix A).

The model has four latent variables: job tension; self-esteem; satisfaction and sales. \$-sales for each individual salesman were taken from company records, which were considered error-free. Therefore the variance of ε_5 was not freely estimated, but set at 0.00, and the '1' on the arrow from F_3 (Factor 3) to ε_5 equalize the two variables—so in reality F_3 is not a latent variable. This has the effect that δ_3 and ε_5 are confounded. Most often ε is assumed to be negligible and the variable is considered measured without error. In this case such an assumption seems reasonable. As you may have guessed, it takes at least two indicators to separate δ_3 and ε_5, and if the assumption of negligible measurement error is not plausible, the problem must be solved in other ways (to which I will return in Chapter 7).

The (other) latent variables were measured by *summated scales* in a questionnaire. A summated scale is constructed by adding scores obtained by answering a series of questions. One of the most popular is the Likert scale: The respondents are asked to indicate their agreement with each of a series of statements by checking a scale from e.g. 1 (strongly disagree) to 5 (strongly agree) and the scores are then added to make up the scale—the scale values being in opposite direction for statements that are favorably worded versus unfavorably worded in regard to the concept being measured. Construction of summated scales is discussed in the next chapter.

In this case the following scales were used:

TEN 1: Eight 5-point scales indicating how frequently the salesman feels bothered with limits of authority, opportunities for advancement, supervisor

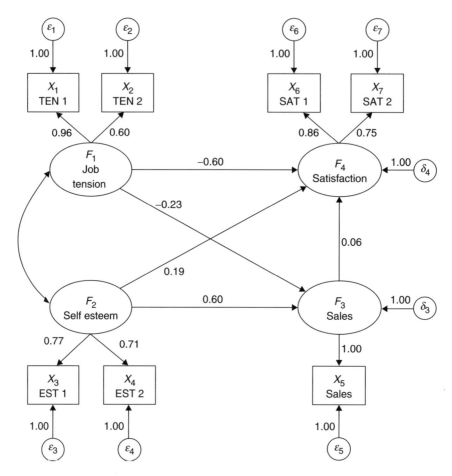

Figure 1.3 Example 2: Bagozzi's model (The figures can be interpreted as standardized regression coefficients—so-called *beta coefficients* (see Appendix A)

demands and decisions, how the amount of work interferes with its quality, and how work interferes with family life.

TEN 2: Seven 5-point scales indicating how frequently the salesperson feels bothered with the scope and responsibilities of the job, work load, the qualifications required for the job, difficulty of obtaining information necessary to perform the job, relations with co-workers, and decisions conflicting with one's values.

EST 1: Two 9-point and one 5-point scales measuring each salesperson's attributions (relative to other salespeople in the company) of the quantity of sales they achieve, the potential for achieving the top 10% sales in their company, and the quality of their performance with regard to planning and management of time and expenses.

EST 2: Three 9-point scales measuring each salesperson's ability to reach quota, feeling as to the quality of customer relations, and self-regard as to knowledge of own products and company, competitors' products and customers' need.

SAT 1: Four 6-point scales measuring degree of satisfaction with promotion, pay, and the overall work situation.

SAT 2: Four 6-point scales measuring satisfaction with opportunity to demonstrate ability and initiative, job security, belief that work is challenging and gives one a sense of accomplishment, and felt degree of control over aspects of job.

The two-headed arrow connecting F_1 and F_2 indicates that the possibility of a *correlation* (see Appendix A) between these two variables as a consequence of factors not included in the model is left open.

The model can also be depicted as a system of equations:

$$F_3 = -0.23F_1 + 0.60F_2 + \delta_3$$
$$F_4 = -0.60F_1 + 0.19F_2 + 0.06F_3 + \delta_4$$
$$X_1 = 0.96F_1 + \varepsilon_1$$
$$X_2 = 0.60F_1 + \varepsilon_2$$
$$X_3 = 0.77F_2 + \varepsilon_3 \quad (1)$$
$$X_4 = 0.71F_2 + \varepsilon_4$$
$$X_5 = F_3$$
$$X_6 = 0.86F_4 + \varepsilon_6$$
$$X_7 = 0.75F_4 + \varepsilon_7$$

The first two equations describe the structural model and the last seven the measurement models.

We see that a hypothesized causal structure can be depicted in two ways:

1. As a graph with variables shown as circles (or ellipses) and squares (or rectangles), (possible) causal links shown as arrows and covariances not explained by the model shown as two-headed arrows.
2. As a system of equations.

Both ways of depicting causal models have their advantages. The graph has great communicative force, and the equations make it possible to use traditional algebraic manipulations. Usually during a causal study you sketch one or more models, and then translate the drawings into equations, which are used as input to calculations. Newer computer programs (such as AMOS) also make it possible to draw a graph of the model, which the program then translates into command statements and carries out the calculations necessary to estimate the parameters.

After the model has been estimated it is tested in various ways and if necessary revised in order to improve its fit and at the same time obtain parsimony. In this example it is tempting to remove the arrow from F_3 to F_4. A coefficient of 0.06 is hardly of any practical importance.

The Basic Problems

From the examples it should be clear that drawing causal conclusions from non-experimental data—a situation in which behavioral and social scientists often find themselves—calls for different statistical techniques than used in sciences where the possibilities for making experiments with well-defined variables are greater.

The problems facing the researcher stem from two conditions:

1. Basing causal conclusions on non-experimental data usually necessitates statistical models comprising several equations, as opposed to traditional regression analysis and analysis of variance, which serve us so well in the simpler situations we meet when we analyze experimental data. Besides, the statistical assumptions underlying the models used are more difficult to fulfill in non-experimental research and, last but not least, the concept of causality must be used with greater care in non-experimental research.
2. The variables with which the social researcher works are usually more diffuse than concepts such as weight, length and the like, for which well-defined and generally accepted measuring methods exist. Rather the social scientist works with concepts such as attitudes, literacy, alienation, social status, etc. Concepts, which are not directly measurable and therefore must be measured indirectly via indicators—be they questions in a questionnaire or some sort of test.

We will now look at these two complications in turn.

2.   The Problem of Non-Experimental Data

As is well known, you are not able to observe causation—considered as a 'force' from cause to effect. What you *can* observe is:

1. *Co-variation*—the fact that two factors *A* and *B* co-vary is an indication for the possible existence of a causal relationship—in one direction or the other.
2. *The time sequence*—the fact that occurrence of *A* is generally followed by the occurrence of *B* is an indication for *A* being a cause of *B* (and not the other way round).

However—and this is the crucial requirement—

3. These observations must be made under conditions that rule out all other explanations of the observations than that of the hypothesized causation.

These three points could be used as building blocks in an operational definition of the concept of causation—even if this concept 'in the real world' is somewhat dim, and perhaps meaningless, except as a common experience facilitating communication between people (Hume, 1739).

It is clear from the above that you can never *prove* a causal relationship; you can only render it probable. It is not possible to rule out all other explanations, but you can try to rule out the ones deemed most 'probable' to the extent that makes the claimed explanation '*A* is the cause of *B*' the most plausible claim.

The extent to which this can be done depends on the nature of the data on which the conclusions are drawn.

The Data

The necessary data can be obtained in one of two different ways:

1. Data can be 'historical' in the sense that they mirror 'the real world,' e.g. the actual consequences a firm's price policy has had on sales.
2. Data can be experimental: You can make your own 'world' in which you can manipulate the variables, the effects of which you want to investigate.

'Historical' data are often called *observational* data in order to point out that, while in an experiment you deliberately manipulate the independent variables, you do not interfere more with the variables in non-experimental research than necessary in order to observe, i.e. measure them.

The Necessity of a Closed System

To rule out all possible explanations except one is of course impossible, and as we can examine only a subset of (possible) explanations it is obvious that causal relationships can only be mapped in isolated systems. Clearly, experimental data are to be preferred to non-experimental data, because in an experiment we create our own world in accordance with an experimental plan designed to reduce outside influences.

It is much more difficult to cut off disturbing effects in a non-experimental study: In an experiment we create our own little world but, when we base our study on the real world, we must accept the world as it is. We deal with historical data and cannot change the past.

While it seems obvious that causality can only be established—or according to Hume (op. cit.) only be meaningful—in a scientific model, which constitutes a closed system, it is a little more complicated to define 'closed.'

In Figure 1.4—inspired by Bass (1969)—some of the factors determining cigarette sales are depicted. There are an enormous number of possible factors influencing cigarette sales—many more than shown in the figure. It would not be very difficult to expand the model to cover several pages of this book. In causal research it is necessary to keep down the number of variables—in this example e.g. (as Bass did) to the variables placed on a gray background.

As any limit on the number of variables must necessarily cut causal relations, we cannot demand that the system must not have any relation to the surrounding world. What we must require is that all effects on a variable in the model from

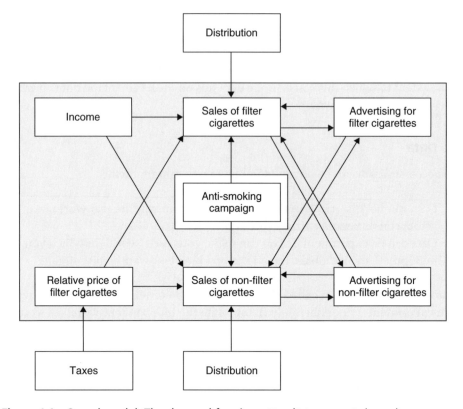

Figure 1.4   Causal model: The demand for cigarettes (δ-terms not shown)

outside the model can be summarized in one variable which is of purely random (i.e. non-systematic) nature, and with a variance small enough not to 'drown' effects from variables in the model in 'noise.' If we use the Greek letter δ (disturbance) to designate the combined effects of excluded independent variables (noise), we write:

$$Y = f(X_1, X_2, X_3, \ldots X_j \ldots, X_p) + \delta \tag{2a}$$

where Y is a dependent variable in the model, and X_j ($j = 1, 2, \ldots, p$) are variables included in the model and supposed to influence Y. If the model is really 'closed,' X_j and δ must be stochastically independent. This is the same as demanding that for one and every value of X_j the expected value of δ is the same and consequently the same as the unconditional expected value of δ. This can be written as

$$E(\delta \mid X_j) = E(\delta) = 0 \text{ for all values of } j \tag{2b}$$

(for a definition of *expected value*, see Appendix A).

   If condition (2b) is not met, a *ceteris paribus* interpretation of the parameters indicating the influence of the various independent variables is not possible, because the effects of variables included in the model are then mixed up with variables *not* included in the model.

Simon (1953; 1954) has given Hume's operational definition of causality a modern formulation.

Example 3

As is well known (Appendix A), least squares estimation in traditional regression analysis forces δ to be independent of the exogeneous variables $X_1, \ldots X_j, \ldots X_p$ *in the model*—and so do the estimation methods used in AMOS. But the point is that this condition must hold in the population and not just in our model. So be careful in specifying your model.

Consider the following model:

$$\text{score obtained at exam} = f \text{ (number of classes attended)} + \delta$$

Think about what variables are contained in δ: intelligence, motivation, age and earlier education—to name a few. Do you think that it is likely that 'number of classes attended' does not depend on any of these factors?

Three Different Causal Models

Figure 1.5 shows three causal models from marketing, depicting three fundamentally different causal structures.

Dominick (1952) reports an in-store experiment concerning the effect on sales of four different packages for McIntosh apples. The experiment ran through four days in four retail stores. The causal model is shown in 1.5a. In order to reduce the noise δ, the most influencing factors affecting sales (apart from the package) were included in the experiment, namely the effects on sales caused by differences among the shops in which the experiment was conducted, the effects caused by variations in sales over time and the varying number of customers in the shops during the testing period.

Aaker and Day (1971) tried to decide which of the two models in 1.5b best describe the buying behavior in regard to coffee. The question is whether buying coffee is considered a *high involvement activity* (in which an attitude towards a brand is founded on assimilated information prior to the actual buying decision), or the buying of coffee is a *low involvement activity* (where the attitude towards the brand is based on the actual use of the product). The non-experimental data came partly from a store panel (market shares and prices), partly from telephone interviews (awareness and attitude). The models in the figure are somewhat simplified compared to Aaker's original models, which additionally included a time-dimension showing how the various independent variables extend their effects over subsequent periods of time.

Bass (1969) analyzed the determinants of cigarette sales using the model in 1.5c based on time series data.

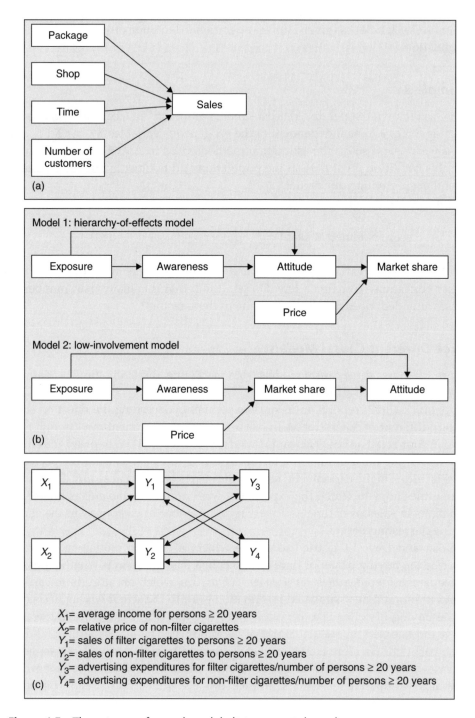

Figure 1.5   Three types of causal models (δ-terms not shown)

The three examples illustrate three types of causal models of increasing complexity.

The model in 1.5a has only one box with in-going arrows. Such models are typical for studies based on experimental data, and the analysis is uncomplicated, since:

1. There is no doubt about the orientation of the arrows—they depart from the variables being manipulated and from variables incorporated in the model in order to reduce the amount of noise.
2. The model can be expressed in only one equation.
3. The parameters in this equation can (subject to the usual assumptions) be estimated with regression analysis or analysis of variance (or in this case analysis of covariance)—simple statistical techniques, which can be found in any introductory statistics text.

In Figure 1.5b and c there are several boxes with both in-going and out-going arrows, so the model translates into more than one equation, because every box with an in-going arrow is a dependent variable, and for every dependent variable there is an equation. For example, the hierarchy-of-effects model can be expressed in the following equations:

$$Awareness = f_1(Exposure) + \delta_1$$
$$Attitude = f_2(Exposure, Awareness) + \delta_2$$
$$Market\ share = f_3(Attitude, Price) + \delta_3$$

Such a system of several equations, where some of the variables appear both as dependent and as independent variables is typical for causal models based on non-experimental data. This complicates the analysis, because it is not obvious *a priori* that the various equations are independent with regard to estimation—and can we then estimate the equations one-by-one using traditional regression analysis?

While the graphs in 1.5b are *acyclic*, i.e. it is not possible to pass through the same box twice by following the arrows, the graph in 1.5c is *cyclic*: You can walk your way through the graph following the arrows and pass through the same box several times. In a way you could say that such a variable has an effect on itself!— a problem that I return to in Chapter 5. In the example the cyclic nature comes from reciprocal effects between advertising and sales: Not only does advertising influence sales (which is the purpose), but sales could also influence advertising through budgeting routines.

We therefore have *two* (possible) causal relationships between advertising and sales, and the problem is to separate them analytically—to *identify* the two relationships.

This identification problem does not arise in acyclic models—at least not under certain reasonable assumptions. The causal chain is a 'one-way street,' just as in an experiment. This means that not only is the statistical analysis simpler, the same applies to the substantive interpretation and the use of the results.

Causality in Non-Experimental Research

Care must be taken in interpreting the coefficients in a regression equation when using non-experimental data.

To take a simple example from marketing research: Suppose a marketing researcher wants to find the influence of price on sales of a certain product. He decides to run an experiment in a retail store by varying the price and noting the amount sold. The data is then analyzed by regression analysis, and the result is

$$\text{sales} = a_0 + a_1(\text{price}) \qquad (3a)$$

where a_0 and a_1 are the estimated coefficients.

Suppose the same researcher also wants to estimate the influence of income on sales of the same product. Now, he cannot experiment with people's income, so he takes a representative sample from the relevant population asking the respondents (among other things), how much they have bought of the product in the last week, and also asking them about their annual income. He then runs a regression analysis, the result of which is

$$\text{sales} = b_0 + b_1(\text{income}) \qquad (3b)$$

How do we interpret the regression coefficients a_1 and b_1 in the two cases?

The immediate answer you would get by asking anyone with a knowledge of regression analysis is that a_1 shows by how many units sales would change if the price was changed one unit and b_1 by how many units sales would change if income was changed one unit.

However, this interpretation is only valid in the first case, where prices were actually changed.

In the second case, income is not actually changed, and b_1 depicts by how many units we can expect a household's purchase to change if it is *replaced* by another household with an income one unit different from the first.

Therefore the word 'causality' must be used with greater care in non-experimental research, if we cannot rule out the possibility that by replacing a household (or whatever the analytical unit may be) with another, the two units could differ on other variables than the one that has your immediate interest.

This is exactly the reason why an earlier name for SEM—'causal modelling'—has now gone out of use.

It is only fair to mention that the use of SEM is in no way restricted to non-experimental research—although this is by far the most common use of it. Readers interested in exploring the possible advantages of using SEM in experimental research are referred to Bagozzi (1977) and Bagozzi and Yi (1994).

However, in this book you will only meet SEM used on non-experimental data, and the point to remember is that SEM analysis is based on relations among the manifest variables measured as covariances, and (as you have probably heard several times before!) 'Correlation is NOT causation.' Therefore—as pointed out at the beginning of Section 2—it takes more than significant relations to 'prove' causation.

If time series data are available you can also use the time sequence to support your theory, but—and this is the crucial condition—you cannot, for pure statistical reasons, rule out the possibility that other mechanisms could have given rise to your observations.

A claimed causal connection should be based on substantiated theoretical arguments.

3.   The Problem of Non-Measurable Concepts

If we compare a SEM with a traditional regression model, such as

$$Y_i = \beta_0 + \beta_1 X_i + \delta_i \qquad (4)$$

it is obvious that the latter is based on an assumption, which is rarely mentioned but nevertheless usually unrealistic; namely that all variables are measured without error. [The assumption of no measurement error always applies to the independent variable, whereas you could assume that δ_i includes measurement error in the dependent variable as well as the effect of excluded variables.]

An assumption of error-free measurements is of course always wrong in principle, but will serve as a reasonable simplification when measuring e.g. weight, volume, temperature and other variables for which generally agreed measurement units and measuring instruments exist.

On the other hand, such an assumption is clearly unrealistic when the variables are life-style, intelligence, attitudes and the like. Any measurement will be an imperfect indicator of such a concept. Using more than one indicator per latent variable makes it possible to assess the connection between an indicator and the concept it is assumed to measure and in this way evaluate the quality of the measuring instrument.

Introducing measurement models has the effect that the estimated parameters in the structural model are cleaned from the influence from measurement errors. Or—put it another way—the errors in the structural model ('errors in equations') are separated from the errors in the measurement model ('errors in variables').

The reader will remember from Example 1 that measurement of suicide was based on only one indicator—the death certificate. When this is the case the error of the indicator is often fixed at 0.00, which means that the latent variable is assumed measured without error. In this case the assumption seems reasonable, but we cannot exclude the possibility that some suicides are masked as other deaths causes—e.g. for religious reasons.

Throughout the book I will use the notation in Figure 1.6.

As in Figure 1.3 latent variables are depicted as circles or ellipses and manifest variables as squares or rectangles. A one-headed arrow depicts a hypothesized relationship between two variables, the arrow pointing from the independent to the dependent variable, while a two-headed arrow indicates co-variance unexplained

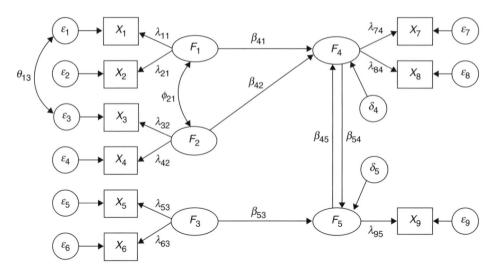

Figure 1.6   Causal model with latent variables

by other variables in the model. β denotes a coefficient in the structural model and λ a coefficient in the measurement model.

Coefficients usually have a subscript with two digits, the first indicating the head of the arrow and the second the foot. However, if no risk of misunderstanding exists only one subscript is used.

Covariances between exogenous (pre-determined) variables are denoted by ϕ and correlations between error-terms are denoted by θ. Subscripts indicate the variables involved. If the two digits of the subscript are the same, it indicates a variance. Variances are not shown in the figure.

The model in Figure 1.6 can also be stated as:

$$F_4 = \beta_{41}F_1 + \beta_{42}F_2 + \beta_{45}F_5 + \delta_4$$
$$F_5 = \beta_{53}F_3 + \beta_{54}F_4 + \delta_5$$

(5a)

$$\begin{array}{lll} X_1 = \lambda_{11}F_1 + \varepsilon_1 & X_4 = \lambda_{42}F_2 + \varepsilon_4 & X_7 = \lambda_{74}F_4 + \varepsilon_7 \\ X_2 = \lambda_{21}F_1 + \varepsilon_2 & X_5 = \lambda_{53}F_3 + \varepsilon_5 & X_8 = \lambda_{84}F_4 + \varepsilon_8 \\ X_3 = \lambda_{32}F_2 + \varepsilon_3 & X_6 = \lambda_{63}F_3 + \varepsilon_6 & X_9 = \lambda_{95}F_5 + \varepsilon_9 \end{array}$$

(5b)

Everywhere it is assumed that error terms are uncorrelated with the exogenous variables, i.e. variables that do not show themselves as dependent variables anywhere in the system of equations.

4.   The Data Matrix and Other Matrices

In the computer output from AMOS you will meet a wide variety of matrices. Therefore a few words about vectors and matrices are in order.

Table 1.2 Data matrix

Variable→ Observation↓	1	2	...	j	...	p
1	X_{11}	X_{12}	...	X_{1j}	...	X_{1p}
2	X_{21}	X_{22}	...	X_{2j}	...	X_{2p}
⋮	⋮	⋮		⋮		⋮
i	X_{i1}	X_{i2}	...	X_{ij}	...	X_{ip}
⋮	⋮	⋮		⋮		⋮
n	X_{n1}	X_{n2}	...	X_{nj}	...	X_{np}

A *matrix* is a rectangular arrangement of numbers in rows and columns. In the data matrix in Table 1.2, X_{ij} is the value of variable j on observation i. In this book the observation is most often a person, and the variable an answer to a question in a questionnaire.

The need to be able to describe manipulations not of single numbers, but of whole data matrices has resulted in the development of *matrix algebra*. Matrix algebra can be considered a form of shorthand, where every single operator (e.g. + or −) describes a series of mathematical operations performed on the elements in the matrices involved. So, matrix algebra does not make it easier to do actual calculations, but it makes it easier to describe the calculations.

In matrix notation the data matrix is:

$$\mathbf{X} = \begin{bmatrix} x_{11} & x_{12} & \cdots & x_{1j} & \cdots & x_{1p} \\ x_{21} & x_{22} & \cdots & x_{2j} & \cdots & x_{2p} \\ \vdots & \vdots & & \vdots & & \vdots \\ x_{i1} & x_{i2} & \cdots & x_{ij} & \cdots & x_{ip} \\ \vdots & \vdots & & \vdots & & \vdots \\ x_{n1} & x_{n2} & \cdots & x_{nj} & \cdots & x_{np} \end{bmatrix} \tag{6}$$

Matrices are denoted by uppercase boldface letters and ordinary numbers (called *scalars*) by lowercase italicized letters. The matrix $\mathbf{X}$ is a $n \times p$ matrix, i.e. it has n rows and p columns.

A single row in the matrix could be looked at as a $1 \times p$ matrix or a *row vector*, the elements of which indicate the coordinates of a point in a p-dimensional coordinate system in which the axes are the variables and the point indicates an observation. In this way we can map the data matrix as n points in a p-dimensional space—the *variable space*. Vectors are denoted by lowercase boldface letters:

$$\mathbf{x}_i = \begin{bmatrix} x_{i1} & x_{i2} & \cdots & x_{ij} & \cdots & x_{np} \end{bmatrix} \tag{7}$$

Alternatively, we could consider the data matrix as composed of *p column vectors*, and map the data as *p* points each representing a variable in a *n*-dimensional coordinate system—the *observation space*—the axes of which refer to each of the *n* observations:

$$\mathbf{x}_j = \begin{bmatrix} x_{j1} \\ x_{j2} \\ \vdots \\ x_{ij} \\ \vdots \\ x_{nj} \end{bmatrix} \tag{8}$$

It is often an advantage to base arguments on such geometrical interpretations.

In addition to the data matrix you will meet a few other matrices.

The *Sum of Cross Products (SCP)* for two variables X_j and X_k is defined as

$$SCP = \sum_{i=1}^{n}(X_{ij} - \overline{X}_j)(X_{ik} - \overline{X}_k) \tag{9}$$

If $j = k$ you obtain the *Sum of Squares (SS)*. The $p \times p$-matrix

$$\mathbf{C} = \begin{bmatrix} SS_{11} & SCP_{12} & \cdots & SCP_{1j} & \cdots & SCP_{1p} \\ SCP_{21} & SS_{22} & \cdots & SCP_{2j} & \cdots & SCP_{2p} \\ \vdots & \vdots & & \vdots & & \vdots \\ SCP_{i1} & SCP_{i2} & \cdots & SCP_{ij} & \cdots & SCP_{ip} \\ \vdots & \vdots & & \vdots & & \vdots \\ SCP_{p1} & SCP_{p2} & \cdots & SCP_{pj} & \cdots & SS_{pp} \end{bmatrix} \tag{10}$$

containing the SCP and—in the main diagonal (the northwest southeast diagonal)— the SS of *p* variables is usually called the sum of squares and cross products *(SSCP) matrix* .

If all elements in **C** are divided by the degrees of freedom $n-1$ (see Appendix A), we obtain the *Covariance Matrix* **S**, containing all covariances and in the main diagonal the variances of the *p* variables.

$$\mathbf{S} = \begin{bmatrix} s_{11} & s_{12} & \cdots & s_{1j} & \cdots & s_{1p} \\ s_{21} & s_{22} & \cdots & s_{2j} & \cdots & s_{2p} \\ \vdots & \vdots & & \vdots & & \vdots \\ s_{i1} & s_{i2} & \cdots & s_{ij} & \cdots & s_{ip} \\ \vdots & \vdots & & \vdots & & \vdots \\ s_{p1} & s_{p2} & \cdots & s_{pj} & \cdots & s_{pp} \end{bmatrix} \tag{11}$$

Are all variables standardized

$$X_{std} = \frac{X_{ij} - \overline{X}_j}{s_j} \tag{12}$$

—where $\overline{X}_j$ is the mean of X_j—to have average 0 and variance 1.00 before these calculations, **S** becomes the *Correlation Matrix* **R**:

$$\mathbf{R} = \begin{bmatrix} 1 & r_{12} & \cdots & r_{1j} & \cdots & r_{1p} \\ r_{21} & 1 & \cdots & r_{2j} & \cdots & r_{2p} \\ \vdots & \vdots & & \vdots & & \vdots \\ r_{i1} & r_{i2} & \cdots & r_{ij} & \cdots & r_{ip} \\ \vdots & \vdots & & \vdots & & \vdots \\ r_{p1} & r_{p2} & \cdots & r_{pj} & \cdots & 1 \end{bmatrix} \tag{13}$$

By default AMOS calculates sample covariance matrices and correlation matrices by dividing by number of observations, n, and not by *degrees of freedom*, $n - 1$ (see Appendix A).

Most often you do not need to input the raw data, but only the covariance matrix. In that case AMOS will assume that the variances and covariances in the input matrix too are calculated using n as denominator. Generally, however, it does not make a great difference which of the two is used as denominator in sample sizes sufficiently large for this kind of analysis.

5. How do We Estimate the Parameters of a SEM Model?

At first it seems impossible to estimate e.g. the regression coefficient β_{41} in Figure 1.6. After all, β_{41} connects two latent, i.e. non-measurable, variables. To give the reader an intuitive introduction to the principle on which estimation of parameters in models with latent variables is based, let us take as a point of departure the simple regression model

$$Y = \beta X + \delta \tag{14}$$

where both X and Y are measurable and we assume—without loss of generality— that both variables are measured as deviations from their average. Under this assumption we have the following *expected values* (see Appendix A) E:

$$E(Y) = E(X) = E(\delta) = 0 \tag{15}$$

and further:

$$Var(Y) = E(Y^2) \tag{16a}$$
$$Var(X) = E(X^2) \tag{16b}$$
$$Cov(YX) = E(YX) \tag{16c}$$

Now:

$$Var(Y) = Var(\beta X + \delta) = \beta^2 \sigma_X^2 + \sigma_\delta^2 \tag{17a}$$

because $E(X\delta) = 0$ following the usual assumption of regression analysis and from (16c) we get:

$$\begin{aligned} Cov(YX) = E(YX) &= E\,[(\beta X + \delta)X] \\ &= \beta E(X^2) + E(X\delta) \\ &= \beta \sigma_X^2 \end{aligned} \tag{17b}$$

We can then write the two covariance matrices:

$$\begin{bmatrix} \sigma_X^2 & \\ \sigma_{YX} & \sigma_Y^2 \end{bmatrix} = \begin{bmatrix} \sigma_X^2 & \\ \beta \sigma_X^2 & \beta^2 \sigma_X^2 + \sigma_\delta^2 \end{bmatrix} \tag{18}$$

The model (14) implies a functional connection between the theoretical covariance matrix and the parameters of the model—here β and σ_δ^2.

If the empirical values are substituted for the theoretical ones, (18) becomes

$$\begin{bmatrix} s_X^2 & \\ s_{YX} & s_Y^2 \end{bmatrix} \cong \begin{bmatrix} s_X^2 & \\ b\,s_X^2 & b^2 s_X^2 + s_\delta^2 \end{bmatrix} \tag{19}$$

The 'nearly equal' sign $\cong$ has been substituted for = because we cannot in general expect the two matrices to be exactly equal, but the better the model describes the data, the more equal the matrices will be.

Let me generalize:

If there is a one-to-one correspondence between the sample covariance matrix and the parameters of a model assumed to have generated the sample (if the model is *identified*)—which is not always the case—then the model can be estimated, its fit tested, and several measures of fit can be calculated based on the difference between the two matrices—the so-called *residual matrix*:

$$\begin{bmatrix} s_X^2 & \\ s_{YX} & s_Y^2 \end{bmatrix} - \begin{bmatrix} s_X^2 & \\ bs_X^2 & b^2 s_X^2 + s_\delta^2 \end{bmatrix} = \begin{bmatrix} 0 & \\ s_{YX} - bs_X^2 & s_Y^2 - b^2 s_X^2 + s_\delta^2 \end{bmatrix} \tag{20}$$

Therefore SEM is often called *analysis of covariance structures*.

In the regression case above, we see that minimizing the elements of the residual matrix leads to the traditional estimates of β and σ_δ^2

$$\beta \approx b = \frac{s_{YX}}{s_X^2} = \frac{SCP_{YX}}{SS_{XX}} \tag{21}$$

$$\sigma_\delta^2 \approx s_y^2 - s_{yx}^2$$

which makes all entries in the residual matrix equal to zero.

You can therefore look at least squares not as a method to minimize the sum of squares for the residuals δ but to minimize the difference between the two matrices in (19).

This is the basis on which estimation in SEM is built: Every model formulation implies a certain form of the covariance matrix of the manifest variables, and the parameters are estimated as the values that minimize the difference between the sample covariance matrix and the implied covariance matrix, i.e. the residual matrix—or to put it more precisely—a function of the residual matrix is minimized.

6. A Short History of SEM

SEM can trace its history back more than 100 years.

At the beginning of the 20th century Spearman laid the foundation for factor analysis and thereby for the measurement model in SEM (Spearman, 1904). Spearman tried to trace the different dimensions of intelligence back to a general intelligence factor. In the thirties Thurstone invented multi-factor analysis and factor rotation (more or less in opposition to Spearman), and thereby founded modern factor analysis, whereby e.g. intelligence, was thought of as being composed of several different intelligence dimensions (Thurstone and Thurstone, 1941; Thurstone, 1947).

About 20 years after Spearman, Wright started the development of the so-called *path analysis* (Wright, 1918, 1921). Based on box-and arrow-diagrams like the ones in Figure 1.5, he formulated a series of rules that connected correlations among the variables with parameters in the assumed data-generating model. Most of his work was on models with only manifest variables, but a few also included models with latent variables.

Wright was a biometrician and it is amazing that his work was more or less unknown to scientists outside this area, until taken up by social researchers in the sixties (Blalock, 1961, 1971; Duncan, 1975).

In Economics a parallel development took place in what was to be known as *econometrics*. However, this development was unaffected by Wright's ideas, and was characterized by absence of latent variables—at least in the sense of the word used in this book. However, in the fifties econometricians became aware of Wright's work, and some of them found to their surprise that he had pioneered estimation of supply and demand functions and in several respects was far ahead of econometricians of his time (Goldberger, 1972).

In the early seventies path analysis and factor analysis were combined to form the general SEM of today. Foremost in its development was Jöreskog, who created the well-known LISREL (Linear Structural Relations) program for analyzing such models (Jöreskog, 1973).

However, LISREL is not alone on the scene. Among other similar computer programs mention can be made of EQS (EQuationS) (Bentler, 1985) and RAM (Reticular Action Model) (McArdle and McDonald, 1984) included in the SYSTAT package of statistics programs under the name RAMONA (Reticular Action Model Or Near Approximation), and of course AMOS (Arbuckle, 1989).

7. —and What Then?

What does it require to perform a SEM analysis? You should know:

1. How to construct a multi-item scale (as e.g. TEN 1 in Figure 1.3).
2. How to construct measurement models, i.e. models that describe connections between a latent variable and its indicators.
3. How to construct a structural model and combine it with the measurement model.

Whether you want to introduce latent variables into a model or not, the variables must be measured. Therefore Chapter 2 will provide an introduction to classical test theory and its fundamental concepts of *reliability* and *validity*.

The use of a many-item scale is based on the assumption that all items measure the same (theoretical) construct—and nothing else: That the items make up a uni-dimensional scale. Chapter 3 will introduce techniques useful for determining the number of dimensions in a dataset. This completes the first part of the book.

The second part of the book will deal with SEM analysis using AMOS, starting with a general introduction in Chapter 4, while the following chapters will demonstrate the use of AMOS in examples covering different types of SEM.

Chapter 5 will cover models with only manifest variables. In Chapter 6 the measurement model—the confirmatory factor analysis model—is introduced, and the last three chapters deal with the complete model with latent variables. Chapter 7 deals with models based on data from one population only and Chapter 8 with models based on data from more than one population in order to compare the populations and examine the extent to which the same model can be used to describe them all.

The last chapter covers two problems: estimation in the face of incomplete data and how to overcome the analysis of non-normal data by bootstrapping.

☞ In this chapter you have met the following concepts:

theory and model	data matrix, SSCP-matrix,
manifest and latent variable	covariance matrix and
structural model and	correlation matrix
measurement model	residual matrix
cyclical and non-cyclical models	

Questions

1. Why should a researcher prefer to work with latent variables? (List all the reasons you can.)
2. Explain the concepts 'measurement model' and 'structural model.'
3. To what extent is it possible to support a hypothesis of causal connections using SEM?
4. Explain the difference between cyclic and a-cyclic models.
5. Explain the various matrices: **X, C, S** and **R**.

Reference List

Aaker, D. A. and D. A. Day (1971) 'A recursive model of communication processes,' in D. A. Aaker (ed.), *Multivariate Analysis in Marketing*, Belmont, Calif.: Wadsworth.

Aaker, D. A. and R. P. Bagozzi (1979) 'Unobservable variables in structural equation models: with an application in industrial selling,' *Journal of Marketing Research*, 16 (May): 65–77.

Arbuckle, J. L. (1989) 'AMOS: Analysis of moment structures,' *The American Statistician*, 43: 66–7.

Bagozzi, R. P. (1976) 'Towards a general theory for the explanation of the performance of salespeople.' Unpublished doctoral dissertation. Evanston, IL: Northwestern University.

Bagozzi, R. P. (1977) 'Structural equation models in experimental research,' *Journal of Marketing Research*, 14: 202–26.

Bagozzi, R. P. and Y. Yi (1994) 'Advanced topics in structural equation models,' in R. P. Bagozzi (ed), *Advanced Methods of Marketing Research*, Oxford: Blackwell.

Bass, F. M. (1969) 'A simultaneous study of advertising and sales—analysis of cigarette data,' *Journal of Marketing Research*, 6(3): 291–300.

Bentler, P. M. (1985) *Theory and Implementation of EQS, A Structural Equation Program.* Los Angeles: BMDP Statistical Software.

Blalock, H. M. (1961) *Causal Inferences in Non-experimental Research.* Chapel Hill: University of North Carolina Press.

Blalock, H. M. (1971) *Causal Models in the Social Sciences.* Chicago: Aldine-Atherton.

Dominick, B. A. (1952) *An illustration of the use of the Latin Square in Measuring the Effectiveness of Retail Merchandising practices.* Ithaca, N.Y.: Department of Agricultural Economics, Cornell University Agricultural Experiment Station, New York State College of Agriculture, Cornell University.

Duncan, O. D. (1975) *Introduction to Structural Equation Models.* New York: Academic Pres.

Durkheim, E. (1897) *Suicide.* Available is e.g. (2002). London: Routledge.

Goldberger, A. S. (1972) 'Structural equation methods in the social sciences,' *Econometrica*, 40: 979–1001.

Hume, D. (1739) *A Treatise of Human Nature: Being an Attempt to Introduce the Experimental Method of Reasoning into Moral Subjects.* Available is e.g. (2000) ed. by D. F. Norton and M. J. Norton. Oxford: Oxford University Press.

Jöreskog, K. G. (1973) 'A general method for estimating a linear structural equation system,' in A. S. Goldberger & O. D. Duncan (ed.), *Structural Equation Models in the Social Sciences*, N.Y.: Seminar Press.

Lavidge, R. C. and G. A. Steiner (1961) 'A model for predictive measurement of advertising effectiveness,' *Journal of Marketing*, 25 (Oct.): 59–62.

McArdle, J. J. and R. P. McDonald (1984) 'Some algebraic properties of the Reticular Action Model for moment structures,' *British Journal of Mathematical and Statistical Psychology*, 37: 234–51.

Simon, H. A. (1953) 'Causal ordering and identifiability,' in W. C. Hood and T. C. Koopmans (eds), *Studies in Econometric Method*, N.Y.: Wiley & Sons; London: Chapman & Hall.

Sinon, H. A. (1954) 'Spurious correlation: a causal interpretation,' *Journal of the American Statistical Association*, 49 (September): 467–79.

Spearman, C. (1904) 'General intelligence, objectively determined and measured,' *American Journal of Psychology*, 15: 201–93.

Thurstone, L. L. (1947) *Multiple Factor Analysis*. Chicago, IL: University of Chicago Press.

Thurstone, L. L. and T. Thurstone (1941) *Factorial Studies of Intelligence*, Chicago, IL: University of Chicago Press.

Wright, S. (1918) 'On the nature of size factors,' *Genetics*, 3: 367–74.

Wright, S. (1921) 'Correlation and causation,' *Journal of Agricultural Research*, 20: 557–85.

2

Classical Test Theory

The concepts in your model will usually be rather diffuse (attitude, skill, preference, democracy)—i.e. concepts for which no generally agreed measuring instruments exist. In such situations, therefore, you have to make your own measuring instruments—be they questions in a questionnaire or some sort of test.

The first requirement for such an instrument is that if you repeat the measurement under identical conditions, then you will end up with nearly the same result: Your instrument must be *reliable*.

Another requirement—which seems just as obvious—is that the instrument shall measure exactly what it is intended to measure and nothing else: The instrument must be *valid*.

Reliability and validity are the two main standards on which we evaluate a measuring instrument.

I will take as my starting point the classical version of the two concepts and show how the use of SEM can illustrate the weaknesses of the classical ways of measuring reliability and validity and perhaps lead to more useful ways of judging these two central concepts.

In Example 2 in the previous chapter you met examples of summated scales. You will also learn how to construct such scales and how special computer programs can be used to that end.

1. Reliability

We evaluate a measuring instrument by its reliability. The reliability of an instrument is its ability to give nearly identical results in repeated measurements under identical conditions; in other words reliability is about reproducibility.

Let me take the simple measurement model in Figure 2.1 as our point of departure.

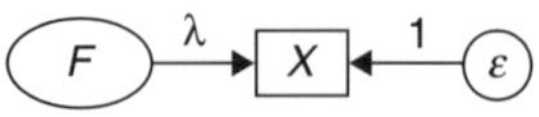

Figure 2.1   A simple measurement model

I can now write

$$X = \lambda F + \varepsilon \qquad \text{(1a)}$$

with the conditions

$$E(\varepsilon) = 0 \quad \text{and} \quad Cov(\varepsilon, F) = 0 \qquad \text{(1b)}$$

The expectation of (1a) is

$$E(X) = E(\lambda F) = \lambda E(F) \qquad \text{(2a)}$$

and the variance

$$Var(X) = Var(\lambda F) + Var(\varepsilon) = \lambda^2 Var(F) + \sigma_\varepsilon^2 \qquad \text{(2b)}$$

While you are able only to observe variation in X, it is of course the latent variable F and its variance—often referred to as the *true variance*—that is the center of our interest. I will now define the *reliability coefficient* ρ_{XX} as the proportion of measured variance that can be traced back to F:

$$\rho_{XX} = \frac{\lambda^2 VAR(F)}{\lambda^2 VAR(F) + \varepsilon} = \frac{\lambda^2 VAR(F)}{VAR(X)} = 1 - \frac{VAR(\varepsilon)}{VAR(X)} = \rho_{XF}^2 \qquad \text{(3a)}$$

It is obvious that (1) is an analog to the simple regression model, and that ρ_{XX} is the squared correlation coefficient in this model. Unlike the traditional regression model, however, the independent variable F is un-observable.

When—as in this case—a latent variable has only one indicator, λ is only a scale factor the value of which is arbitrary. Usually λ is then taken to have the value 1.00, in which case (3a) can be written:

$$\rho_{XX} = \frac{VAR(F)}{VAR(X)} = 1 - \frac{VAR(\varepsilon)}{VAR(X)} \qquad \text{(3b)}$$

Variances, Covariances and Reliability

Analysis of quantitative empirical data is basically analysis of variation and co-variation. By how much do the attributes vary among observations, and to what extent do they co-vary?

Suppose you are interested in measuring the structural correlation $\rho_{F_1 F_2}$ between the two latent variables F_1 and F_2 in Figure 2.2. However, being able to only observe

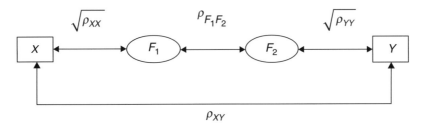

Figure 2.2 Correlation and reliability

the empirical correlation r_{XY} between the manifest variables X and Y, you will underestimate the structural co-variation.

As you can read from the figure

$$\rho_{XY} = \sqrt{\rho_{XX}}\, \rho_{F_1F_2} \sqrt{\rho_{YY}} = \rho_{F_1F_2} \sqrt{\rho_{XX}\rho_{YY}} \tag{4}$$

From which you get

$$\rho_{F_1F_2} = \frac{\rho_{XY}}{\sqrt{\rho_{XX}\rho_{YY}}} \tag{5}$$

As the denominator is generally smaller than one you underestimate the structural correlation, the size of underestimation depending on the reliability of the two measurements. It is therefore quite possible to overlook an existing correlation because of unreliable measuring instruments.

In order to develop satisfactory measuring instruments we must find a way to estimate the reliability of such instruments. This, however, necessitates that we have at least two measurements, as shown in Figure 2.3.

From (3a) the reliability coefficients of the two measurements X_1 and X_2 are $\rho_{X_1X_1} = \rho_{X_1F}$ and $\rho_{X_2X_2} = \rho_{X_2F}$, respectively. However, as F is non-observable you cannot use (3a) for computation.

From Figure 2.3 it is evident that X_1 and X_2—both being influenced by F—must correlate, and the more they correlate with F, the stronger their mutual correlation. It should therefore be possible to judge the reliabilities of the two measurements based on the empirical correlation between X_1 and X_2.

We can now write:

$$\begin{aligned} X_1 &= \lambda_1 F + \varepsilon_1 \\ X_2 &= \lambda_2 F + \varepsilon_2 \end{aligned} \tag{6a}$$

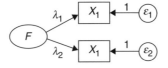

Figure 2.3 A measurement model with two indicators

with the usual regression assumptions:

$$E(\varepsilon_1) = E(\varepsilon_2) = 0$$
$$Cov(\lambda_1, \varepsilon_1) = Cov(\lambda_2, \varepsilon_2) = 0 \tag{6b}$$

to which we add one further assumption:

$$Cov(\varepsilon_1, \varepsilon_2) = 0 \tag{6c}$$

This leaves us with four possibilities:

$$\left.\begin{array}{l} \lambda_1 = \lambda_2 \\ \sigma_{\varepsilon_1}^2 = \sigma_{\varepsilon_2}^2 \end{array}\right\} \text{ the measurements are (strictly) parallel}$$

$$\left.\begin{array}{l} \lambda_1 \neq \lambda_2 \\ \sigma_{\varepsilon_1}^2 = \sigma_{\varepsilon_2}^2 \end{array}\right\} \text{ the measurements are (weakly) parallel}$$

$$\left.\begin{array}{l} \lambda_1 = \lambda_2 \\ \sigma_{\varepsilon_1}^2 \neq \sigma_{\varepsilon_2}^2 \end{array}\right\} \text{ the measurements are tau-equivalent} \tag{7}$$

$$\left.\begin{array}{l} \lambda_1 \neq \lambda_2 \\ \sigma_{\varepsilon_1}^2 \neq \sigma_{\varepsilon_2}^2 \end{array}\right\} \text{ the measurements are congeneric}$$

If the measurements are strictly parallel or tau-equivalent, the values of λ are arbitrary and are usually set to 1.00—a tradition I will follow.

In classical test theory the latent variables F are not formally taken into account, which means that the coefficients λ are not known.

Consequently, classical theory builds on strictly parallel (and to a lesser extent tau-equivalent) measurements, where values of λ can be set to 1.00. Therefore, unless otherwise stated, parallel in the following means *strictly* parallel.

Parallel Tests

Setting $\lambda = 1$, it follows from (6) and (7) that if X_1 and X_2 are parallel measurements, then

$$E(X_1) = E(X_2) = E(F)$$
$$Var(X_1) = Var(X_2) = Var(F) + Var(\varepsilon) \tag{8}$$
$$Cov(X_1, X_2) = Var(F)$$

It should be possible to use parallel measurements to evaluate the reliability. I will therefore calculate their correlation:

$$\rho_{X_1 X_2} = \frac{\sigma_{X_1 X_2}}{\sigma_{X_1} \sigma_{X_2}} = \frac{\sigma_{X_1 X_2}}{\sigma_{X_1}^2} = \frac{\sigma_{X_1 X_2}}{\sigma_{X_2}^2} = \frac{\sigma_F^2}{\sigma_F^2 + \sigma_\varepsilon^2} \tag{9}$$

or—read from right to left:

$$\rho_{X_1 X_1} = \rho_{X_2 X_2} = \rho_{X_1 X_2} \tag{10}$$

In other words: Parallel measurements have the same reliability, which is equal to their correlation.

If you are able to create parallel measurements, you can then estimate their reliability. In the following paragraphs, I will show three different ways of doing so.

'Test-Retest'

The obvious way to create parallel measurements is to repeat the measurement using the same instrument on the same respondents with a shorter or longer interval, and then estimate the reliability as the correlation coefficient between the two. The problem with this method is that it is difficult to say whether we are measuring reliability or changes in the latent variable: If the value of the latent variable has changed between the two points in time the correlation could be small, even if the measurements are reliable.

Besides, the correlation could be large if the respondent could remember her answer to the first measurement, when the second is taken.

'Alternative Form Method'

In order to rule out the possibility that the respondents at the second measurement remember their answer to the first—which will contradict assumption (6c)—it is necessary to construct another measuring instrument, which is parallel to the first, and use that in the second round.

If e.g. you intend to measure the skills of children in arithmetic by administering a test comprising various arithmetical problems, you can let them have another test with different problems at a later time. Of course the two tests have to be of the same difficulty in order to obtain parallelism. One way to secure the same difficulty in both tests is to split the pool of problems between the two tests by randomization.

If you are interested in measuring attitudes or other more diffuse concepts it is difficult enough to construct one measuring instrument—and to construct two parallel ones can be a formidable task.

'Split-Halves Method'

Both the above-mentioned methods require that two measurements are taken at shorter or longer intervals.

This is a drawback, and instead you can randomize the indicators of the latent variable in question into two equal-sized parts and calculate the correlation between these two 'part-measures.' This can be looked upon as an approximation to the 'alternative-form method.'

Let the two indicators X_1 and X_2 in Figure 2.3 be the results obtained by splitting the pool of arithmetic problems (after they have been administered) in the above-mentioned example into two. If the two measurements can be considered parallel, the correlation between them is an estimate of the reliability of the two separate tests. However, we are interested in the reliability of the combined test. How then is the connection between the reliability of the two part-tests and the total—the combined—test?

This, of course, depends upon how the two half-tests are combined, but if the combination is a simple addition $X = X_1 + X_2$, the reliability can be expressed as

$$\rho_{XX} = \frac{2\rho_{X_1 X_2}}{1 + \rho_{X_1 X_2}} \tag{11}$$

This is the so-called *Spearman–Brown-formula*. We see that—other things being equal—the longer the test, the larger the reliability.

Let the correlation coefficient between the number of correct answers to the two part-tests be 0.75. This being an estimate of the reliability of the part-tests, the reliability of the total test will—according to the Spearman-Brown-formula—be:

$$\rho_{XX} = \frac{2 \times 0.75}{1 + 0.75} = 0.86 \tag{12}$$

A drawback with the split-halves method is that the estimated reliability depends on how the test battery is split. I shall return later to a possible solution to that problem.

2. Summated Scales

Adding together the number of correct answers to a test is an example of a *summated scale*: The answers are coded as '0' if the answer is wrong and as '1' if it is correct, and the total score is then taken to be the sum of the *item scores*.

We met other summated scales in Example 2 in chapter (1.2) where concepts such as 'job tension,' 'self-esteem' and 'satisfaction' were measured in this way. It is unrealistic to expect one question in a questionnaire to uncover all facets of complicated concepts like these. The solution to the problem is to use several questions—or *items* as they are called in this connection—per concept and to combine the scores obtained on each item into one measurement, usually by adding together the separate scores.

Among several different techniques of this sort, the one in most widespread use is the *Likert scale*.

The respondents are asked to make up their minds about a number of statements by checking a five-point scale such as:

| strongly disagree | moderately disagree | neither agree nor disagree | moderately agree | strongly agree |

Each of these alternatives are given a number from 1 to 5, the scale values being oriented in opposite direction for statements which are positive and negative, respectively, in relation to the latent variable you intend to measure.

A respondent's scale is then obtained by summing over the checked positions: The larger value of the sum, the more 'job tension' (still referring to Example 1.2):

$$X_1 + X_2 + X_3 + \cdots + X_p = L \tag{13}$$

Usually you will try to have nearly the same number of 'positive' and 'negative' statements (why?).

Prior to the main study, a pilot study is carried out with 50–200 items, which are sorted by 'positive' and 'negative' for the purpose of the orientation of the scale values. Only those items which differentiate respondents with high and low total scores are used in the main study.

By adding several item-scores we obtain a larger differentiation in the measurements: While a variable measured on a single five-point scale can have five different values (usually the values 1–5), a variable measured by summing over ten five-point scales can take on 41 different values (usually the values 10–50).

A further advantage is that while several objections could be raised against treating the separate items as interval scaled or even as normally distributed, things look different when it comes to the sum of several items:

The central limit theorem (Appendix A) states that under fairly general conditions the sum of several stochastic variables will approach a normal distribution (and consequently be interval scaled) as the number of addends grows toward infinity.

However, objections against the use of summated scales have been raised:

1. The simple summation of item scores presupposes that all items are equally good in measuring the underlying concept.
2. The respondents are scaled solely on their total score irrespective of how this score is obtained. Consequently different respondents could have obtained the same score in very different ways—and are they then similar with regard to the attribute we intend to measure?

The last question can also be formulated: 'Do the various items in the battery measure one and the same concept, or do they measure more concepts than one?' In the latter case it could—depending on the circumstances—be meaningless to add item scores that measure different concepts.

Constructing Summated Scales

As the use of summated scales is so widespread we need examine in more detail how to construct a 'good' summated scale.

'Good' items require:

1. Large variances.
2. Expected values near the middle value.

3. All items should be positively correlated, and all the correlations should have about the same magnitude.
4. All items should correlate with the sum of the rest.

The more these conditions are met, and the more items make up the scale, the larger the reliability.

Analysis of empirical data is basically analysis of variation and co-variation: By how much does a measurement vary across respondents and to what extent does it co-vary with other measurements? If a variable does not vary it is of no interest, because then it is part of the definition of the elements making up the population—and if a variable does not vary it cannot co-vary!

If the average of a variable is near one of the endpoints of a scale, we have denied respondents with more extreme attitudes to express their opinion. If a reformulation of the item brings the average nearer the midpoint of the scale, this will in most cases also increase the variance.

In a summated scale the inter-item correlations must necessarily all be positive. If an item shows negative correlations with the other items the most obvious reason is that you have forgotten to reverse the scale of an item, which is worded in an opposite direction to the others. Another possibility is that the majority of respondents have failed to see a negation in the item. This risk is of course largest if only a few items have negations, so that the respondents do not get used to them. Good advice is to avoid negations altogether. An item having both positive and negative correlations to other items should be discarded.

The positive correlations should have about the same size. Two items having a larger correlation between them than the rest indicate that they—apart from measuring the intended concept—also measure something else not measured by the other items, i.e. the scale is not uni-dimensional.

Point 4 above is, of course, a logical consequence of point 3. Nevertheless, I mention it as a separate point, as it expresses in a single number the value of adding an item to a scale.

A Few Requirements More

Statistical techniques will usually require the sum L to be normally distributed, and if the separate items are going to enter into statistical calculations—which is often the case in SEM—the separate items should follow normal distributions—or at least have nearly symmetrical distributions with a kurtosis (see Appendix A) near zero.

The Reliability of Summated Scales

In connection with the 'split-half-method' at the end of Section 1, mention was made of the Spearman-Brown formula:

$$\rho_2 = \frac{2\rho}{1 + \rho} \tag{14}$$

You can consider (14) to express the reliability of a scale which has twice the length (therefore ρ_2) of a scale with reliability ρ: If a summated scale has a reliability coefficient of 0.75, a scale of double length will have a reliability of 0.86, provided the items are parallel.

(14) is a special case of the general formula:

$$\rho_k = \frac{k\rho}{1 + (k-1)\rho} \tag{15}$$

expressing the reliability of a summated scale with k times the length of a scale with reliability ρ. If a summated scale has reliability 0.40, then the reliability of a scale five times as long has a reliability of

$$\rho_5 = \frac{5 \times 0.40}{1 + (5-1)0.40} = 0.77 \tag{16}$$

assuming parallel measurements.

Cronbach's α

Let the reliability of a single item X_i be ρ. The reliability of a scale made by simple summation of k items is then

$$\rho_k = \frac{k\rho}{1 + (k-1)\rho_{ii}} \tag{17}$$

If we use the simple correlation coefficient r_{ij} between two arbitrary items as an estimate for ρ, we can estimate the reliability of the summated scale as

$$\hat{\rho}_k = \frac{kr_{ij}}{1 + (k-1)r_{ij}} \tag{18}$$

In other words, in a test battery of n items we can calculate $n(n-1)/2$ different estimates of the reliability of the summated scale. But, even if the tests are parallel these estimates will differ, and it is natural to insert the average correlation $\bar{r}$ in equation (18):

$$\hat{\alpha}_{std} = \frac{k\bar{r}}{1 + (k-1)\bar{r}} \tag{19}$$

This is *Cronbach's α* (Cronbach, 1951). The subscript std (for standardized) indicates that Cronbach's α also exists in an un-standardized version based, not on correlations but on covariances. It is possible to prove that α_{std} equals the average of the $n(n-1)/2$ reliability coefficients that can be computed using (18).

If the measurements are not parallel the standardized version of α is of course not appropriate, and an un-standardized version based on the covariance matrix is to be preferred.

Then (19) becomes:

$$\alpha = \frac{k\bar{c}}{\bar{v} + (k-1)\bar{c}} \tag{20}$$

where $\bar{v}$ is the average of the elements in the main diagonal and $\bar{c}$ is the average of the off-diagonal elements in the covariance matrix for X_i. If (20) is used on a correlation matrix, we get (19).

(20) is a measure of the reliability of a summated scale whether the measurements are parallel or only tau-equivalent. Moreover, (20) can be proved to indicate a lower limit of the reliability if the measurements are only congeneric (Bollen, 1989).

Usually (20) is written as

$$\alpha = \frac{k}{k-1} \frac{\sigma_L^2 - \sum \sigma_i^2}{\sigma_L^2} \tag{21}$$

I leave it to the reader to demonstrate the equality of (20) and (21).

3. Computer-Based Item Analysis

The process of choosing the 'best' items from a pool of items to be used in a research project is called *item analysis* or *reliability analysis*. Item analysis is usually done on a computer, and routines for this sort of analysis are found in some of the most widespread statistics packages, e.g. Stata, SPSS and SYSTAT, but—strangely enough—not in SAS.

Example 1

The consumption of fresh fish is much smaller in Denmark than in the surrounding countries, in spite of the fact that no Dane has more than 60 miles to the sea.

Therefore a research project was launched in order to map the possible barriers for an increase in consumption of fresh fish (Bredahl and Grunert, 1995; Grunert et al., 1995). Part of the project was a survey of the Danish population's attitudes towards fish and the use of fish in the household; one variable of interest was 'general experience/competence regarding preparation of fish.' Respondents were presented with the questionnaire in Table 1, and asked to check their agreement with the sentences on a scale from 1 (strongly agree) to 7 (strongly disagree). After reversion of item 36 the seven points were added, and the sum was proposed as a measure of a respondent's 'general experience/competence.'

You can now open the SPSS file containing the data from the book's website. You choose Analyze/Scale/Reliability Analysis as shown in Figure 2.4, and the dialog box shown in Figure 2.5a pops up.

You select the items in the left column and click the little triangle (or double-click the selected items), whereby they are moved to the right column. In the model pane

Table 2.1 Example 1: Extract from questionnaire

35.	I don't feel quite sure of how to clean fish:	❏
36.	It is quite natural for me to clean and fillet fish:	❏
37.	I think that fresh fish are unpleasant to touch:	❏
38.	I don't like the smell of fish:	❏
39.	I only rarely clean fresh fish:	❏
40.	If I want fresh fish, I usually get the fishmonger (or somebody else) to clean the fish, so that I don't have to handle it myself:	❏
41.	When I buy fish, I prefer ready-made dishes, so that I don't have to do anything myself:	❏
42.	I have never learned how to clean and fillet fish:	❏

you choose Alpha (the default) and click Statistics, which forces the dialog box in 2.5b to pop up. As you can see SPSS offers a wide range of possibilities, which you can explore on your own. In order to keep things simple you check only the three boxes shown, which results in the output shown in Table 2.2, which I shall briefly comment on:

1. First in the output is Cronbach's α in un-standardized and standardized form. The two are of about equal size as a consequence of the items having nearly the same standard deviations.

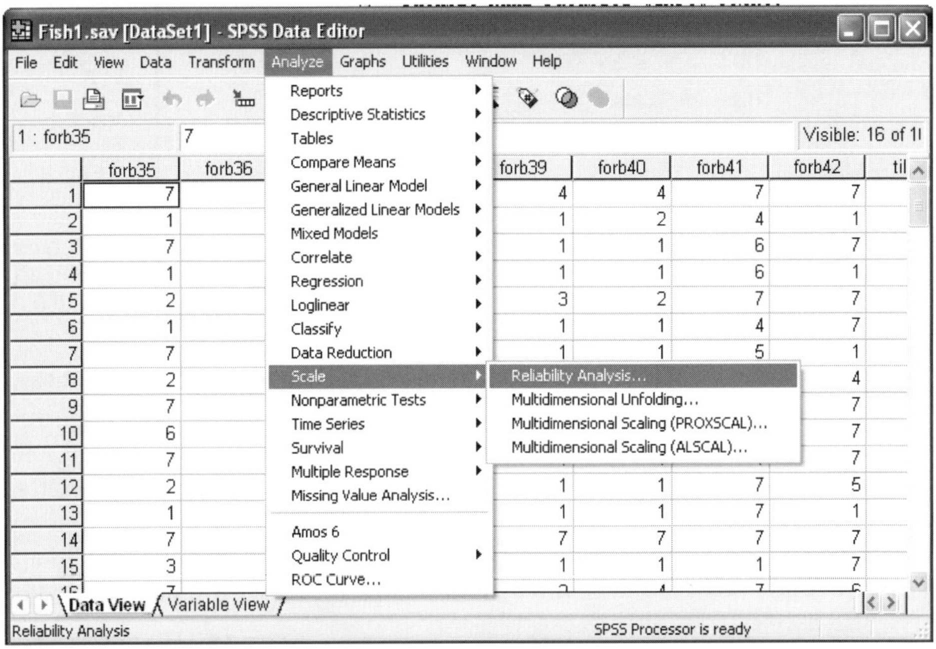

Figure 2.4 Example 1: Reliability analysis using SPSS

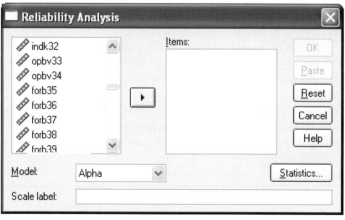

(a)

(b)

Figure 2.5   Example 1: Reliability analysis using SPSS: Main window and dialog boxes

2. Then average, standard deviation and number of answers to every single item
   are stated. We see that item 41 has a small standard deviation and therefore
   is a candidate for exclusion. On a seven-point scale a minimum standard
   deviation of 1.5 should be obtainable. The average is very extreme, so perhaps
   a re-formulation of the item would be a good idea. The two items 37 and 38
   also have extreme averages.
3. Next the correlation matrix is shown. All the correlations are positive after
   reversal of item 36 (therefore 36r). However, item 41 correlates poorly with

Table 2.2　Example 1: Reliability analysis using SPSS

Reliability Statistics　　(1)

Cronbach's Alpha	Cronbach's Alpha Based on Standardized Items	N of Items
.831	.823	8

Item Statistics　　(2)

	Mean	Std. Deviation	N
forb35	3.93	2.662	89
forb36r	3.00	2.454	89
forb37	5.56	2.164	89
forb38	5.22	2.152	89
forb39	2.31	2.156	89
forb40	2.57	2.235	89
forb41	6.15	1.736	89
forb42	4.21	2.643	89

Inter-Item Correlation Matrix　　(3)

	forb35	forb36r	forb37	forb38	forb39	forb40	forb41	forb42
forb35	1.000	.607	.326	.245	.538	.442	.179	.698
forb36r	.607	1.000	.439	.310	.689	.541	.240	.604
forb37	.326	.439	1.000	.524	.276	.280	.153	.249
forb38	.245	.310	.524	1.000	.264	.370	.171	.237
forb39	.538	.689	.276	.264	1.000	.691	.209	.484
forb40	.442	.541	.280	.370	.691	1.000	.119	.385
forb41	.179	.240	.153	.171	.209	.119	1.000	.043
forb42	.698	.604	.249	.237	.484	.385	.043	1.000

Item-Total Statistics　　(4)

	Scale Mean if Item Deleted	Scale Variance if Item Deleted	Corrected Item-Total Correlation	Squared Multiple Correlation	Cronbach's Alpha if Item Deleted
forb35	29.03	109.783	.671	.570	.795
forb36r	29.967	109.283	.760	.635	.782
forb37	27.40	127.016	.463	.375	.823
forb38	27.74	128.717	.429	.343	.827
forb39	30.65	117.389	.690	.632	.795
forb40	30.39	119.696	.605	.524	.805
forb41	26.82	142.263	.218	.111	.846
forb42	28.75	113.620	.598	.561	.806

the other items, and a few of the correlations are a little too high compared to the rest—e.g. (forb35, forb42) and (forb39, forb40).
4. Towards the end of the output you meet the most interesting results of the analysis, where you can evaluate the consequences of deleting an item from the battery: For each item is first shown mean and variance for the summated scale if the item is deleted. 'Corrected Item-Total Correlation' is the simple correlation between the item and the sum of the rest, and 'Squared Multiple Correlation' is the coefficient of determination when the item is regressed on the others. Finally, the last column shows the size of (un-standardized) α, if the item is deleted.

If you remove item forb41, you can expect α to increase from 0.831 to 0.846. Also notice that the corrected item-total correlation and squared multiple correlations are very small for this item. Often a minimum of 0.40 for the two is used as a rule of thumb.

If you remove item 41 and repeat the analysis, you get the output shown in Table 2.3.

I will leave it to the reader to convince himself that α can be further increased (to 0.866) by deleting both item 37 and 38.

It is worth noting that these two items—together with item 41—are the only ones that mention reasons for (low) experience with preparation of fish; namely that they are unpleasant to touch and do not smell good—and in the case of item 41 that you prefer ready-made dishes. This is not the reason in the majority of cases (cf. the high means); therefore the rather small corrected item-total correlations and squared multiple correlations of these items.

Now, you could make a long list of reasons why a person would avoid preparing fish, but there is no reason a priori to expect that the various reasons should correlate with each other or with any other item in the battery.

The three items should never have entered into the scale in the first place.

A final warning: Remember that the last column in Table 2.3 shows the expected change in α if a single item is removed. Sometimes α cannot be increased by removing just one item, but can still be increased if more than one item is

Table 2.3 Example 1: Reliability Analysis using SPSS (second run)

	Scale Mean if Item Deleted	Scale Variance if Item Deleted	Corrected Item-Total Correlation	Squared Multiple Correlation	Cronbach's Alpha if Item Deleted
forb35	22.89	99.419	.674	.564	.814
forb36r	23.82	99.308	.755	.627	.801
forb37	21.26	116.148	.460	.375	.845
forb38	21.60	117.971	.421	.334	.850
forb39	24.51	106.935	.688	.630	.814
forb40	24.25	108.597	.615	.520	.824
forb42	22.61	101.991	.623	.545	.823

removed simultaneously. Therefore also look at the corrected item-total correlations and the squared multiple correlations.

As mentioned 'Alpha' is the default in SPSS, but it is also possible (in the window in Figure 2.5a) to specify other measurement models:

1. *Split-half* calculates the split-half coefficient between the first and the second half of the items. In addition the Spearman-Brown-coefficient (12) and the Guttman-Rulow-coefficient, which only assumes tau-equivalence, are calculated.
2. *Guttman's lower bound on true reliability* calculates lower bounds for test-retest reliability under six different sets of assumptions, which are all weaker than the traditional assumption of parallel measurements. Besides, they are based on only one sample (Guttman, 1945).
3. *Parallel* estimates reliability under the assumption of weak parallel measurements and tests this hypothesis.
4. *Strictly parallel* estimates reliability under the assumption of strictly parallel measurements and tests this hypothesis.

It should be mentioned that the way SPSS calculates split-half is not the wisest one, as there could be a fatigue factor. It is preferable to calculate split-half between odd and even numbered items.

As should be evident, there is no such thing as 'the true reliability.' The various methods for calculating reliability measures different aspects of reliability: 'test-retest' is a measure of the *stability* of the measuring instrument, whereas 'alternative forms' measures the *equivalence* of two measuring instruments. In a way split-half measures the equivalence of the two halves of the same measuring instrument and alpha the equivalence of the separate items. In that way 'split-half' and alpha are measures of the *internal consistency* of the measuring instrument.

4. Validity

It is of course not sufficient that a measuring instrument is reliable, it must also be valid—it must measure what is intended. If your instrument is not reliable it measures only *uncertainty* or *noise*—and then it is of course meaningless to ask whether the instrument is valid. If, on the contrary, your measuring instrument is reliable, it measures something—but what? In other words, in order to be valid, a measurement must be reliable.

I have hitherto assumed that a measurement measures one and only one concept. However, this is not always the case. Often an indicator is connected to more than one latent variable, as is pictured in Figure 2.6.

This is not a problem if you can name the two factors, which usually can be done only if they both have several indicators. If, however, the measurement X_1, in addition to measuring the factor F, is also influenced by the unknown factor F_*,

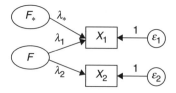

Figure 2.6   An indicator measures two different factors

for which it is the only indicator, then things become more complicated. A factor such as F_* is called measurement X_1's *specific factor*.

The answer to the question: 'How many times in the last five years have you been stopped by the police for drunken driving?' will not only be influenced by the 'true' driving habits of the respondent (F), but also by his tendency to play down his drunk-driving (F_*). We can write:

$$X_1 = \lambda_1 F + \lambda_* F_* + \varepsilon_1 \tag{22a}$$

with expected value:

$$E(X_1) = \lambda_1 E(F_1) + \lambda_* E(F_*) \tag{22b}$$

and variance:

$$Var(X_1) = \lambda_1^2 Var(F) + \lambda_*^2 Var(F_*) + Var(\varepsilon_1) \tag{22c}$$

$\lambda_1^2 Var(F)$ is called the *common variance* or *communality*. It is that part of the variables variance that it shares with the other variables, measuring the same factor (or factors). $\lambda_*^2 Var(F_*)$ is called the *specific variance*, as it relates to the specific factor, and $Var(\varepsilon_1)$ is the *error variance*.

In this notation

$$\rho_{X_1 X_2} = \frac{\lambda_1^2 Var(F) + \lambda_*^2 Var(F_*)}{Var(X_1)} \tag{23}$$

constitutes the reliable share of the variance, while only a share of

$$\frac{\lambda_1^2 Var(F)}{Var(X_1)} \tag{24}$$

is valid.

If the measurements are strictly parallel or tau-equivalent the λs are usually fixed at 1.00, which simplifies the equations.

As the validity of a measuring instrument expresses the agreement of the reading of the instrument with the 'true value,' you could—at least in principle—judge the validity by comparing the imperfect measurement with that of a one hundred pct. valid instrument. For example, the validity of the question: 'How many times in the last five years have you been stopped by the police for drunken driving?' can be judged by comparing the answers with police reports.

However, this method presupposes that:

1. A one hundred pct. valid measuring instrument exists, and
2. It is possible to get access to it.

Usually at least one of these conditions will not be met. In such situations the concept of validity becomes ambiguous, and you talk about:

1. Content validity,
2. Criterion validity, and
3. Construct validity.

A measurement has large *content validity* if it covers all (or many) aspects of the concept being measured. A trivial example is a test to measure children's ability in arithmetic. Such a test has content validity if it covers all of the examination requirements. On the other hand, if the test only covers a small part of the requirement, the content validity is low. Now, this example is special, because the content of the concept 'examination requirement' is laid down in the curriculum. It is, however, very seldom that you are that lucky. In most cases content validity is evaluated in discussions with colleagues or other experts.

Criterion validity of a measuring instrument is evaluated by comparing the actual measurement with a criterion variable. We distinguish between *concurrent validity*, where the criterion is measured at the same time as the variable we wish to evaluate, and *predictive validity*, where the criterion is measured at a later time. A concurrent criterion is usually a measurement of the same concept with a different measuring instrument, while an example of a predictive criterion is the final exam result from a university as predicted by the entrance examination.

If a measurement is a valid measurement of construct F_1 it should correlate— positively or negatively—with measurements of other constructs $(F_2, F_3, F_4, \ldots)$ with which concept F_1 is causally related, in exactly the same way as the constructs $F_1, F_2, F_3, F_4, \ldots$ etc. are expected to correlate, based on theory. A measuring instrument which stands such a test is said to have (a large) *construct validity*.

You could say that content validity is theoretically based and usually not measurable, while criterion validity is purely empirical, and construct validity is theoretically as well as empirically based.

Weaknesses of Traditional Validity Measures

Criterion validity is fundamentally an empirical concept without much theoretic content. Concurrent validity is measured by the correlation coefficient between two or more simultaneous measurements assumed to measure the same theoretical construct. Let X_1 be the measurement the validity of which you want to judge, and X_2 the criterion. Then it is apparent that the correlation between the two, apart from the reliability of X_1, also depends on the reliability of X_2, and that the correlation could be inflated if the two measurement methods are not sufficiently different.

Construct validity suffers from many of the same weaknesses as criterion validity: Let F_1 with indicator X_1 and F_2 with indicator X_2 be two theoretical constructs, which—based on sound, substantiated theory—are expected to correlate. However, the correlation between X_1 and X_2 depends not only on the correlation between X_1 and F_1, but also on the correlation between X_2 and F_2, and the correlation between F_1 and F_2.

Convergent and Discriminant Validity: the Multitrait–Multimethod Technique

Cambell and Fiske (1959) have proposed the so-called *multitrait–multimethod technique* for assessing validity: Each of several concepts (traits) is measured by several methods.

Let three traits (latent variables) each be measured by two methods (manifest variables), and let the correlation matrix be as shown in Table 2.4.

In order for the methods to be valid, Cambell and Fiske state the following requirements:

1. *Convergent validity*: The correlations of measurements of the same traits using different methods should be statistically significant and 'sufficiently large.' In this case these so-called convergent correlations are ρ_{41}, ρ_{52} and ρ_{63}.
2. *Discriminant validity*: Convergent correlations should be larger than correlations among measurements of different traits using same method. In this case ρ_{41}, ρ_{52} and ρ_{63} should be larger than ρ_{21}, ρ_{31} and ρ_{32}.
3. *Discriminant validity*: Convergent correlations should be larger than correlations of measurements having neither trait, nor method in common, i.e. ρ_{41}, ρ_{52} and ρ_{63} should be larger than ρ_{51}, ρ_{61}, ρ_{42}, ρ_{52}, ρ_{43} and ρ_{53}.
4. The pattern of correlations among traits should be the same across methods.

The multitrait–multimethod technique is an attempt to support the researcher in evaluating construct validity, but some of the fundamental problems still persist.

Table 2.4   Multitrait–multimethod matrix

	X_1	X_2	X_3	X_4	X_5	X_6
method 1, trait 1 X_1	1,00					
method 1, trait 2 X_2	ρ_{21}	1,00				
method 1, trait 3 X_3	ρ_{31}	ρ_{32}	1,00			
method 2, trait 1 X_4	ρ_{41}	ρ_{42}	ρ_{43}	1,00		
method 2, trait 2 X_5	ρ_{51}	ρ_{52}	ρ_{53}	ρ_{54}	1,00	
method 2, trait 3 X_6	ρ_{61}	ρ_{62}	ρ_{63}	ρ_{64}	ρ_{65}	1,00

This is easiest to see if we sketch the method in a SEM-diagram, as shown in Figure 2.7.

Assuming all variables are standardized, we can write:

$$\rho_{X_1 X_4} = \lambda_{11}\lambda_{41} + \lambda_{14}\lambda_{45}\phi_{45} \tag{25}$$

and we see that the convergent correlation $\rho_{X_1 X_4}$ does not only depend on F_1's influence on X_1 and X_4, which is implicit in the MTMM-philosophy, but also on the correlation ϕ_{45} between the two methods and their effects on X_1 and X_4.

The fundamental problem with the classical methods of validity assessment discussed so far is that they are all based exclusively on relations among manifest variables without explicitly taking the latent variables into account.

In Chapter 6 you will learn how SEM by introducing latent variables opens up for evaluations of reliability and validity that are based directly on the theoretical definition of these concepts.

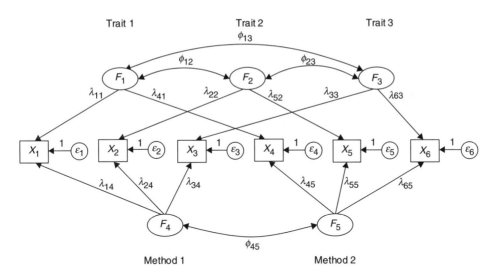

Figure 2.7 SEM-model of multitrait–multimethod validation

☞ In this chapter you have met the following concepts:

reliability and reliability coefficient
parallel, tau-equivalent and
   congeneric measurements
summated scale

item analysis
validity
content, criterion and concept validity
convergent and discriminant validity

Questions

1. Define reliability and validity.
2. Discuss the various ways in which you can judge the reliability of a measuring instrument.
3. Discuss the demands an item should meet in order to be included in a summated scale.
4. List the various steps you would go through in constructing a summated scale.
5. Explain the concepts 'common variance,' 'specific variance' and 'error variance.'
6. Explain the various forms of validity.

Reference List

Bollen, K. A. (1989) *Structural Equations with Latent Variables*, N.Y.: Wiley.

Bredahl, L. and K. L. Grunert (1995) 'Determinants of the consumption of fish and shellfish in Denmark: An application of the theory of planned behaviour,' in *International Seafood Conference: Seafood from Producer to Consumer, Integrated Approach to Quality*, Noordwijkerhout.

Cambell, D. T. and D. W. Fiske (1959) 'Convergent and discriminant validation by the multitrait–multimethod matrix,' *Psychological Bulletin*, 56: 81–105.

Cronbach, L. (1951) 'Coefficient alpha and the internal structure of tests,' *Psychometrika*, 16: 297–334.

Grunert, K. G., S. Bisp, L. Bredahl, E. Sørensen, and N. A. Nielsen (1995) En undersøgelse af danskernes køb af fisk og skaldyr. Århus: Aarhus School of Business. MAPP project paper.

Guttman, L. (1945) 'A basis for analyzing test-retest reliability,' *Psychometrika*, 10(4): 255–82.

3

Exploratory Factor Analysis

Ideally we require that a summated scale measures one and only one concept—that the scale is uni-dimensional. Therefore this chapter will introduce two classical techniques for mapping the dimensionality of a data set.

The first technique is (*principal*) *components analysis*, whereby a set of manifest variables (e.g. items) are transformed into new and fewer uncorrelated variables called *principal components*, each representing a dimension in the data.

The other is *exploratory factor* analysis, where the roles, so to speak, are inverted: Instead of the 'new' variables being functions of the original manifest variables, the original variables are considered to be indicators (and thus functions) of underlying dimensions called *factors*.

This last-mentioned technique will, however, only be scantily treated as an introduction to *confirmatory factor analysis* treated in Chapter 7. The reason being that components analysis is less complicated and usually will give the same results as exploratory factor analysis. As the reason is purely pragmatic, the reader will no doubt find several examples on the use of components analysis, where factor analysis would have been more 'correct.'

Most often both techniques go under the name of factor analysis, hence the name of the chapter.

1. Optimal Scales

In connection with Figure 1.3, mention was made of summated scales as a means for measuring latent variables, and in Chapter 2, you saw how item analysis based on a pilot sample could help you pick the 'best' items for use in the main study.

It was mentioned that a large variance is an essential attribute of a 'good' scale: As the aim is to study variations and co-variations in variables across respondents or other objects, you could in fact consider the variance of a variable as an expression of the amount of information contained in that variable. The larger the variance, the larger the amount of information.

[A digression: This, perhaps, sounds a bit strange to the reader, who is used to looking at the variance as a measure of uncertainty or noise; the larger the variance, the larger the uncertainty, and thereby the less information. This, however, is only correct as long as we talk about the variance of a sampling distribution for an estimator (see Appendix A), but in scale construction we are interested in the variance in the population.

If all objects had the same value on a variable (in which case the variance was 0), measurement of this variable was of no interest, because then the population was partly defined as the collection of objects having that value on the variable.]

Let us now have a look at the variance of L in the expression:

$$X_1 + X_2 + X_3 + \cdots + X_p = L \tag{1}$$

and ask the question: Is it possible to obtain a larger variance (and thus a larger amount of information) by using a weighted sum:

$$Y_1 = a_{11}X_1 + a_{12}X_2 + \cdots + a_{1j}X_j + \cdots + a_{1p}X_p \tag{2}$$

The answer is yes, and a simple example will illustrate the idea.

Example 1

A class has obtained the marks shown in Figure 3.1 in an exam in French (measured on a 13 point scale as used in Denmark until 2007).

Most often the average of the two marks will appear on the certificate, i.e.:

$$Y = 0.5X_1 + 0.5X_2 \tag{3}$$

A look at the graph in Figure 3.1 will convince the reader that the points are more spread out along the X_1-axis than along the X_2-axis.

X_1 has a variance of 6.37 and X_2 a variance of 2.79. The written exam does a better job in discriminating between the students, and should it then not also count more in the calculation of the combined mark for French?

In the figure a line is drawn through the cluster of points in such a way that the points are spread out more along this line than along any other line that could be drawn. If you project the points onto this line and provide a suitable scale, you, perhaps, have a better expression of the students' abilities in French than if you use an un-weighed average, which is tantamount to projecting the points on to the dotted 45° line.

The Y_1 line has the equation

$$Y_1 = 0.64X_1 + 0.36X_2 \tag{4}$$

and expresses the optimal weighting scheme for the two variables. Y_1 is called *the first principal component*.

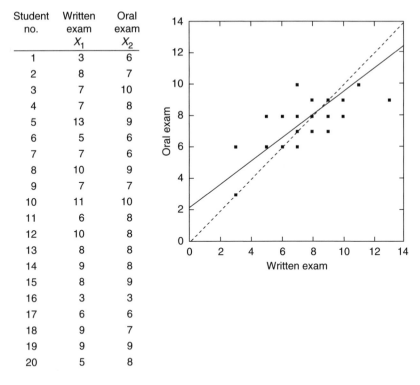

Student no.	Written exam X_1	Oral exam X_2
1	3	6
2	8	7
3	7	10
4	7	8
5	13	9
6	5	6
7	7	6
8	10	9
9	7	7
10	11	10
11	6	8
12	10	8
13	8	8
14	9	8
15	8	9
16	3	3
17	6	6
18	9	7
19	9	9
20	5	8

Figure 3.1 Example 1: Data and graphics

Note that the Y_1 line is *not* the regression line. We can estimate two regression lines: The regression of X_2 on X_1, and the regression of X_1 on X_2. The first of these is placed so that the sum of squared *vertical* distances from the points to the line is minimized, and the second so that the sum of the squared *horizontal* distances is minimized. Both these lines pass through the point $(\overline{X}_1, \overline{X}_2)$. The Y_1 line also passes through this point, minimizing the sum of squared *orthogonal* distances from the points to the line. See Figure 3.2.

So, a correlation (see Appendix A) between two or more variables could be considered a sign of a cause-effect relation—as in the structural part of a SEM model—in which case you can use regression analysis to map the relationship, or it could be interpreted as a sign that the variables measure the same underlying concept—as in the measurement part of the model—in which case the measurements could be combined to include as much information as possible from the original variables, using *principal components analysis.*

2. Principal Components Analysis

In Example 1 marks obtained in written and oral exams in French were combined into a single mark using the formula $Y_1 = 0.64X_1 + 0.36X_2$. In doing so we treat

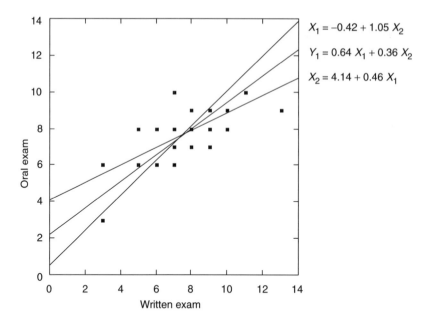

Figure 3.2   Example 1: The two regression lines and the (first) principal component

the observations as if they were all placed on the Y_1 line, and thereby ignore the information contained in the distance from the various points to the Y_1 line.

   This information can be utilized by introducing a Y_2 line perpendicular to the Y_1 line and thereby constructing a new coordinate system, as shown in Figure 3.3.

   It is obvious that Y_1 (by a suitable choice of scale) has a much larger variance than Y_2 (and any of the two original variables). Therefore, Y_1 discriminates better among

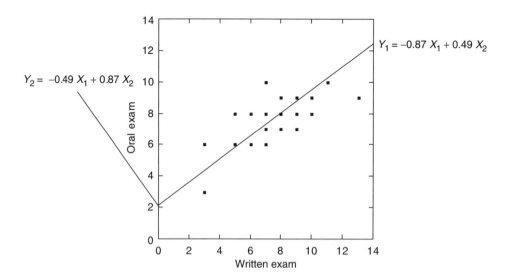

Figure 3.3   Example 1: The two principal components

the students than any of the three other variables—it thus has the largest amount of information of the four variables and Y_2 the least. Also observe that Y_1 and Y_2—contrary to X_1 and X_2—are un-correlated (a regression line would coincide with the Y_1-axis).

The two components have the equations:

$$Y_1 = 0.87X_1 + 0.49X_2$$
$$Y_2 = -0.49X_1 + 0.87X_2 \tag{5}$$

The first equation describes the same line as (4), because only the relative size of the coefficients matters.

If we measure the amount of information in the data by the variances of the variables, then the total amount of information in the X-variables is:

$$VAR(X_1) + VAR(X_2) \tag{6}$$

As the Y-coordinate system is just a rotation of the X-system, this transformation should not change the information contained in the data, and consequently the coefficients in (5) are chosen so that

$$VAR(X_1) + VAR(X_2) = VAR(Y_1) + VAR(Y_2) \tag{7}$$

In the present case:

$$6.37 + 2.78 = 8.00 + 1.15$$

If we disregard Y_2 we will still keep

$$8.00/(8.00 + 1.15) = 87\% \tag{8}$$

of the total amount of information in the X-variables.

The primary goal of components analysis is to reduce a number of correlating variables (i.e. variables sharing a certain amount of information) to a smaller number of—usually uncorrelated—variables. The p original variables X_j are transformed to p new variables Y_i called *principal components*:

$$Y_1 = a_{11}X_1 + a_{12}X_2 + \ldots + a_{1j}X_j + \ldots + a_{1p}X_p$$
$$Y_2 = a_{21}X_1 + a_{22}X_2 + \ldots + a_{2j}X_j + \ldots + a_{2p}X_p$$
$$\vdots$$
$$Y_i = a_{i1}X_1 + a_{i2}X_2 + \ldots + a_{ij}X_j + \ldots + a_{ip}X_p \tag{9}$$
$$\vdots$$
$$Y_p = a_{p1}X_1 + a_{p2}X_2 + \ldots + a_{pj}X_j + \ldots + a_{pp}X_p$$

The total amount of information in the original variables (the X-variables) is then the sum of their variances, and the scales of the new variables (the Y-variables) are chosen to make

$$\sum_{i=1}^{p} Var(Y_i) = \sum_{j=1}^{p} Var(X_j) \tag{10}$$

in order to preserve the amount of information measured in this way. We have, therefore, not reduced the amount of data *unless we disregard some of the Y-variables*.

If we choose to keep only Y_1, then the coefficients a_{1j} are chosen so as to maximize the amount of information in Y_1 (i.e. to maximize $Var(Y_1)$ under the restriction (10)). If we also wish to keep the second principal component Y_2, then a_{2j} must be chosen so as to maximize $Var(Y_2)$, under the restriction that Y_2 is not correlated with Y_1 so that Y_2 only contains new information—and of course also under the restriction (10). This process is then continued with $Y_3, Y_4 \ldots$ etc.

In other words: The coefficients are chosen so that the principal components, the Y-variables, are not correlated and are ordered by decreasing variance. The values of the Y-variables are called *component scores*, the coefficients a_{ij} are called *component score coefficients* and the covariances or correlations (depending on whether the analysis is based on a covariance or a correlation matrix) between the Y-variables and the X-variables are called *component loadings*.

The whole process groups the X-variables according to which component they correlate strongest with, *load most on*. By examining the variables loading on the same component it should be possible to interpret the component, i.e. to name it.

If the variables entering into a component analysis are very different in size (size of household, income, amount spent on a certain product or activity) it could be advantageous to standardize the variables to a variance of 1.00 before the analysis, because the variables with the largest variances would otherwise have the strongest influence on the outcome. This is tantamount to basing the analysis on the correlation matrix instead of the covariance matrix.

Although several good statistical reasons could be given in favor of basing component analysis on the covariance matrix (Anderson, 1984) the use of correlations is almost universal—at least in the social and behavioral sciences.

Example 2

The correlations in Table 3.1 are based on measurement of eight physical variables on 305 individuals (Harman, 1976).

From a correlation matrix of eight variables you can extract eight principal components, but the real question is: How many of these shall you keep in order to retain most of the information in the data? You can find some support for this decision in Figure 3.4.

The sum of the component variances is equal to the number of components. This comes as no surprise, as the original variables were standardized to have variance 1.00.

Table 3.1 Example 2: Correlations of eight physical measurements

	1	2	3	4	5	6	7	8
1. Height	1.000							
2. Arm span	0.846	1.000						
3. Forearm length	0.805	0.881	1.000					
4. Lower leg length	0.859	0.826	0.801	1.000				
5. Weight	0.473	0.376	0.380	0.436	1.000			
6. Bitrochanteric diameter	0.398	0.326	0.319	0.329	0.762	1.000		
7. Chest girth	0.301	0.277	0.237	0.327	0.730	0.583	1.000	
8. Chest width	0.382	0.415	0.345	0.365	0.629	0.577	0.539	1.000

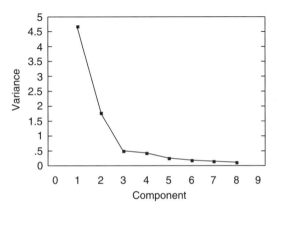

Component	Variance	Variance in pct.
1	4.67	58
2	1.77	22
3	0.48	6
4	0.42	5
5	0.23	3
6	0.19	2
7	0.14	2
8	0.10	1
Total	8.00	100

Figure 3.4 Example 2: Component variances and elbow plot (or scree plot)

When deciding how many of the components to retain, the following rules of thumb are often used as starting points:

1. Extract components until a satisfactory share of the total information has been picked up. From the figure we see that by extracting one component we keep 58% of the information (variance), while extraction of two components brings this figure up to 80%:

$$\left(\frac{4.67 + 1.77}{8.00}\right) 100\% = 58\% + 22\% = 80\%$$

2. From component 3 the variances are smaller than the average variance of the original variables (in this case 1.00). In other words: The last six components each contain less information than an average X-variable, and should therefore be discarded. According to this so-called *Kaiser criterion* only the first two components should be retained.

3. If we look at the discarded components as uncertainty or noise, we shall extract components until the next component is mainly made up of noise. But when is that? Usually you consider remaining components to be noise, when the component variances begin to level off and have about the same size. This point is easier to find if the variances are depicted in an *elbow plot* (or *scree plot* as it is called in SPSS), as shown in Figure 3.4. The curve has a distinctive bend—an elbow—after the second component. According to this criterion a two-component solution should be chosen.

In this case the last two rules (and possibly also the first) lead to the same conclusion: extraction of two components. We measure two different attributes and not one or eight.

However, these are only rules of thumb—in the end the decision of how many components to retain depends on whether the components are substantively meaningful.

The transformation from the original variables to the two principal components is:

$$Y_1 = 0.40X_1 + 0.39X_2 + 0.38X_3 + 0.39X_4 + 0.35X_5 + 0.31X_6 + 0.29X_7 + 0.31X_8$$
$$Y_2 = 0.28X_1 + 0.33X_2 + 0.34X_3 + 0.30X_4 - 0.39X_5 - 0.40X_6 - 0.44X_7 - 0.31X_8$$
$$(11)$$

Rotation of components

In order to interpret the components—to name them—the *X*-variables are grouped according to which component they correlate strongest with—*load most on*. The variables loading on the same component should have something in common, which could be used to name the component and thereby give it a substantive meaning. However, more often than not, the picture will, be rather confusing.

The transformation (11) from *X*-variables to *Y*-variables is a mechanical process, and there is no reason to believe that the new variables should have any substantive meaning.

You would expect the variables to load most on the first component, and a look at the component loadings in Figure 3.5a shows that not a single variable load is highest on component 2—so are there really two *meaningful* components?

In Figure 3.5b the component loadings are depicted graphically, and you see that they fall into two separate groups. There are in fact *two* components—the upper depicting the last four variables and the lower one the first four. However, our coordinate system is not able to disclose this unless we resort to a graph.

It is easily seen that a rotation of the coordinate system could bring the axes to pass nearer the two point clusters. By doing so, you obtain a simpler component structure, in that each variable has a large loading on one of the components and only a small loading on the other (or the others if there are more than two components). The result of this so-called *Varimax rotation* is shown in Figure 3.6.

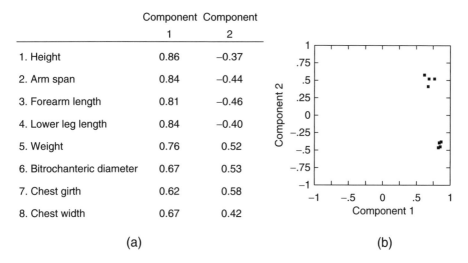

	Component 1	Component 2
1. Height	0.86	-0.37
2. Arm span	0.84	-0.44
3. Forearm length	0.81	-0.46
4. Lower leg length	0.84	-0.40
5. Weight	0.76	0.52
6. Bitrochanteric diameter	0.67	0.53
7. Chest girth	0.62	0.58
8. Chest width	0.67	0.42

(a)   (b)

Figure 3.5 Example 2: Original component structure

You could name the first component 'bone structure' and the second 'flesh structure' (or 'height' and 'breadth').

It is possible, however, to let the axes go right through the point clusters of Figure 3.6, if we relax the restriction of orthogonal Y-axes. Such an *oblique rotation* is shown in Figure 3.7.

An oblique rotation means that the two components are no longer un-correlated. In this case the correlation is 0.50. Whether to prefer an orthogonal or an oblique

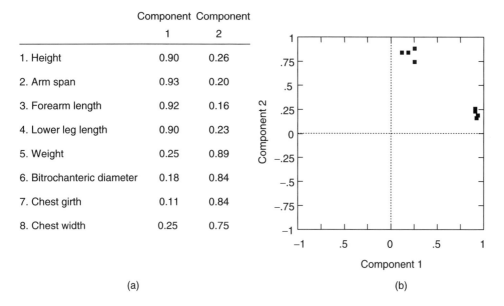

	Component 1	Component 2
1. Height	0.90	0.26
2. Arm span	0.93	0.20
3. Forearm length	0.92	0.16
4. Lower leg length	0.90	0.23
5. Weight	0.25	0.89
6. Bitrochanteric diameter	0.18	0.84
7. Chest girth	0.11	0.84
8. Chest width	0.25	0.75

(a)   (b)

Figure 3.6 Example 2: Varimax-rotated component structure

	Component 1	Component 2
1. Height	0.80	0.03
2. Arm span	0.84	−0.04
3. Forearm length	0.84	−0.07
4. Lower leg length	0.80	0.00
5. Weight	0.00	0.80
6. Bitrochanteric diameter	−0.05	0.77
7. Chest girth	−0.13	0.79
8. Chest width	−0.04	0.66

(a)

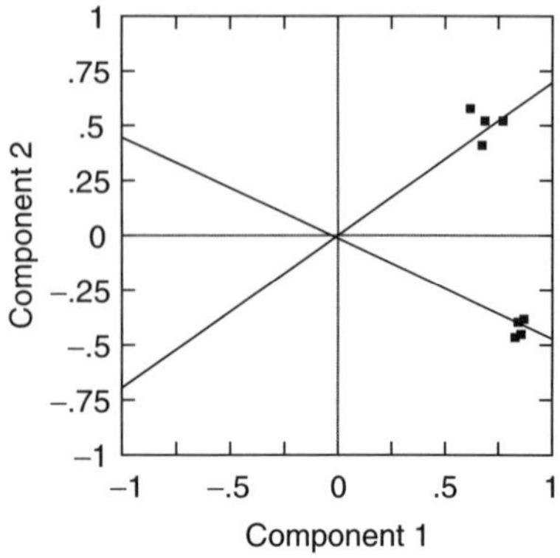

(b)

Figure 3.7   Example 2: Oblique rotated component structure

structure is not a question of fit and figures, but a substantive question: Is it more reasonable to assume 'bone structure' and 'flesh structure' to be correlated, or is the opposite assumption more reasonable?

It is worth noting that in more complex cases there could be more than one among the infinite number of rotations that had meaningful but different substantive interpretations.

It is worthy of note that SPSS (unfortunately!) does not allow you to use a covariance or correlation matrix as input when using roll-down menus. You have to write a command syntax. You can see how to do that on pages 421–22 in Norušis (2005).

Component Analysis as Item Analysis

A summated scale is supposed to be one-dimensional and, furthermore, each item is assumed to be just as good as any other item in measuring the underlying concept. If a number of items make up a reliable summated scale, a component analysis should result in the following:

1. The first (un-rotated) component should account for a large share of the total variance in the data.
2. Each of the following components should account for about the same variance.
3. Each item should have about the same weight in the calculation of the component score.

Fulfillment of the first two conditions is usually considered an indication of uni-dimensionality, and if the last condition is also fulfilled, the simple summation of item scores is an adequate approximation to component scores.

While nowadays—where we do not use hand calculation—it is just as easy to calculate a component score as a summated score, one strong point against using component scores could be put forward: If the scale is expected to be used repeatedly in several studies, you could argue that the simple summated scale is a more robust instrument than a weighted scale, because the weights (the component score coefficients) could vary across the studies.

Example 3

(Continued from Example 2.1) After having opened the SPSS data editor, you choose Analyze/Data Reduction/Factor (see Figure 3.8a), and the dialog box in panel (b) pops up. You select the variables in the left column and, by clicking, the little triangle move them to the right panel. Then you click Extraction, and, in the dialog box in panel (c), you are given the choice whether you want your analysis to be based on the correlation matrix (the default) or the covariance matrix. You choose the covariance, because all of your variables are measured on the same scale, check 'unrotated factor solution' and 'scree plot' and set the number of factors to be extracted to 1. Then you click 'Continue', return to the dialog box in Figure 3.8b and click 'Scores'. When the dialog box (d) pops up, you check 'Display factor score coefficient matrix,' click 'Continue' and when you return to the box in 3.8(b), you click 'OK.'

Part of the output from the analysis is shown in Table 3.2.

1. First in the output are the communalities. Remember: The communality is that part of the variance of a measurement that it has in common with the latent variables—or in this case the one latent variable—it is supposed to measure (and thus with all other variables supposed to measure that same latent variable). In principal components analysis, there is neither specific variance nor error variance as opposed to the model in equations (2.22). Consequently *all* variance is common variance if all components are extracted, and the raw initial communalities are just the variances of the various items, while the extracted communalities are the variances shared with the extracted component(s).

   The rescaled communalities are the same variances, after rescaling the initial communalities to have the value 1.00 (e.g. for the first item: $4.882/7.086 = 0.689$).

   Forb41 catches the eye, because it only shares 6% of its variance with the extracted component. This item is therefore a candidate for exclusion and so are forb37 and forb38, the communalities of which are also much lower than the majority of items.

2. Then comes a listing of the principal components with their respective variances followed by an elbow plot that confirms the existence of only one component. You should compare this part of the output with Figure 3.4.

   Notice that the variances of the principal components are called *eigenvalues*. Every symmetric $p \times p$ matrix (and that includes covariance matrices) has

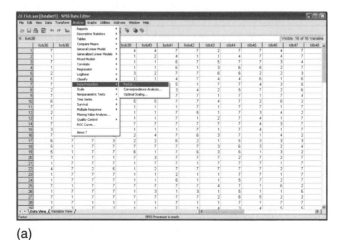

(a)

(b)

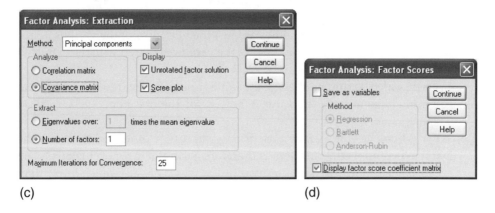

(c)

(d)

Figure 3.8   Example 3: First steps in principal component analysis in SPSS

Table 3.2 Example 3: Part of output from component analysis extracting one component (SPSS)

Communalities (1)

	Raw		Rescaled	
	Initial	Extraction	Initial	Extraction
forb35	7.086	4.882	1.000	.689
forb36r	6.023	4.412	1.000	.733
forb37	4.681	1.283	1.000	.274
forb38	4.631	1.045	1.000	.226
forb39	4.650	2.864	1.000	.616
forb40	4.997	2.474	1.000	.495
forb41	3.013	.175	1.000	.058
forb42	6.988	4.382	1.000	.627

Extraction Method: Principal Component Analysis.

Total Variance Explained (2)

	Initial Eigenvalues(a)			Extraction Sums of Squared Loadings		
Component	Total	% of Variance	Cumulative %	Total	% of Variance	Cumulative %
Raw						
1	21.517	51.148	51.148	21.517	51.148	51.148
2	5.825	13.847	64.995			
3	4.276	10.164	75.158			
4	3.106	7.382	82.541			
5	2.535	6.025	88.566			
6	2.165	5.145	93.711			
7	1.459	3.468	97.179			
8	1.187	2.821	100.000			

Extraction Method: Principal Component Analysis.

Scree plot

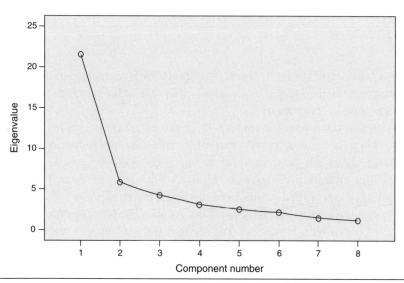

(Continued)

Table 3.2   Cont'd

Component Matrix[a]			(3)

	Raw Component	Rescaled Component
	1	1
forb35	2.210	.830
forb36r	2.101	.856
forb37	1.133	.524
forb38	1.022	.475
forb39	1.692	.785
forb40	1.573	.704
forb41	.418	.241
forb42	2.093	.792

Extraction Method: Principal Component Analysis.

[a] 1 components extracted.

Component Score Coefficient Matrix[a]		(4)

	Component
	1
forb35	.273
forb36r	.240
forb37	.114
forb38	.102
forb39	.170
forb40	.163
forb41	.034
forb42	.257

Extraction Method: Principal Component Analysis.

[a] Coefficients are standardized.

associated with it p eigenvalues. An eigenvalue is a function of the matrix. It is a mathematical concept, which just in this case is interpreted as the variance of a principal component.

The first component extracts 51% of the variance, which is more than the 40% often recommended as a rule-of-thumb. Also the following components extract about the same amount of variance. So, the first two of the three conditions mentioned above are fulfilled. What about the third?

3. Next are the so-called component loadings, the covariances and correlations between the original variables and the component scores—compare this part of the output with Figure 3.5. We see that the loading of forb41 is extremely small and therefore measures a different concept, and the loadings forb37 and forb38 are also smaller than the rest.

4. We could therefore expect forb41 to have a very small influence on the component score. Looking at the component score coefficients—or weights—our expectation is confirmed. This item should be left out, as should forb37 and forb38. Running another component analysis after having left out these three items results in the output in Table 3.3.

The first component now extracts 66% of the variance (not shown). All rescaled loadings are above the often-recommended minimum value of 0.40, and the scale would now be considered one-dimensional according to that rule. We also see that the component score coefficients are roughly located in the interval 0.20–0.30, and all three conditions are fulfilled.

This is the same result we obtained in Example 2.1, based on traditional item analysis. From this, it is tempting to conclude that Cronbach's alpha is a measure of uni-dimensionality, but this is not the case: Rather, *uni-dimensionality is a precondition for alpha.*

Uni-dimensionality means that correlations among items assumed to measure the same concept are only due to that concept, i.e. controlling for the effect of the concept, there should be no excess correlation among the items.

Table 3.3 Example 3: Component analysis, second run

Component Matrix[a]

	Raw Component	Rescaled Component
	1	1
forb35	2.264	.850
forb36r	2.088	.851
forb39	1.723	.799
forb40	1.560	.698
forb42	2.182	.825

Extraction Method: Principal Component Analysis.

[a] 1 components extracted.

Component Score Coefficient Matrix[a]

	Component
	1
forb35	.307
forb36r	.261
forb39	.189
forb40	.177
forb42	.294

Extraction Method: Principal Component Analysis.

[a] Coefficients are standardized.

Example 4

In the same study, measurement of the respondents 'involvement' in procuring and serving fish was also required. The items used in a Likert scale are shown in Table 3.4 and the data can be found on the book's website.

Mean and standard deviations are—after reversing items 5–8, 10 and 21—shown in Table 3.5. If we require the standard deviation to be at least 1.5 and the mean to be in the interval 2.5–5.5, the following items are candidates for exclusion: 4, 5r, 16, 20 and 21.

Table 3.4 Example 4: Extract from the questionnaire

1. Fish is something I can talk about at length:	❏
2. I know so much about fish that I am able to evaluate the suitability of various types of fish for various dishes and various occasions:	❏
3. Fish is a product that interests me:	❏
4. I prefer some kinds of fish to others:	❏
5. Fish is a product or food product category which I don't believe that I have any use for:	❏
6. On the whole I don't know anything about fish:	❏
7. When I buy fish I usually buy the same kind every time:	❏
8. If I have decided to buy a certain type of fish, it is very possible that I change my mind if I have to go out of my way to get it:	❏
9. If somebody told me that the type of fish I have decided to buy was full of bones or maybe difficult to cook, I would stick to my decision no matter what:	❏
10. If I cannot get my favourite kind of fish where I usually shop, I don't mind buying another kind:	❏
11. Eating and serving fish add to the picture of me that I find ideal:	❏
12. Eating fish helps me live the life I strive for:	❏
13. There are many occasions and experiences in my life that I some way or another can connect to fish or eating fish:	❏
14. Fish is clearly something that I like:	❏
15. When I look at (fresh) fish or dishes made from (fresh) fish, there is a whole bunch of properties that I match them against:	❏
16. Eating fish is to a high degree something I do to express my 'ego':	❏
17. Personally it is of great importance to me to eat fish:	❏
18. On the basis of my personal values, I feel that I must eat fish:	❏
19. Eating and serving fish helps me to express a way of life that I want:	❏
20. On the basis of what other people think, I feel that fish and eating fish is something I ought to be interested in:	❏
21. There is not much difference in the various types of fish that can be bought:	❏

Table 3.5 Example 4: average and standard deviation for the 21 items

	Mean	Std. deviation
involv1	4.45	2.06
involv2	4.18	2.26
involv3	3.85	2.13
involv4	1.45	.99
involv5r	1.44	1.22
involv6r	2.34	1.86
involv7r	4.75	2.22
involv8	3.70	2.50
involv9	4.03	2.50
involv10	2.84	2.14
involv11	5.40	1.97
involv12	4.67	2.25
involv13	4.25	2.39
involv14	2.22	1.86
involv15	3.69	2.20
involv16	6.02	1.46
involv17	4.10	2.08
involv18	3.61	2.17
involv19	4.89	2.31
involv20	5.68	1.82
involv21	6.34	1.36

Items having extreme means should be reformulated in order to bring the mean towards the middle of the scale; this will usually also increase the variance.

Cronbach's alpha is 0.81 and successive removal of items 10r, 8r, 20, 21r, 9, 4, 18, 7r and 5r brings alpha up to 0.89, which by any standard is considered *very* satisfactory. Inter-item correlations and item-rest correlations are shown in Table 3.6. All inter-item correlations are positive (as they should be), and the smallest item-rest correlation is 0.49, so they too are satisfactory according to common norms.

It is, however, possible to find clusters of items with satisfying intra-cluster correlations but with very small correlations to other clusters. For example, items 1, 2 and 3 seem to form a cluster, which is only very weakly linked to another cluster consisting of items 11, 12, 17 and 19. So, perhaps these two parts of the scale measure two different latent variables—and maybe there are more than two?

If so, the scale is not uni-dimensional despite the very satisfying alpha and, perhaps, it would be a good idea to perform a principal component analysis in order to find out whether the items really make up a uni-dimensional scale, and if not, how many dimensions it contains?

Now, as uni-dimensionality is a precondition for calculation of Cronbach's alpha, it is perhaps safest to run the component analysis on all the variables, and not on the ones left *after* the item analysis—although in my experience this will usually (but not always!) give the same result.

Table 3.6 Example 4: Inter-item- and item-rest-correlations after traditional item analysis

	1	2	3	6r	11	12	13	14	15	16	17	19
involv1	1.00											
involv2	.65	1.00										
involv3	.77	.69	1.00									
involv 6r	.47	.56	.56	1.00								
involv 11	.37	.29	.40	.33	1.00							
involv 12	.43	.35	.44	.34	.61	1.00						
involv 13	.44	.42	.42	.25	.36	.34	1.00					
involv 14	.49	.45	.59	.43	.37	.46	.26	1.00				
involv 15	.51	.61	.57	.49	.21	.27	.44	.45	1.00			
involv 16	.32	.19	.31	.26	.58	.59	.33	.33	.24	1.00		
involv 17	.35	.40	.44	.34	.31	.49	.26	.56	.27	.37	1.00	
involv 19	.26	.21	.23	.26	.53	.47	.29	.36	.13	.59	.45	1.00
Item-rest	.69	.66	.74	.57	.58	.63	.51	.64	.56	.55	.56	.49

As in the last example, you choose Analyze/Data Reduction/Factor and select the variables. In the Extraction Window you choose to base your analysis on the covariance matrix, check the 'scree plot' box and leave everything else at the default values, because, at present, you are only interested in finding out how many dimensions are present in your data. Then you click 'Continue', return to the dialog box in Figure 3.8b, and click 'OK.'

In Figure 3.9 you see the scree plot, which indicates the existence of three dimensions.

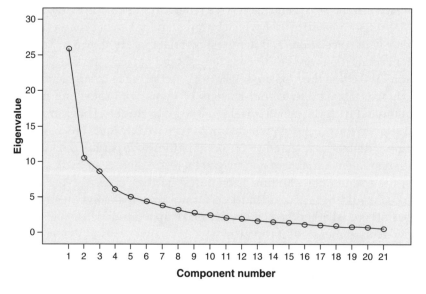

Figure 3.9 Example 4: Principal component analysis, 1st run: Elbow plot (SPSS)

So, let us try a three-component solution:

You start all over again, and when the dialog box shown in Figure 3.8c pops up you choose to extract 3 factors, click 'Continue' and when you return to the dialog box in Figure 3.8b, you click 'Rotation'. In the dialog box in Figure 3.10a you check 'Varimax' (the default method) and 'Display rotated solution', and click 'Continue'.

When you again return to the box in Figure 3.8b, you open the dialog box in Figure 3.10b by clicking 'Options'. You check 'Sorted by size' and choose to 'Suppress absolute values less than .40'. Then you click 'Continue,' and, after returning to the Factor Analysis box, you click 'OK.'

The result of all your clicking is the output in Table 3.7, on which I shall briefly comment:

The first component extracts 29.968% of the variance, the second 12.194% and the third 9.906%. Taken together the first three principal components account for 52.909% of the variance in the data.

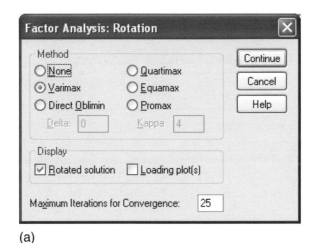

(a)

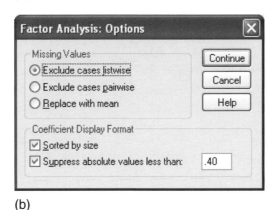

(b)

Figure 3.10 Example 4: Principal component analysis: Dialog boxes for second run

The rotated component matrix shows the relations between the various items and each of the three components in raw (covariances) and in rescaled (correlations) form.

The first component is an expression of personal knowledge, interests and behavior, while the second is some sort of life style dimension incorporating psychological and social elements such as consumption of fish as a signal to other people. The third component includes only two nearly identical items expressing the person's determination or the strength of his preferences.

As calculation of Cronbach's alpha across different dimensions is meaningless, it is customary to do an item analysis for each dimension. This is left to the reader as an exercise.

However, the reader is warned that exploratory techniques such as principal component analysis or exploratory factor analysis is not always the most efficient way to uncover the structure of a dataset. Confirmatory techniques will (as shown in Chapter 6) often do a better job.

Table 3.7   Example 4: Principal component analysis. Selected output from second run

Total Variance Explained

Component		Initial Eigenvalues[a]			Rotation Sums of Squared Loadings		
	Total	% of Variance	Cumulative %	Total	% of Variance	Cumulative %
Raw 1	25.911	29.968	29.968	20.221	23.388	23.388
2	10.543	12.194	42.162	15.071	17.431	40.819
3	8.568	9.909	52.071	9.729	11.252	52.071
4	6.130	7.091	59.162			
5	4.982	5.762	64.924			
6	4.413	5.104	70.028			
7	3.794	4.388	74.416			
8	3.191	3.691	78.107			
9	2.750	3.180	81.287			
10	2.459	2.844	84.131			
11	2.073	2.398	86.529			
12	1.935	2.238	88.767			
13	1.590	1.839	90.607			
14	1.515	1.752	92.359			
15	1.425	1.649	94.007			
16	1.139	1.318	95.325			
17	1.023	1.183	96.508			
18	.958	1.108	97.616			
19	.773	.894	98.510			
20	.731	.846	99.356			
21	.557	.644	100.000			

Extraction Method: Principal Component Analysis.

Table 3.7 Cont'd

Rotated Component Matrix(a)

	Raw Component			Rescaled Component		
	1	2	3	1	2	3
involv2	1.802			.799		
involv3	1.659			.781		
involv15	1.585			.719		
involv1	1.476			.716		
involv14	1.219			.655		
involv6r	1.100			.591		
involv7r	1.256			.565		
involv9	1.356			.542		
involv13	1.151			.481		
involv5r						
involv19		1.743			.755	
involv12		1.686			.750	
involv16		1.044			.714	
involv11		1.351			.686	
involv18		1.374			.634	
involv17		1.108			.532	
involv20		.941			.516	
involv21r						
involv8r			−2.153			−.864
involv10r			−1.503			−.703
involv4						

Extraction Method: Principal Component Analysis.

Rotation Method: Varimax with Kaiser Normalization.

[a]Rotation converged in 6 iterations.

3. Exploratory Factor Analysis

The principal components Y_i are linear functions of the manifest variables X_j, as expressed in equations (9), which in a more compact form can be written:

$$Y_i = \sum_{j=1}^{p} a_{ij}X_j \quad \text{for} \quad i = 1, 2, \ldots, p \tag{12}$$

This is an exact mathematical transformation with a one-to-one correspondence between X- and Y-variables. Principal component analysis is therefore *not* a statistical model, the parameters of which have to be estimated. Therefore, it is possible to isolate the X-variables on the left side of the equality sign, and consider them functions of the Y-variables:

$$X_j = \sum_{i=1}^{p} b_{ji}Y_i \quad \text{for} \quad j = 1, 2, \ldots, p \tag{13}$$

In this way the principal components are seen as latent variables, the values of which are mirrored in the manifest X-variables.

If there are theoretical reasons to assume that only $k < p$ Y-variables are 'significant,' we can write:

$$X_j = \sum_{i=1}^{k} \lambda_{ji} F_i + \lambda F_{spec} + \varepsilon_j \quad \text{for} \quad j = 1, 2, \ldots, p \tag{14}$$

This is the so-called *factor model*, where the 'significant' Y-variables are designated F_i. The 'non-significant' Y-variables are then either considered to express that an X-variable apart from measuring the *common factors* F_i also measures a *specific factor* F_{spec}—i.e. a factor which is measured only by the X-variable in question—or they express purely stochastic uncertainty or noise ε_j.

It is not possible to isolate the specific factor in cross-sectional data and it will therefore be included in the error-term. This means that the error term will not be purely stochastic, even if it is usually treated as such and attributed the assumptions:

$$E(\varepsilon_j) = 0$$
$$Cov(\varepsilon_j \varepsilon_l) = 0 \quad \text{for} \quad j \neq l \tag{15}$$
$$Cov(\varepsilon_j F_{ji}) = 0 \quad \text{for all} \quad i \text{ and } j$$

Contrary to (13), (14) is a hypothetical model, often based on theoretically founded *a priori* assumptions—e.g. regarding the number of common factors. Contrary to (13) it is also a *statistical* model, as it includes a stochastic error ε_j, and its parameters therefore need to be estimated.

Note that while we can go from (12) to (13) and vice versa, the same simple operation is not possible on (14) because of the stochastic term ε_j. Factor scores can therefore not be calculated in a simple way, but have to be estimated. Several estimation methods exist, but none of them are very satisfying. The reason is that the factor model contains more parameters than there are data points—a rare situation in statistics! As a consequence you can estimate an unlimited number of factor models (and factor scores), all having the same mathematical properties. This is the so-called 'factor indeterminacy problem'—see e.g. Thurstone (1947) or McDonald and Mulaik (1979).

The variance of X_j is

$$Var(X_j) = \sum_{i=1}^{k} \lambda_{ij}^2 Var(F_i) + \lambda_{spec}^2 Var(F_{spec}) + Var(\varepsilon) \tag{16}$$

Leaving out the specific factor, the exploratory factor model can be depicted as shown in Figure 3.11, where the principal component model is also shown for comparison.

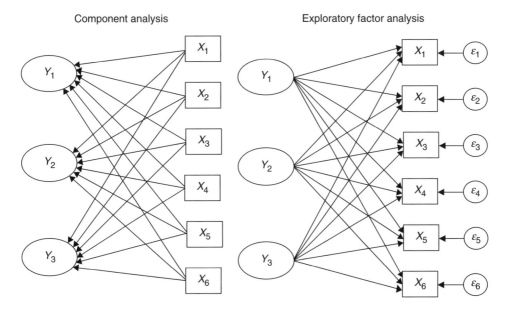

Figure 3.11 The exploratory factor analysis model

If you compare (14) to equation (2.22a) and (16) to (2.22c) it is obvious that the factor model is an extension of the traditional measurement model from Chapter 2 to the case of several factors.

It is also obvious that the exploratory factor model is more in accordance with the measurement models of SEM than the principal component model is. Indeed, it only differs from the ideal measurement model in that the various indicators are related to *all* the latent variables (factors) in the model—as in principal components analysis.

Therefore it would have been more 'correct' to use factor analysis instead of component analysis in the examples above. However, as mentioned in the introduction to this chapter, the two techniques will usually give nearly the same results (even if there is a tendency for factor analysis to extract fewer factors than component analysis), and component analysis is in many ways less complicated—e.g. there is no 'factor indeterminacy problem.'

The factor model resembles the traditional regression model but differs from this in that the independent variables (the F-variables) are not directly measurable. The word factor analysis covers a rather large number of different estimation and rotation techniques (and usually component analysis is included under the same hat). Consult Kim and Mueller (1978a, b) for a short introduction and Harman (1976) or Mulaik (1972) for a deeper treatment of the subject.

As the main purpose of factor analysis is to connect the X-variables to the common factors, it is clear that you cannot base the analysis on the variances of the variables, as stated in the main diagonal of the covariance matrix. These variances must be reduced by that part of the variance caused by the specific factor and the random error ε_j, so that only the common variances (the communalities) form the basis for the calculations.

Usually factor analysis is based on standardized variables, i.e. on the correlation matrix, and the treatment here will follow that tradition. Analogous reasoning can, however, be used if the analysis is based on the covariance matrix.

In most estimation methods the communalities are estimated first, so that they can be substituted for the 1s in the main diagonal of the correlation matrix. The estimation is usually done by an iterative process, using as starting values R^2 from a regression of the variable in question on all other variables.

Usually this process will initially result in a matrix in which the smallest eigenvalues are negative. This is not very fortunate, as the eigenvalues are the variances of the factors (cf. comments to Table 3.3). Therefore the correlations outside the diagonal have to be 'regulated' so as to secure non-negative eigenvalues. This is done 'automatically' by the computer program.

As mentioned several times, the name 'factor analysis' covers a suite of different algorithms varying in the ways communalities and factor structure are estimated.

The most popular technique today is, perhaps, *maximum likelihood estimation.*

The maximum likelihood principle is based on calculation of the *likelihood function*, which expresses the probability of obtaining the present data (covariance or correlation matrix) as a function of the parameters of the model. Then the parameters are estimated as the values of the parameters that maximize the likelihood function—in other words, parameters estimated by maximum likelihood are the values that have the largest probability of producing the covariance or correlation matrix on which the estimation is based. In maximum likelihood estimation, invented by Lawley (see e.g. Lawley and Maxwell (1971)) in the forties, communalities are not estimated at the beginning of the process, but are a product of the estimation of the number of factors.

The likelihood function can be deduced from the assumption that the common factors and the error terms are multivariate normally distributed. As maximum likelihood estimates—besides other nice properties, to be mentioned in the next chapter—are asymptotically normally distributed, it enables statistical testing to be carried out.

It is, however, only fair to mention that e.g. Morrison (1967) shows several examples of statistical testing in principal components analysis too.

As you will see exploratory factor analysis is a step from classical measurement theory towards the measurement model of SEM, both with regard to introducing several common factors and with regard to estimation, as maximum likelihood estimation is also the preferred estimation method in SEM analysis.

Component Analysis or Factor Analysis?

Which should then be the preferred technique: component analysis or factor analysis?

The two techniques have had their followers, and it is not too much to say that at times the arguments between the two groups have developed into 'wars' (Velicer and Jackson, 1990). However, a simple answer to the question can be found in the structure of the covariance matrix on which the analysis is based. In principal component analysis, the main diagonal constitutes of variances and the components are extracted in decreasing order of variance. In factor analysis, the diagonal elements are the communalities, i.e. that part of each variable's variance that is shared with the common factors (and in that way with all other variables), and the factors are extracted in decreasing order of co-variation with the other variables.

Therefore the answer is:

If you are interested in summarizing a number of correlating variables in a few new variables with the smallest possible loss of information, then component analysis is the answer.

If you are interested in explaining the correlations in a data set as a result of a few underlying factors, then factor analysis is the answer.

In most situations component analysis and factor analysis will give nearly identical solutions, although factor analysis has a (very!) weak tendency to find a solution in fewer dimensions than component analysis. If you want to calculate scores, I would definitely recommend component analysis because of the unsatisfactory estimation methods offered by factor analysis.

☞ In this chapter you have met the following concepts:

(principal component) analysis	Kaiser criterion
principal component	elbow plot
component scores, component score	rotation
coefficients component loading	exploratory factor analysis
	maximum likelihood estimation

Questions

1. Explain the purpose and the principles of principal component analysis.
2. Define the following: principal component, component score, component score coefficient, component loading and communality.
3. What is the role of eigenvalues in component analysis?
4. What is rotation?
5. How do you use a component analysis as item analysis?
6. What are the main differences between component analysis and (exploratory) factor analysis?

Reference List

Anderson, T. W. (1984) *Introduction to Multivariate Statistical Analysis*, 2nd edn, New York: Wiley.

Harman, H. (1976) *Modern Factor Analysis*, 3rd edn, Chicago: University of Chicago Press.

Kim, J.-O. and C. W. Mueller (1978a) *Introduction to Factor Analysis: What it is and how to do it*, Beverly Hills, Calif.

Kim, J.-O. and C. W. Mueller (1978b) *Factor Analysis: Statistical Methods and Practical Issues*, Beverly Hills, Calif.: Sage.

Lawley, D. N. and A. E. Maxwell (1971) *Factor Analysis as a Statistical Method*, 2nd edn, American Elsevier: Butterworths.

McDonald, R. and S. A. Mulaik (1979) 'Determinacy of common factors: a nontechnical review,' *Psychological Bulletin*, 86: 297–306.

Morrison, D. F. (1967) *Multivariate Statistical Methods*, New York: McGraw-Hill.

Mulaik, S. A. (1972) *The Foundations of Factor Analysis*, N.Y.: McGraw-Hill.

Norušis, M. J. (2005) *SPSS 14.00 Statistical Procedures Companion*, Upper Saddle River NJ: Prentice Hall.

Thurstone, L.L. (1947) *Multiple Factor Analysis*, Chicago, IL: University of Chicago Press.

Velicer, W. F. and D. N. Jackson (1990) 'Component analysis versus common factor analysis: some issues in selecting an appropriate procedure,' *Multivariate Behavioural Research*, 25: 1–28.

Section II

Modelling Reality

4

SEM-Analysis and AMOS

In this chapter you are led through the various steps of SEM analysis. On your way you will meet several problems that are connected with SEM analysis.

Among the questions the analyst has to answer are: Are there enough data to estimate the models? Which estimation method should be used? How do I get the computer to do what I want it to do? How shall I react to error messages? How do I interpret the computer output?

As a soft introduction to AMOS, a traditional multiple regression model is programmed and the output is shown and commented upon.

All through the chapter a number of concepts, which will be used during the remaining pages of the book, will be introduced and defined.

1. How Do You Proceed?

A SEM-analysis is usually done by going through the following steps:

1. Statement of research questions.
2. Formulation of a SEM-model, which (hopefully!) will answer the research questions.
3. Examination of whether the model can be estimated—the so-called identification problem, which was briefly mentioned in connection with the model in Figure 1.5c.
4. If necessary, a reformulation of the model in order to make it estimable.
5. Data collection and estimation of the model.
6. Examination of computer output.
7. If necessary, modification of the model based on interpretation of computer output.
8. Provisional acceptance of the model.

9. Test of the model on new data.
10. Acceptance or rejection of the model.

The first two points above are problem-specific and are therefore treated in connection with various examples later on. The rest are taken up in this chapter.

Even if it is difficult to say much on model specification without reference to a specific problem, a warning is in place.

Always remember that SEM is not all about statistics and technicalities. When starting up a new project, learn as much as possible from published theory and earlier research on the subject. If you start modelling too early, there is a great risk that you will end up with a misspecified model that would (at the very least!) bias the estimates of the parameters.

Read Example 1.3 once more—and think about it!

2.   Identification

In connection with Bass's model (Figure 1.5c) in Section 1.2, the identification problem was briefly touched upon and formulated: Is there enough data to estimate the parameters in the model?

Intuitively, the data should contain at least as many data points as there are parameters to estimate. A simple analogy will illustrate the idea.

Let β_1 and β_2 in the equation

$$\beta_1 + \beta_2 = 10 \tag{1}$$

be two parameters and let the number '10' be the collected data. It is clear that there is not enough data for estimation. The equation has an unlimited number of solutions for β_1 and β_2, and the model is *under-identified*. If we add another equation to get

$$\beta_1 + \beta_2 = 10$$
$$\beta_1 - \beta_2 = 2 \tag{2}$$

the two equations have one and only one solution:

$$\beta_1 = 6$$
$$\beta_2 = 4 \tag{3}$$

and the model is *just-identified*. However, this model will agree with any dataset— implying that it cannot be tested. If we add the equation

$$\beta_1 \times \beta_2 = c \tag{4}$$

we have 'one piece of information' left over for testing of the model, which is now *over-identified*. If $c = 24$, the data is in agreement with the model, but if c is 'very' different from 24, the model is not supported by the data and must be rejected.

The number of surplus 'pieces of information' is called the *degrees of freedom* for the model. If the degrees of freedom are positive the model can be estimated and tested, and the more degrees of freedom the more precise the estimation and the more powerful the tests.

As—in most cases—the only data needed as input is the sample covariance matrix, a model is identified if there are at least as many non-redundant elements in the covariance matrix as there are parameters to be estimated.

The so-called *t-rule*: that the number of 'pieces of information' shall be at least as large as the number of parameters to be estimated for the estimation to be possible, is, however, a necessary but *not* a sufficient condition. As was demonstrated in Section 1.5 a postulated model implies a special form of the covariance matrix, as the elements of this matrix are functions of the parameters of the model. This should make it possible to estimate the parameters from the covariance matrix, but, even if the number of equations is at least as large as the number of unknown, a system of equations can still have more than one solution.

In principle, it is possible to determine whether a model is identified or not by examining the structure of the implied covariance matrix and finding out whether the resultant system of equations has more than one solution for each and every parameter. This can be a very complicated process, and a general necessary and sufficient condition for identification would be very useful.

Such a condition does not exist. What we have is a series of conditions for special model types, but these are all either necessary or sufficient—but not both.

Two conditions must, however, always be satisfied for a model to be identified:

1. The *t*-rule must be met.
2. All latent variables must have assigned a scale. This is also true for the error terms (ε or δ). You cannot simultaneously estimate the coefficient and the variance of an error term. Usually (as in ordinary linear regression analysis) the coefficient is fixed at 1.00 and the variance is estimated. By fixing the coefficient at 1.00, the error term is measured in the same units as the dependent variable.

Remember: A model's parameters are regression coefficients—or *regression weights* as they are called in AMOS—and variances and covariances of the exogenous variables. An *exogenous variable* is a variable that does not appear as a dependent variable anywhere in the model. All other variables are called *endogenous variables*. Variances and covariances of endogenous variables are not parameters of the model, but consequences of the model.

What to Do if a Model Is Not Identified?

If a model is not identified, it must be made identified by increasing the number of manifest variables or by reducing the number of parameters to be estimated.

Reduction in the number of parameters to be estimated is done by *fixing* one or more parameters. Parameters are either *free* or *fixed*. A free parameter is a parameter that is 'free' to take on any value, and such a parameter is to be estimated. A fixed parameter is a parameter, the value of which is restricted in some way. In AMOS a parameter can be restricted in three ways:

1. The parameter can be restricted *a priori* to take on a certain value.
2. Two or more parameters can be restricted to have the same unspecified value.
3. The parameter can be missing in the model, because such a parameter is restricted to having the value 0.

I strongly recommend examination of the model in order to find out whether it is identified prior to data collection. One reason for that is that you can often attain identification by introducing more manifest variables.

Consider the measurement model in Figure 4.1a.

After having fixed the coefficients of the error terms to 1.00, the assignment of a scale to the latent variable F remains. We have two possibilities: (1) We can fix one of the coefficients (λ_1 or λ_2) at 1.00 in which case F will have the same scale as the X-variable in question, or (2) we can fix the variance of the latent variable at some arbitrary value—usually 1.00. Whatever we do, we have four parameters to estimate:

$$
\begin{array}{ccccc}
\lambda_2 & & \lambda_1 & & \lambda_1 \\
Var(\varepsilon_1) & & Var(\varepsilon_1) & & \lambda_2 \\
Var(\varepsilon_2) & \text{or} & Var(\varepsilon_2) & \text{or} & Var(\varepsilon_1) \\
Var(F) & & Var(F) & & Var(\varepsilon_2)
\end{array}
$$

However, we have only three pieces of information: The variances of the two manifest variables and their covariance. Our model is under-identified.

Adding another indicator X_3 gives us one further coefficient λ_3 and one variance $Var(\varepsilon_3)$ to estimate, but adds three new 'pieces of information': the variance of the new indicator and its covariances with the two other indicators—see panel (b). The model is just-identified.

In panel c of the model, we have four indicators and consequently $(4 + 1)4/2 = 10$ 'pieces of information' on which to base our estimation of the 9 parameters:

$$
\begin{array}{lll}
\lambda_1 & Var(\varepsilon_1) & \phi_{12} \\
\lambda_2 & Var(\varepsilon_2) & \\
\lambda_3 & Var(\varepsilon_3) & \\
\lambda_4 & Var(\varepsilon_4) &
\end{array}
$$

assuming that the variances of the two latent variables are fixed. The model is over-identified with one degree of freedom.

However, suppose that ϕ_{12} is estimated to have a value near zero, then—because of rounding errors—you could end up in a situation similar to (a). This is an example of *empirical under-identification*. The problem is not with the model, but with the data, and is therefore more difficult to foresee. The lesson learned is: Always have at least four indicators per latent variable in order to obtain an over-identified

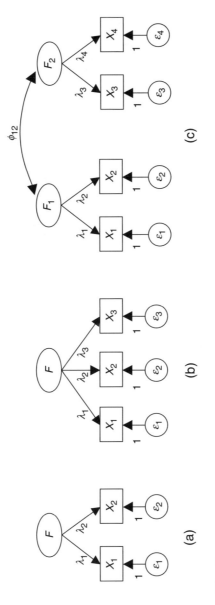

Figure 4.1 Identification

measurement model, and avoid estimation problems—and do not under-estimate the problems with formulating good items. It is not unusual for half of them not to pass item analysis!

Due to lack of a general necessary and sufficient condition for identification of SEM models, you often have to fall back on empirical methods, i.e. try to estimate a proposed model, and await AMOS' error messages.

You could say that this is a little too late to find out that a model is under-identified, but it is not impossible to use this method prior to data collection!

Just sketch your model, and construct one or more covariance matrices that are comparable with your model, run the model in AMOS and await AMOS' answer. If the model seems to be identified, run the analysis again with the implied covariance matrix as input. In your first run you place the statement

```
Sem.ImpliedMoments
```

in the AMOS program (more on programming in AMOS in Section 4 below).

In order to improve your safety, you could run the analyzes several times with different *start values* (the values that the computer takes as initial 'guestimates' of parameter values and steadily improve until the final solution—more about this below) and check that you obtain the same parameter estimates.

The identification problem is a consequence of the formulation of the model. However, sometimes the computer will tell you that the model is not identified even if all sufficient conditions for identification are fulfilled. This could happen if computing problems arise: Because of rounding errors you could end up in calculations that are not defined, such as dividing by zero or taking the logarithm of zero. This is called *empirical under-identification*.

3. Estimation

In Section 1.5, I wrote that the model is estimated in such a way that the difference between the empirical covariance matrix and the covariance matrix implied by the model is minimized. It is more correct to say that you minimize a function of that difference:

$$F = f(\mathbf{S} - \mathbf{\Sigma}(\mathbf{\theta})) \tag{5}$$

where $\mathbf{S}$ is the empirical covariance matrix and $\mathbf{\Sigma}(\mathbf{\theta})$ is the covariance matrix implied by a model with the parameters $\mathbf{\theta}$.

The fit-function F can have many forms, as each estimation method has its own special F-function. At present (version 16) AMOS offers the following estimation methods:

1. Maximum likelihood (ML)
2. Unweighted least squares (ULS)

3. Generalized least squares (GLS)
4. Scale free least squares (SLS)
5. Asymptotically distribution-free estimation (ADF)

All five estimation methods are so-called *full-information methods*; i.e. they estimate the parameters of the whole system in one go using all available data, while *limited-information methods* estimate one equation at a time. While full-information methods are generally more effective, they have two drawbacks:

1. It can sometimes give difficulties in solving estimation problems, because specification problems in one corner of the model can have its roots in another corner of the model.
2. It is not possible to introduce non-identified relations in the model solely to obtain identification of other relations. The whole model must be identified for the estimation to work.

I shall say a few words about the various estimation methods. A deeper treatment can be found in the literature listed at the end of the chapter.

Maximum Likelihood

As mentioned in Section 3.3 maximum likelihood estimation is the preferred estimation method in SEM. Parameters are estimated as the values that have the largest probability of producing the sample covariance matrix **S**.

The likelihood function can be deduced from an assumption of multivariate normality of the manifest variables (it can, however, also be deduced under less demanding assumptions (Browne, 1982; Bollen, 1989)).

ML-estimation has a number of favorable qualities: ML-estimation is consistent, i.e. the estimates $\hat{\theta}$ approach the parameter values θ asymptotically by increasing n. The ML-estimator is furthermore asymptotically unbiased, asymptotically sufficient and asymptotically normally distributed. Also, $C = (n - 1) F_{ML}$—where n is the sample size—is asymptotically distributed as χ^2 (Chi-square, see Appendix A) with $p(p + 1)/2 - t$ degrees of freedom, where p the number of manifest variables and t the number of free parameters. This makes it possible to test the model against the data.

Note that all these are asymptotic qualities, and therefore cannot be guaranteed to hold in small samples.

Finding the parameter values that maximize the likelihood function is too complicated to be done in an exact way. Instead the maximum is located by an iterative procedure, whereby the computer makes an initial 'guess' on the values of the parameters and then improves this initial guess step by step.

In a way you could compare this process with the process of locating the top of a hill by the feeling in your feet, when you are blindfolded.

From this picture it is obvious that the iterative process is not always successful in finding 'the top of the hill': A curling landscape could have more than one hilltop, and perhaps the procedure does not find the highest one—or it does not find any top at all.

Unweighted Least Squares

ULS is analogous to ordinary least squares (OLS) in traditional regression: OLS minimizes the sum of squared errors and ULS minimizes the sum of squared values in the residual matrix. Like OLS, ULS does not make any distributional assumptions, and ULS is consistent (and so are all the estimation methods listed above), but it is not asymptotically most efficient.

As you cannot be sure that $C = (n - 1)F_{ULS}$ is not even asymptotically distributed as χ^2, the output in AMOS does not contain χ^2-test and other test statistics or measures of fit based on such statistics. For the same reason neither standard deviations nor test statistics for the various parameters are reported. Browne (1982) shows some possibilities for making various tests if ULS-estimation has been used, but these are not at present implemented in AMOS.

ULS also uses an iterative procedure (as do all estimation methods in AMOS).

Generalized Least Squares

Just as ULS is analogous to OLS, GLS is analogous to weighted least squares (WLS) in traditional regression.

OLS gives equal weight to all observations in calculating the regression coefficients. This will result in inefficient estimates if all observations do not have about the same error variance. The solution to this problem is WLS, where each observation is given a weight proportional to the reciprocal of the error variance $Var(\varepsilon_i)$. In much the same way GLS weights all elements in the residual matrix taking variances and covariances of the elements into consideration.

GLS has the same asymptotic qualities as ML, and consequently the same tests can be performed. It is worth noting that GLS can be derived under less restrictive assumptions than ML.

Scale Free Least Squares

You could say that SLS is ULS based on the correlation matrix (and not the covariance matrix), and the two algorithms will therefore give identical results if the correlation matrix is used for ULS estimation.

If used on the covariance matrix SLS is scale-invariant while ULS is not, i.e. if using ULS, linear transformations of scale for manifest variables will result in solutions that are not directly comparable.

I cannot think of any situation where SLS would be the natural choice.

Asymptotically Distribution-Free Estimation

The heading seems promising as such an estimation method should make it possible to avoid building analysis and conclusions on doubtful assumptions.

Asymptotically distribution-free (ADF) estimation requires that the manifest variables have an eight-moment matrix, and it requires a sample size measured in thousands. Bootstrapping (treated in Chapter 9) could be a solution to the problem of ill-behaved distributions if the sample is too small to allow for ADF.

A Few Remarks on Discrete (Ordinal) Variables

When ADF makes such large demands on the sample size, how do we then treat discrete (ordinal) data from the very popular 5- or 7-point scales?

A special problem with ordinal scales is that the usual covariances cannot be used, and therefore special measures of co-variation must be calculated. These methods are not at present implemented in AMOS, and besides, they all assume that the ordinal measurements cover underlying variables that fulfill the assumption of multivariate normality—a rather strong assumption.

Alternatively you can treat the ordinal variables as if they were normally distributed interval scaled variables. This will be most realistic if:

1. The variables can take on 'many' values,
2. The variables are 'nearly normal,' i.e. symmetric with kurtosis (see Appendix A) near 0, and
3. A possible (limited) skewness goes to the same side for all variables.

If a scale has at least 5 possible values, the first condition can usually be taken as fulfilled.

I your scale is shorter, you can use *parceling*: Let a test consist of five Yes/No questions. If you let 'No' count as '0' and 'Yes' as '1' summating the scores will give you a scale ranging from zero to five. See e.g. Bandaleros and Finney (2001).

It deserves mentioning that the present version of AMOS (AMOS 16) offers some special methods for handling ordinal data. These methods can, however, only be approached through the graphic interface and is therefore outside the scope of this book.

4. Programming in AMOS

AMOS has one of the user-friendliest interfaces for this type of computer program. As in a few other programs the analysis can be done in two different ways:

1. You can write your program (in Visual Basic or C+).
2. You can sketch the model in a user-friendly drawing environment, where most of the drawing is done in a few mouse-clicks. AMOS then translates the drawing to a written program and performs the necessary calculations.

If you are a beginner (or have formula-phobia), you will probably prefer the graphic interface. However, I have chosen here to use the programming interface (and Visual Basic) for three reasons:

1. The exact model formulation stands out more precisely—and with less use of space—in a program, so that alterations in the model during the analysis are easier to follow, and necessitate less explanation than would be the case with drawings.
2. Drawing the program could be problematic with complicated models, because the drawing easily becomes messy.
3. The programming is so simple that there is no reason for not using it.

All programs in this book are written in Visual Basic (VB). I will, however, show a single example of graphic programming in Appendix B.

A simple example will introduce you to AMOS programming:

Example 1

Bredahl (2001) uses SEM in a cross-national study of factors influencing consumers' attitudes and buying intentions towards genetically modified food products.

I will use part of Bredahl's German data to illustrate programming and estimation of a simple regression model. It must be emphasized, however, that this is not the way Bredahl analyzed her data.

The model is shown in Figure 4.2 exactly as it would look if the graphic interface were used for programming. The two-headed arrows indicate (possible) co-linearity among the independent variables. As the reader can imagine, more

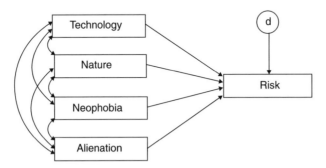

Variable name	Description	Measurement
Risk	Perceived risk by using gm food	Six-item summated scale
Technology	Attitude to genetic modification in food production	Five-item summated scale
Nature	Attitude to nature	Six-item summated scale
Neophobia	Food neophobia	Five-item summated scale
Alienation	Alienation to the market place	Nine-item summated scale

Figure 4.2   Example 1: Model

complicated models will give rise to a large number of such two-headed arrows, which will contribute to the messiness of the drawing.

When you open the program editor, it looks like Figure 4.3a, and you write your program in place of the comment: 'Your code goes here.' Observe that the comment begins with a single opening quote. This forces AMOS to skip that line and not consider it as part of the program. You can therefore use single quotes to place comments in your programs, and you are advised to do so in order to keep track of various versions of the programs in your project. Figure 4.3b shows a visual basic (VB) program for estimation of the model.

The program statement 'Sem.Dispose' releases resources used by the Sem object and the 'Try/Finally/End Try' secures that the 'Sem.Dispose' statement will be executed even if the program runs into trouble.

In a way you could say that the program is placed between 'Try' and 'Finally.'

The first line is a title, which will be printed in the output, and it is followed by a comment.

The next line tells AMOS to find the data in the sheet 'Manifest' in the Excel file 'Bredahl.xls.' AMOS reads data from text files, and from various other formats such as Excel, SPSS, dBase, FoxPro, Lotus 1-2-3, and Access.

The line Sem.TextOutput forces AMOS to show the resulting output in a window on the screen after calculations. Otherwise the calculations will be executed and saved to a temporary file but *not* shown on the screen.

We estimate the model by maximum likelihood (the default) and order the output to include standardized parameter values (Sem.Standardized) and the squared multiple correlation coefficient (Sem.Smc).

Then the model is described (Sem.AStructure). Note that every arrow in the program corresponds to an arrow in Figure 4.2, and thereby indicates that these regression coefficients—or *regression weights* as they are called in AMOS—will be estimated. However, these five structure lines can be replaced by

```
Sem.AStructure ("Risk = Technology + Nature
                      + Neophobia + Alienation + d")   (6)
```

saving a good deal of writing, especially in more complicated models involving several regression functions.

Then the statement 'Sem.FitModel' fits the model.

As you can see, the correlations among the exogenous variables are not specified in the program as such correlations are default in AMOS when you use the programming interface. However, in the graphic interface the correlations must be specified, because here 'what you see is what you get.'

Also note that no constant is specified. This does not mean that AMOS cannot estimate models with explicit constant terms—as we shall see in Chapter 8—but usually the constant is of less interest and can be omitted. Therefore the only input needed is the covariance matrix arranged as in Figure 4.4 (the means will not be used in this example). Remember the underline after 'rowtype' and 'varname,' otherwise AMOS will not read the file.

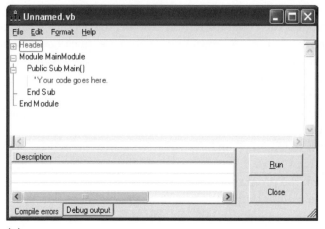

(a)

(b)

Figure 4.3   Example 1: (a) New program editor and (b) program for 1. Run

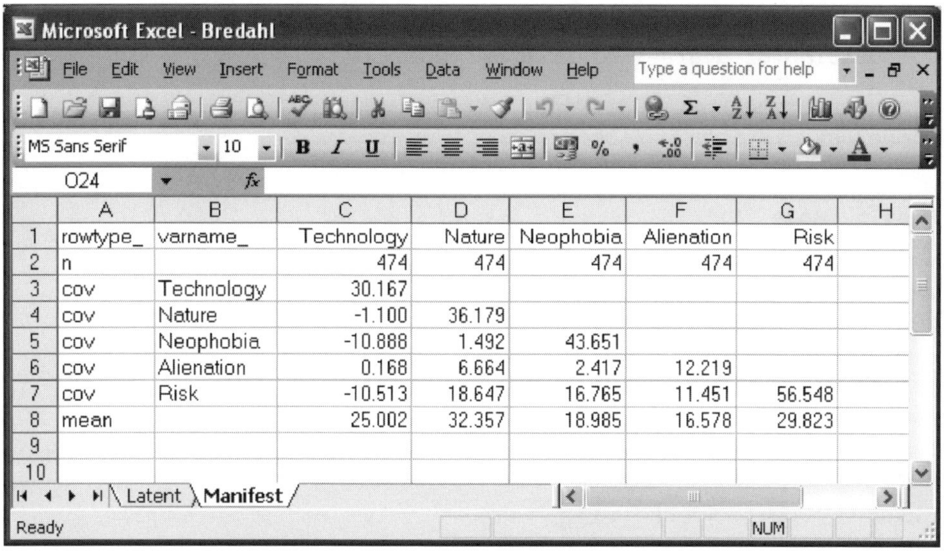

	A	B	C	D	E	F	G	H
1	rowtype_	varname_	Technology	Nature	Neophobia	Alienation	Risk	
2	n		474	474	474	474	474	
3	cov	Technology	30.167					
4	cov	Nature	-1.100	36.179				
5	cov	Neophobia	-10.888	1.492	43.651			
6	cov	Alienation	0.168	6.664	2.417	12.219		
7	cov	Risk	-10.513	18.647	16.765	11.451	56.548	
8	mean		25.002	32.357	18.985	16.578	29.823	
9								
10								

Figure 4.4 Example 1: Data

Unfortunately the estimation could not be done. Part of the output is shown in Table 4.1, from which you see that the regression weight and the variance of the error term are both unidentified. The reason is that we have forgotten to supply a scale to the latent variable d. Accordingly the last line in the program is replaced by

$$\text{Sem.AStructure ("Risk<--d"(1))} \qquad (7)$$

Or if you use the equation method in (6):

$$\text{Sem.AStructure ("Risk = Technology + Nature}$$
$$\text{+ Neophobia + Alienation + (1)d")}$$
$$(8)$$

and you have learned that in AMOS a parameter is fixed to have a certain value by writing that value in parentheses next to the variable.

This change results in the output in Table 4.2 on which I shall make a few comments:

1. First, information is given on time and date for the run and the (possible) name of the project.
2. Then the title is shown.
3. Next is the number of the group. In this case there is only one group of respondents—the German—while Bredahl, in her cross-national study, analyzes data from several groups (countries).
4. We are told that the model is recursive (roughly meaning that it has no 'loops' such as those in the model in Figure 1.5c) and that the sample size is 474.

Table 4.1   Example 1: Output 1. Run (extract)

Computation of degrees of freedom (Model 1)

```
        Number of distinct sample moments:     15
Number of distinct parameters to be estimated:  16
               Degrees of freedom (15-16):     -1
```

Result (Model 1)

The model is probably unidentified. In order to achieve
identifiability, it will probably be necessary to impose 1
additional constraint.

Scalar Estimates (Germany—Model 1)

The (probably) unidentified parameters are marked.

Regression Weights: (Germany—Model 1)

Risk	<---	Technology	
Risk	<---	Nature	
Risk	<---	Neophobia	
Risk	<---	Alienation	
Risk	<---	d	unidentified

Covariances: (Germany—Model 1)

Technology	<-->	Nature
Technology	<-->	Neophobia
Nature	<-->	Neophobia
Technology	<-->	Alienation
Nature	<-->	Alienation
Neophobia	<-->	Alienation

Variances: (Germany—Model 1)

Technology	
Nature	
Neophobia	
Alienation	
d	unidentified

5. Then comes a summary of variables and parameters. The variables are listed and classified as exogenous (pre-determined) and endogenous (post-determined). The parameters are classified as fixed (the regression weight of the error term) or labeled, i.e. provided with a name, which can be used when referred to. If AMOS needs labels for reference purposes, AMOS will itself label the parameters.

6. As it is possible to estimate several models in the same run, the model number is shown next—in this case only one model is estimated; consequently the model number is 1.

Table 4.2   Example 1: Output 2. Run

Analysis Summary	(1)

Date and Time

Date: Friday, February 17,2006
Time: 8:39:22 AM

Title	(2)

Example 4.1

Groups	(3)

Group number 1 (Group number 1)

Notes for Group (Group number 1)	(4)

The model is recursive.
Sample size = 474

Variable Summary (Germany)	(5)

Your model contains the following variables (Germany)

Observed, endogenous variables
Risk

Observed, exogenous variables
Technology
Nature
Neophobia
Alienation

Unobserved, exogenous variables
d

Variable counts (Germany)

Number of variables in your model:	6
Number of observed variables:	5
Number of unobserved variables:	1
Number of exogenous variables:	5
Number of endogenous variables:	1

Parameter summary (Germany)

	Weights	Covariances	Variances	Means	Intercepts	Total
Fixed	1	0	0	0	0	1
Labeled	0	0	0	0	0	0
Unlabeled	4	6	5	0	0	15
Total	5	6	5	0	0	16

(Continued)

Table 4.2 Cont'd

Models	(6)

Model 1 (Model 1)

Notes for Model (Model 1)

Computation of degrees of freedom (Model 1)	(7)

Number of distinct sample moments: 15
Number of distinct parameters to be estimated: 15
Degrees of freedom (15—15): 0

Result (Model 1)	(8)

Minimum was achieved
Chi-square = .000
Degrees of freedom = 0
Probability level cannot be computed

Germany (Germany—Model 1)

Estimates (Germany—Model 1)	(9)

Scalar Estimates (Germany—Model 1)

Maximum Likelihood Estimates

Regression Weights: (Germany—Model 1)

			Estimate	S.E.	C.R.	P	Label
Risk	<---	Technology	−.240	.052	−4.636	***	
Risk	<---	Nature	.371	.048	7.805	***	
Risk	<---	Neophobia	.274	.043	6.328	***	
Risk	<---	Alienation	.684	.082	8.324	***	

Standardized Regression Weights: (Germany—Model 1)

			Estimate
Risk	<---	Technology	−.175
Risk	<---	Nature	.297
Risk	<---	Neophobia	.240
Risk	<---	Alienation	.318

Covariances: (Germany—Model 1)

			Estimate	S.E.	C.R.	P	Label
Technology	<-->	Nature	−1.098	1.517	−.724	.469	
Technology	<-->	Neophobia	−10.865	1.738	−6.250	***	
Nature	<-->	Neophobia	1.488	1.825	.816	.415	
Technology	<-->	Alienation	.168	.881	.190	.849	
Nature	<-->	Alienation	6.650	1.012	6.571	***	
Neophobia	<-->	Alienation	2.411	1.065	2.263	.024	

Table 4.2 Cont'd

Correlations: (Germany–Model 1)

			Estimate
Technology	<-->	Nature	−.033
Technology	<-->	Neophobia	−.300
Nature	<-->	Neophobia	.038
Technology	<-->	Alienation	.009
Nature	<-->	Alienation	.317
Neophobia	<-->	Alienation	.105

Variances: (Germany–Model 1)

	Estimate	S.E.	C.R.	P	Label
Technology	30.103	1.957	15.379	***	
Nature	36.103	2.348	15.379	***	
Neophobia	43.559	2.832	15.379	***	
Alienation	12.193	.793	15.379	***	
d	34.615	2.251	15.379	***	

Squared Multiple Correlations: (Germany–Model 1)   (10)

	Estimate
Risk	.387

7. Then follows the degrees of freedom account: There are 15 variances and covariances in the input, and 15 parameters to estimate. So the model has 0 degrees of freedom. The model is just-identified and will fit any data set.
8. The χ^2-test cannot be carried out because no degrees of freedom are left over for testing.
9. Then follows the estimates of the parameters (as we have not specified an estimation algorithm AMOS uses maximum likelihood by default), their standard errors and *CriticalRatios* (C.R.). C.R. is the estimates divided by their standard errors. C.R. should be asymptotically standard normally distributed.

   The last column shows the P-values of a two-sided test of the various parameters. The null hypothesis is the usual one, that the parameter in question is 0. *** means that the P-value is less than it is possible to express in the number of decimal places chosen for the output—in this case less than 0.0001.
10. The coefficient of determination (multiple coefficient of correlation squared) follows.

We observe that even if all the regression weights are highly significant, the four independent variables taken together explain less than 40% of the variation in Risk.

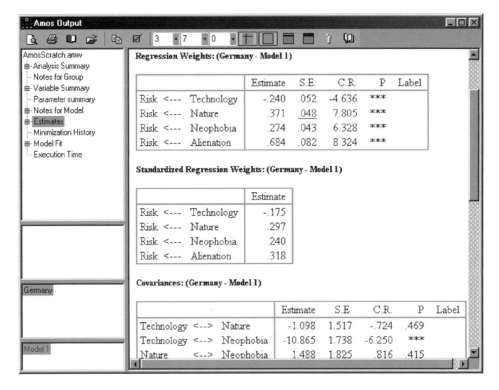

Figure 4.5 Example 1: Output from second run as seen on the screen

As will be shown in Chapter 7 this is partly due to the fact that the measurements are not fully reliable.

Table 4.3 shows the output as it appears after being copied from AMOS to a word processing program. On the screen the output appears as shown in Figure 4.5.

5. Examining AMOS Output

Examination of AMOS output starts by looking for error-messages, to see whether AMOS has had troubles during the estimation process. Examples of such problems are:

1. Parameters that (probably) are not identified.
2. The program fails to converge.
3. Negative variance estimates.
4. Covariance matrices that are not positive definite.

Point 1 was treated in Section 2 above; the other points on the list will have a few comments in the following.

Convergence Problems

If the program fails to converge, the cause most often is that the sample is too small, or that the model is extremely miss-specified, so that correlations among indicators for different latent variables are larger than correlations among indicators for the same concept.

In both cases the cure is simple: Collect more data and/or reformulate the model.

Another cause for failing convergence could be that the variances of the manifest variables are too different in size—e.g. family's yearly income in dollars and family size. In this case the solution is just as simple: change the measurement scale from dollars to 1,000 dollars or 10,000 dollars or whatever is necessary to obtain nearly comparable variances for the variables.

Extreme non-normal data can also give convergence problems.

Computer programs such as AMOS are generally very good in finding start values for the iterations, but if bad start values should be the problem, you can supply your own start values for some or all the parameters yourself. In AMOS you just label the parameter in question followed by a colon and the wanted start value—e.g. to label the variable 'nature' with the letter 'b' and specify the start value 0.5 in equation (8), you write:

```
SEM.AStructure ("Risk = Technology + (b:0.5) Nature
                    + Neophobia + Alienation + (1)d")
```

Convergence problems could also arise as a consequence of the sample covariance matrix not being positive definite, a subject that is dealt with below.

Negative Variances

Negative variances are of course impossible. Most often, it is the estimated variances of error terms (ε and δ) that are negative. The reason could be a sample that is too small. Often the reason is that existing correlations among some of the indicators for the same latent variables have not been taken care of. Such correlations will emerge in situations where there have been problems in formulating items that are sufficiently different—but never-the-less different enough to measure the same concept.

Reformulating the model by introducing the relevant correlations can solve the problem. The perfectionist will look at such a correlation as a blemish, as the ideal is that the only cause for correlation among the items is the latent variable itself. If two correlating indicators are very similar, you could omit one of them.

If a negative variance is numerically small, you could fix it to have a small positive value.

Correlating ε or δ across latent variables in models based on cross-sectional data are difficult to defend, and should be avoided by reformulation of the model (c.f. Example 6.2).

Covariance Matrices That Are Not Positive Definite

Every symmetric $p \times p$ matrix—and that includes covariance and correlation matrices—has associated with it p *eigenvalues* (some of which could be identical). If the eigenvalues are all positive, the matrix is said to be *positive definite* (if they all negative, it is *negative definite*).

In component analysis (Chapter 3) we met a special interpretation of the eigenvalues of the covariance or correlation matrix; namely as variances of the principal components. As a variance cannot be negative, covariance and correlation matrices cannot be negative definite.

But can they have one or more eigenvalues being zero (in which case the matrix is described as being *positive semidefinite*)? Yes, that is possible. It means that the data can be fully described in fewer than p dimensions. However, certain calculations, which could occur in the fit function, are not defined for semidefinite matrices (e.g. because they lead to division by zero).

From equation (5) we see that the fit function F contains two covariance matrices S and $\Sigma(\theta)$ to which we can add a third matrix, namely a weight matrix W used, e.g. in ADF estimation. As W shall also be positive definite, all three matrices could cause problems for the estimation process, and cause the error message.

If it is S that is not positive definite, then either you have used pairwise deletion (see Chapter 9), or one or more of the of the variables is a linear function of one or more of the other.

If you cannot 'repair' the input and a positive semidefinite S makes sense in the situation, I recommend using ULS, as ML estimation then requires the calculation of the logarithm of 0 and and GLS requires division by zero—and as you know both these operations are undefined.

In this connection I must point out that, because of rounding errors, strong colinearity among manifest variables will lead to the same problems as if this matrix was semidefinite. Be prepared, therefore, to face problems if you have correlations larger than 0.80 among the manifest variables. However, there could also be more subtle colinearities involving more than two variables at a time. A simple way to get indications of such multivariate colinearities is to calculate the multiple correlation coefficient for each variable when regressing it on the remaining variables. Large correlations signal colinearity problems—but say nothing about their nature. To detect such colinearities can be a challenging job. SPSS and other statistics packages have advanced output to assist you in such efforts. A simple explanation of the methods as implemented in SYSTAT (and SPSS!) can be found in Wilkinson et al. (1996).

What if it is the estimate $\hat{\Sigma}(\theta)$ that is not positive definite? It could be that the first guess on $\Sigma(\theta)$ is not positive definite. If this happens, AMOS will, in most instances, iterate to a positive definite $\hat{\Sigma}(\theta)$ in a few steps. If this does not happen, there is a risk that the process will not find the global maximum of the fit function. As you can imagine, most often problems with $\hat{\Sigma}(\theta)$ can be traced back to problems with S—after all the whole idea is to minimize the discrepancy between the two matrices. Another reason could be that your model is 'very wrong,' and in that case you have to re-specify your model.

If the problem arises with a matrix that emerges as a result of the calculations, i.e. covariance matrices of ε or δ, it can often be traced back to variances being estimated as negative (see above). Sometimes, however, a positive semidefinite covariance matrix is a natural consequence of the model. In such a case you can of course neglect the warning.

Last, but not least, it should be pointed out that any of the three matrices could cause problems if the sample is too small.

Outliers and Non-Normality

Many of the problems mentioned above can be traced back to the causes making out the heading—and even if they do not result in error messages, estimates and the validity of the tests can—depending on the estimation method—be severely influenced by outliers and by data not being multivariate normal. Therefore, it is recommendable to examine the raw data very carefully before any calculation is done.

Outliers are observations, which take on values that are very different from the main part of the data. As long as we consider each variable separately, it is not too difficult to locate outliers. A simple way to do so is to standardize all variables and then examine observations with one or more variables having values numerically larger than e.g. 4.00. But, when we look at two variables, we already encounter problems.

In Figure 4.6 the first two variables from Example 3.4. are depicted. A small amount of error is added to the values so that all observations can be seen, even

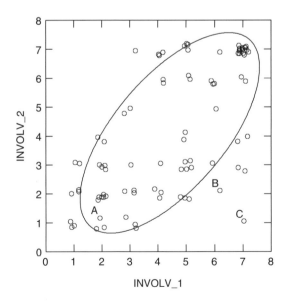

Figure 4.6 Example 3.4: Identifying Outliers

if they take on the same values. A contour ellipse, including about 68% of the observations, is also shown.

Three observations (A, B and C) are marked. Observation C is longer from the centroid than A and B, but which is farthest from the centroid A or B?

By traditional standards A is further from the centroid than B, but B has a *combination* of the variable values that is more unusual than those of A. You could therefore argue that B is farther away from the centroid if we use a measure, where the units are smaller, in directions where the Euclidian distance from the center to the 'limits' of the cluster of observations is small. Such a measure is *Mahanalobis' squared distance D^2*.

AMOS calculates D^2 for every observation as well as diagnostics to check normality assumptions.

Including the order:

```
Sem.NormalityCheck
```

in the program in Figure 4.3 (and also basing the analysis on the raw data and not on the covariance matrix) returns the additional output shown in Table 4.3.

As can be seen from the table, the following are shown for each variable: minimum value; maximum value skewness and kurtosis—and as far as the two last-mentioned statistics regards; critical values (supposing the statistics to be standard normally distributed) are also presented. For a symmetric distribution skewness is 0. If the distribution has a long upper tail, the skewness is positive, and if it has a long lower tail, it is negative. Kurtosis is a measure of the 'peakiness' of

Table 4.3   Example 1: Checking for normality and outliers

Assessment of normality (Germany)

Variable	min	max	skew	c.r.	kurtosis	c.r.
alienati	4	21	−.720	−6.447	.236	1.055
neophobi	5	35	.209	1.869	−.416	−1.863
nature	12	42	−.315	−2.820	−.485	−2.173
tech	7	35	−.359	−3.215	.028	.124
risk	7	42	−.553	−4.950	−.225	−1.008
Multivariate					4.021	5.270

Observations farthest from the centroid (Mahalanobis distance) (Germany)

Observation number	Mahalanobis d-squared	p1	p2
185	27.719	.000	.020
354	22.608	.000	.016
198	22.103	.001	.002
473	20.868	.001	.001
206	18.293	.003	.009

(only first five observations shown)

the distribution. For a normal distribution the kurtosis is 0, if the distribution is flatter than the normal, the kurtosis is negative, and if it is peakier, the kurtosis is positive. In the last line in this section Mardia's measure of multivariate kurtosis (Mardia, 1970, 1974) is shown.

Severe non-normality biases parameter estimates, test results and fit measures.

Unfortunately, this section of the output is of limited value. The statistical significance depends on the sample size, and the null hypotheses of zero skewness and kurtosis are bound to be rejected with sample sizes relevant for SEM analysis. Of course, you could discard the critical values, and just look at the statistics themselves, but it is difficult to judge from them whether the deviations from normality are serious enough to invalidate SEM estimation or testing.

I would rather recommend using graphical methods, such as histograms and normal probability plots, to judge whether it is necessary to transform a variable to obtain normality.

In the next panel the observations are shown in order of decreasing D^2 distance from the centroid. The column p1 shows that the probability that any arbitrary observation should have a larger distance from the centroid than 27.719 is 0.000, and in column p2 we see that the probability that the *largest* distance from the centroid should exceed 27.719 is 0.020. In the second line we see that the probability of any observation being farther away from the centroid than 22,608 is also 0.000, while the probability that the *second largest* distance should exceed 22,608 is 0.016 and so on.

You should expect small p1-values, whereas small p2-values indicate outliers.

It must be remembered, however, that the probability calculations are based on the assumption of multivariate normality, and in this case this assumption is far from fulfilled. As a consequence of this most p2-values are small, and cannot be used to locate outliers. However, observe that there is a rather large drop in d-squared from observation 185 to 354, so no doubt observation 185 is an outlayer.

My advice would therefore be:

1. Judge the univariate normality of the variables based on histograms and probability plots.
2. If necessary transform non-normal variables to (near) normality. Often this will also bring outliers nearer the main body of the data.
3. After transformations, use AMOS to detect outliers.

I am well aware that in theory normality of marginal distributions does not guarantee multivariate normality. However, in my experience in practice you can in general assume multivariate normality if all marginal distributions are normal.

In addition: If the data are multivariate normal, all bivariate regression functions are linear. This could also be used as a check for multivariate normality—but note that this is also a necessary and not a sufficient condition.

The Following Steps

After having dealt with the problems that caused the error messages, you move on to examining the output.

The first step is to look at the coefficients (and other parameters): Do they have the expected signs, and is their numerical magnitude in agreement with grounded theories, earlier empirical studies and common sense?

Are any of the standard errors extremely large—causing uncertainties of the magnitude of the parameter estimates? Or are they perhaps extremely small— which could cause problems with the calculation of the test statistics?

Next, you usually look at the global χ^2-test for the model as a whole and the long list of fit measures (not shown in Table 4.2). If the model fit is unsatisfactory you try to improve the fit—usually by adding more parameters to the model—and if the fit is 'too good' the model can perhaps be simplified by fixing or deleting parameters. In both cases you can order output that can help you with these modifications.

In this way you can reach a model step by step, which with as few parameters as possible gives a satisfactory description of the data, but at the same time is theoretically sound and substantively meaningful—a so-called *parsimonious* model.

I would like to emphasize the importance of simple models: The simpler the model, the more generalizable the model.

Exploratory Use of SEM

This process is not without problems. The more revisions you go through, the larger the risk that you will profit by peculiarities in the sample at hand, and that your model will not fit any other comparable data set.

In principle SEM is a confirmatory procedure, by which you test a model formulated *a priori*. However, the continual 'improvement' of the model is more exploratory and invalidates the 'testing': You test hypotheses on the same data that have given birth to them—a circular argument!

In this way the *P*-values lose their proper meaning and can only be used descriptively. This is the reason for including stages 9 and 10 in the list at the beginning of this chapter. Judged by published research this cross-validation is very seldom done, and if you forego it, it is extra important

1. that your original model is based on well-grounded substantive theory, and
2. that stepwise alterations of the model are few and also based on substantive thinking.

AMOS 5 introduced a whole range of methods to automate revision of models and search for the 'best' model. No doubt this development will continue in future versions.

I will not treat these methods, but remember: The more you rely on automation, the larger the risk that you will neglect serious thinking based on substantive considerations. This is artificial intelligence in its worst form!

6. A Few Problems of SEM Analysis

I would like to end the chapter by pointing out three problems that you should always keep in mind when doing SEM analysis: (1) The 'reverse' use of statistical tests, (2) the dependence of the χ^2-test on sample size and (3) the existence of *equivalent models* that all have the same fit to the data.

The 'Reverse' Testing Procedure

As is well known, the philosophy of traditional statistical testing is the following: You formulate two hypotheses, a null hypothesis H_0 and an alternative hypothesis H_1. H_0 is the hypothesis that represents status quo, while H_1 is the hypothesis you want to support. If the data does not support H_0, this hypothesis is rejected and H_1 is accepted—not as *true*, but as a *better* description of the data-generating process than H_0.

We accept H_1, not because we prove it is true, but because we reject a competing hypothesis. Statistical inference is 'the science of disproof.'

In SEM this logic is reversed: H_0 states that the model you actually want to support is true and H_1 that is not.

In a broader perspective this procedure is in conflict with the basic philosophy of scientific discovery: That a new model proposed to explain an empirical phenomenon is only accepted if its explanation is better than the one taken to be 'true' hitherto. It is not 'true' in any absolute sense, but only 'more true' than the old one—but will in all probability give way for an even 'better' model at some point in the future.

R.A. Fisher (1890–1962), 'the greatest statistician of all time', often cited Thomas Fuller (1654–1734): 'Nothing is good or bad but by comparison,' but this comparison very seldom takes place in SEM analysis, except the implicit comparisons with the usually very unrealistic models that are the basis for fit measures.

There will in general be several processes that could be hypothesized to have generated the data at hand. It is therefore a good idea to start out with several models, which are substantively meaningful (based on prior theory or common sense), compare them and judge their relative ability to explain the data.

Based on published research this is very seldom done, in which case the researcher runs a risk of overlooking other plausible explanations of the data.

The example in Figure 1.5b is a positive exception to the usual way SEM analysis is carried out.

The χ^2-test and the Sample Size

It is a well-known fact that the χ^2-test depends on sample size. In the case of SEM the test is based on $C = (n - 1)F$ where F is the fit function. If the sample size is sufficiently small you will always accept H_0, and if it is sufficiently large you will always reject H_0.

The combination of the 'reversed' test procedure and the dependence of χ^2 on sample size are therefore rather grotesque: Even if we know that our model is not literally 'true,' we will accept it at small sample sizes and reject it at large sample sizes.

This is the main reason for the invention of a long series of fit indices (some of them analogous to the well-known R^2), you will meet in the next chapter.

Indeed this is the problem with all two-sided tests, where a sharp null hypothesis is tested against a diffuse alternative: The null hypothesis is always false; it is only a matter of taking a sufficiently large sample to prove it is false!

This is one of several good reasons for using one-sided tests when testing estimated parameters.

Equivalent Models

If we estimate a simple regression model:

$$y = \alpha_0 + \alpha_1 x + \delta_y \qquad (9a)$$

we will obtain exactly the same fit as in

$$x = \beta_0 + \beta_1 y + \delta_x \qquad (9b)$$

and in SEM where several equations and variables are involved, it will *always* be possible to find several different models with exactly the same fit but with different theoretical implications. While all such *equivalent models* will include different parameters and different parameter values, they will show exactly the same values on all figures in the output used to measure the (global) 'goodness' of the model, including the χ^2-test and fit measures.

Figure 4.7 shows a few of the models that will fit the data of a model with three manifest variables equally well: They are *equivalent*. In simple SEM-models you may only have a limited number of equivalent models, but in larger models the number of equivalent models may be counted in hundreds or even thousands (in Figure 4.7 the models are just-identified, and all just-identified models are equivalent).

Even if most of the equivalent models are usually without any substantive meaning, there will in most cases exist a number of meaningful equivalent models. It is therefore the researcher's duty to explain why he prefers one meaningful equivalent model to others.

Judged from published work this is very seldom done.

It can be a cumbersome job to specify all equivalent models (Lee, 1990; Herschberger, 1994), and a special computer program TETRAD has been invented for this job (TETRAD Project homepage http://www.phil.cmu.edu/projects/tetrad/).

Questions

1. Sketch the various steps in a typical SEM analysis.
2. Explain the identification problem, and what can be done with an under-identified model.

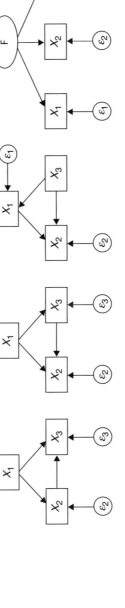

Figure 4.7 Equivalent models (in this case the models are just-identified—and all just-identified models are equivalent)

☞ In this chapter you have met the following concepts:

identification

t-rule

fixed and free parameters

maximum likelihood (ML)

unweighted least squares (ULS)

generalized least squares (GLS)

scale free least squares (SLS)

asymptotically distribution-free (ADF)

parceling

convergence

positive definite and positive

   semidefinite covariance matrices

equivalent models

Besides you have learned the following AMOS statements:

Sem.TextOutput

Sem.Standardized

Sem.Smc

Sem.BeginGroup

Sem.GroupName

Sem.AStructure

Sem.NormalityCheck

Sem.ImpliedMoments

3. Give a short description of the five estimation methods currently available in AMOS.
4. How would you go along examining AMOS output?

Reference List

Bandaleros, D. L. and S. J. Finney (2001) 'Item parceling issues in structural equation modeling,' in G. A. Marcoulides and R. E. Schumacker (eds), *New Developments and Techniques in Structural Equation Modeling*, Mahwah, NJ: erlbaum.

Bollen, K. A. (1989) *Structural Equations with Latent Variables*, NY: Wiley.

Bredahl, L. (2001) 'Determinants of consumer attitudes and purchase intentions with regard to genetically modified foods—Results of a cross-national survey,' *Journal of Consumer Policy*, 24: 23–61.

Browne, M. W. (1982) 'Covariance structures,' in D. M. Hawkins (ed.), *Topics in Multivariate Analysis*, Cambridge: Cambridge University Press.

Herschberger, S. I. (1994) 'The specification of equivalent models before the collection of data,' in A. E. von Eye and C. C. Clog (eds), *Latent Variables Analysis*, Thousand Oaks, CA: Sage.

Lee, S. (1990) 'A simple rule for generating equivalent models in covariance structure modeling,' *Multivariate Behavioral Research*, 25: 313–34.

Mardia, K. V. (1970) 'Measures of multivariate skewness and kurtosis with applications,' *Biometrika*, 26: 47–558.

Mardia, K. V. (1974) 'Applications of some measures of multivariate skewness and kurtosis in testion normality and robustness studies,' *Sankhya, Series B*, 36: 115–28.

Wilkinson, L., B. Grant, and C. Gruber (1996) *Desktop Data Analysis with SYSTAT*, Upper Saddle River, NJ: Prentice-Hall.

5

Models with Only Manifest Variables

I **n this chapter** you will be introduced to acyclic and cyclic models with only manifest variables.

I start with the acyclic models; mentioning two sufficient rules for identification, and then go through a very simple example, which is also used to explain how to interpret the very extensive output from an AMOS analysis, including the various fit indices.

Then I turn to cyclic models. The identification problem—which is much more of a problem in this kind of model—is illustrated using the cigarette-advertising example from Chapter 1.

The very meaning of 'two-way causation' is discussed, and final advice is given: Avoid cyclical models if at all possible!

1. Identifying and Estimating Acyclic Models

Of the few rules for identification in acyclic models with manifest variables only two are mentioned here.

The Zero B-rule

A model with no variable that has both in-going and out-going arrows is always identified.

The Recursive Rule

If the regression weights can be arranged in a lower triangular matrix:

$$
\begin{aligned}
X_1 &= \delta_1 \\
X_2 &= \beta_{21}X_1 + \delta_2 \\
X_3 &= \beta_{31}X_1 + \beta_{32}X_2 + \delta_3 \\
X_4 &= \beta_{41}X_1 + \beta_{42}X_2 + \beta_{43}X_3 + \delta_4 \\
X_5 &= \beta_{51}X_1 + \beta_{52}X_2 + \beta_{53}X_3 + \beta_{54}X_4 + \delta_5
\end{aligned}
\tag{1a}
$$

and

$$
\text{Cov}(\delta_i, \delta_j) = 0 \quad \text{for all } i \text{ and } j
\tag{1b}
$$

the model is said to be *recursive* and it is always identified. If some of the regression weights are zero, the model is over-identified.

The condition (1b) loosens any tie among the equations as far as estimation is concerned. Consequently, the equations can be estimated independently of each other—e.g. using OLS, if the other conditions for that procedure are fulfilled.

It should be mentioned that models satisfying the zero B-rule are also called recursive by AMOS, while all other models are called non-recursive.

Example 1

If in the hierarchy-of-effects model—first met in Figure 1.5b—we let

$$
\begin{aligned}
X_1 &= \text{exposure} \\
X_2 &= \text{price} \\
X_3 &= \text{awareness} \\
X_4 &= \text{attitude} \\
X_5 &= \text{market share}
\end{aligned}
$$

the model can be written as (1a), where

$$
\beta_{21} = \beta_{32} = \beta_{42} = \beta_{51} = \beta_{53} = 0.
\tag{2}
$$

If the condition (1b) is met, the model is (over-)identified according to the recursive rule. It is left to the reader to verify whether the low-involvement model is identified. The models are shown in Figure 5.1.

Example 2

Wheaton et al. (1977) made a panel study covering the years 1966–1971 in order to study e.g. the stability of alienation, as measured on two summated scales

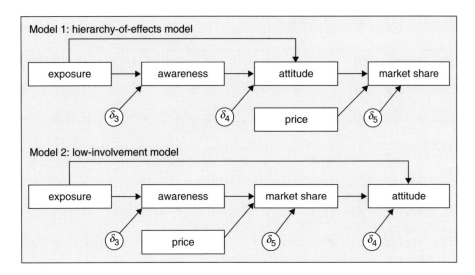

Figure 5.1   Example 1: A-cyclical causal models (from Figure 1.5b)

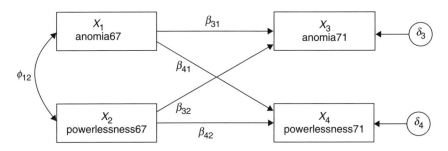

Figure 5.2   Example 2: Model

called 'anomia' and 'powerlessness.' Like several others—e.g. Jöreskog & Sörbom (1984), Bentler (1995) and Browne and Mels (2002)—I will use the Wheaton data to illustrate SEM analysis and to acquaint you with the extensive AMOS output.

The study included several background variables, but here I will concentrate on two variables, 'anomia' and 'powerlessness' and the two years 1967 and 1971.

Figure 5.2 from Bentler (1995) shows a so-called cross-lagged panel design with 932 respondents.

With four variables there are $(4+5)/2 = 10$ variances/covariances, on which to base the estimation, and the number of parameters to be estimated is $4+4+1=9$ (number of coefficients + number of variances + number of covariances). The model is therefore possibly identified with one degree of freedom. The identification is confirmed by the zero-B-rule.

Table 5.1 shows the data and a program for estimation of the model.

Table 5.1   Example 2: Data and Program

	X_1	X_2	X_3	X_4
X_1	11.834			
X_2	6.947	9.364		
X_3	6.819	5.091	12.532	
X_4	4.783	5.028	7,495	9.986

```
Sub Main()
  Dim sem As New AmosEngine
  Try
     Sem.Title ("Example 5.2")
     'Data from Wheaton (1977)
     Sem.TextOutput()
     Sem.Standardized()
     Sem.ResidualMoments()
     Sem.BeginGroup ("Wheaton.xls", "Sheet1")
     Sem.AStructure ("anomia71 = anomia67 + powerlessness67 + (1) d3")
     Sem.AStructure ("powerlessness71 = anomia67 + powerlessness67 + (1) d4")
     Sem.FitModel()
  Finally
     Sem.Dispose()
  End Try
End Sub
```

We estimate the model by maximum likelihood (the default) and order the output to include standardized parameter values (Sem.Standardized) and the residual covariance matrix (Sem.ResidualMoments), mentioned in Section 1.5.

A few comments on the output in Table 5.2:

1. You are told that the model is recursive and that the sample size is 932.
2. Then comes a listing and classification of the variables and parameters.
3. The number of degrees of freedom is calculated at 1.
4. The global χ^2-test of the model has a P-value of 0.000. *The null hypothesis is that the model is correct.* This means that there is practically no chance of getting a sample like ours, or one that is less consistent with the model, if the model is true. As mentioned in the last chapter, in SEM analysis the null hypothesis is not performing its usual part as a 'straw man,' so we are interested in getting *large* values of P. On the other hand very large P-values could be an indication of over-fitting, in which case the model should be simplified.
5. Then follows the parameter estimates in raw and standardized form. All parameters are statistically significant by traditional norms.
6. Next is the residual covariance matrix in raw and standardized form. As mentioned earlier the residual covariance matrix is the difference between the sample covariance matrix and the covariance matrix implied by the model. The smaller the elements in the residual covariance matrix, the more the model is supported by the data—and the smaller the χ^2-value.

Table 5.2 Example 2: Output (to be continued in Table 3)

Analysis Summary

Date and Time
Date: Monday, February 20, 2006
Time: 8:30:36 AM
Title

Groups

Group number 1 (Group number 1)

Notes for Group (Group number 1) (1)
The model is recursive.
Sample size = 932

Variable Summary (Group number 1) (2)
Your model contains the following variables (Group number 1)

Observed, endogenous variables
anomia71
powerlessness71

Observed, exogenous variables
anomia67
powerlessness67

Unobserved, exogenous variables
error_1
error_2

Variable counts (Group number 1)
Number of variables in your model: 6
Number of observed variables: 4
Number of unobserved variables: 2
Number of exogenous variables: 4
Number of endogenous variables: 2

Parameter summary (Group number 1)

	Weights	Covariances	Variances	Means	Intercepts	Total
Fixed	2	0	0	0	0	2
Labeled	0	0	0	0	0	0
Unlabeled	4	1	4	0	0	9
Total	6	1	4	0	0	11

Models

Model 1 (Model 1)

Notes for Model (Model 1)

Computation of degrees of freedom (Model 1) (3)

Number of distinct sample moments: 10
Number of distinct parameters to be estimated: 9
Degrees of freedom (10−9):   1

(Continued)

Table 5.2 Cont'd

Result (Model 1)   (4)

```
Minimum was achieved
Chi-square = 341.863
Degrees of freedom = 1
Probability level = .000
```

Group number 1 (Group number 1—Model 1)

Estimates (Group number 1—Model 1)

Scalar Estimates (Group number 1—Model 1)

Maximum Likelihood Estimates   (5)

Regression Weights: (Group number 1—Model 1)

	Estimate	S.E.	C.R.	P Label
anomia71 <--- anomia67	.455	.037	12.407	***
anomia71 <--- powerlessness67	.206	.041	4.988	***
powerlessness71<--- anomia67	.158	.034	4.658	***
powerlessness71<--- powerlessness67	.420	.038	11.042	***

Standardized regression weights: (Group number 1—Model 1)

	Estimate
anomia71 <--- anomia67	.443
anomia71 <--- powerlessness67	.178
powerlessness71 <--- anomia67	.172
powerlessness71 <--- powerlessness67	.407

Covariances: (Group number 1—Model 1)

	Estimate	S.E.	C.R.	P Label
anomia67 <--> powerlessness67	6.940	.413	16.806	***

Correlations: (Group number 1—Model 1)

	Estimate
anomia67 <--> powerlessness67	.660

Variances: (Group number 1 - Model 1)

	Estimate	S.E.	C.R.	P	Label
anomia67	11.821	.548	21.575	***	
powerlessness67	9.354	.434	21.575	***	
d3	8.370	.388	21.575	***	
d4	7.113	.330	21.575	***	

Table 5.2 Cont'd

Matrices (Group number 1—Model 1)

Residual Covariances (Group number 1—Model 1) (6)

	powerlessness67	anomia67	powerlessness71	anomia71
powerlessness67	.000			
anomia67	.000	.000		
powerlessness71	.000	.000	.000	
anomia71	.000	.000	4.277	.000

Standardized Residual Covariances (Group number 1—Model 1)

	powerlessness67	anomia67	powerlessness71	anomia71
powerlessness67	.000			
anomia67	.000	.000		
powerlessness71	.000	.000	.000	
anomia71	.000	.000	11.225	.000

The standardized residual variances and covariances (the variances/covariances divided by their standard errors) are asymptotically distributed as standard normal.

7. Last in the output is a wide assortment of fit indices (not shown). I shall not comment on them here, but only point out that they are far from satisfying. I shall return to the fit measures in the next section.

As is evident from Figure 5.2 our model states that the covariance between Anomia71 and Powerlessness71 can be explained as a result of Anomia67 and Powerlessness67.

This hypothesis cannot be maintained, as a χ^2-value of about 342 is significant by any reasonable criterion—even if the sample is 'large.'

The usual remedy in such a case, to introduce additional parameters, is not possible here. The only way to do so would be to allow δ_3 and δ_4 to correlate, and this would eat up our only degree of freedom, after which we would be left with a just-identified, i.e. a non-testable model.

Nevertheless, let us have a look at the output. All coefficients are statistically significant according to traditional criteria, and anomie seems to be slightly more stable than powerlessness. The two cross-effects are small and not very different in their standardized form. However, these conclusions must be taken with a grain of salt, as they are based on an incorrect model.

The residual matrix shows clearly where the problem is located: The model can reproduce the sample covariance matrix except the covariance between the two 71-variables.

As the residual covariance of Powerlessness71 and anomie71 is positive, the model under-estimates the covariance between the two variables. As mentioned above, allowing the two variables to correlate more than caused by the exogenous variables would eat up our only degree of freedom.

As it is impossible to patch up the model, I will (in Chapter 7) construct a new one based on latent variables.

2.   Fit Indices

As pointed out earlier the χ^2-test has the weakness that if the sample is sufficiently small we will accept any model, and if it is sufficiently large any model will be rejected. To put it sharply: We test a hypothesis that we know *a priori* is false—and if the sample is large enough the test will show what we expect it to show!

In order to overcome this problem a large number of fit indices has been constructed to help evaluate to what extent the model is supported by the data. Some of these indices take on values in the interval 0.00–1.00—just as a determination coefficient—and the closer to 1.00, the better the fit. However, the coefficient of determination has the advantage of having a certain interpretation, namely as the share of variance of a dependent variable that can be 'explained' by one or more independent variables. Unfortunately most fit indices lack such an interpretation, so only experience can tell what is necessary for a specific fit index to show a good fit.

Fit indices are different ways of expressing the 'distance' between the sample covariance matrix **S** and the estimated implied covariance matrix $\hat{\Sigma}(\theta)$, i.e. they are functions of the residual matrix $\mathbf{S} - \hat{\Sigma}(\theta)$; but how do we measure this distance and express it in one number only?

As is evident from Table 5.3, this can be done in several ways. The many fit measures can be classified as shown in Table 5.4, where they are shown in the same order as in the output.

Absolute fit measures judge the fit of a model *per se* without reference to other models that could be relevant in the situation. This means that there is no standard or basis relative to which the actual model could be judged, for again, as Fisher says: 'Nothing is good or bad but by comparison.' In a way you could say that a model is judged relative to no model at all.

Relative fit measures introduce an explicit basis model, which usually is rather unrealistic, but which nevertheless serves the purpose: to make it possible to judge the fit of different models on a common basis.

Parsimony adjusted measures introduce a 'punishment' for complicating the model by increasing the number of parameters in order to improve the fit.

Fit measures based on the non-central Chi-square distribution have as their starting point the fact that no model is 'correct'—it can only be 'approximately correct.'

Fit measures based on information theory are not used for judging the fit of a single model, but are used in situations where you have to choose among several realistic but different models.

The *Hoelter measure*—falling in a class of its own—pinpoints the connection between sample size and significance of χ^2.

Table 5.3 Example 2: Fit measures (continuation of output from Table 5.2)

Model Fit Summary

CMIN

Model	NPAR	CMIN	DF	P	CMIN/DF
Default model	9	341.863	1	.000	341.863
Saturated model	10	.000	0		
Independence model	4	1563.944	6	.000	260.657

RMR. GFI

Model	RMR	GFI	AGFI	PGFI
Default model	1.353	.867	−.332	.087
Saturated model	.000	1.000		
Independence model	4.738	.515	.192	.309

Baseline comparisons

Model	NFI Delta1	RFI rho1	IFI Delta2	TLI rho2	CFI
Default model	.781	−.312	.782	−.313	.781
Saturated model	1.000		1.000		1.000
Independence model	.000	.000	.000	.000	.000

Parsimony-Adjusted Measures

Model	PRATIO	PNFI	PCFI
Default model	.167	.130	.130
Saturated model	.000	.000	.000
Independence model	1.000	.000	.000

NCP

Model	NCP	LO 90	HI 90
Default model	340.863	283.736	405.393
Saturated model	.000	.000	.000
Independence model	1557.944	1431.609	1691.640

FMIN

Model	FMIN	F0	LO 90	HI 90
Default model	.367	.366	.305	.435
Saturated model	.000	.000	.000	.000
Independence model	1.680	1.673	1.538	1.817

(Continued)

Table 5.3 Cont'd

RMSEA

Model	RMSEA	LO 90	HI 90	PCLOSE
Default model	.605	.552	.660	.000
Independence model	.528	.506	.550	.000

AIC

Model	AIC	BCC	BIC	CAIC
Default model	359.863	359.960	403.399	412.399
Saturated model	20.000	20.108	68.373	78.373
Independence model	1571.944	1571.987	1591.294	1595.294

ECVI

Model	ECVI	LO 90	HI 90	MECVI
Default model	.387	.325	.456	.387
Saturated model	.021	.021	.021	.022
Independence model	1.688	1.553	1.832	1.688

HOELTER

Model	HOELTER .05	HOELTER .01
Default model	11	19
Independence model	8	11

Execution time summary

Minimization:	.070
Miscellaneous:	1.222
Bootstrap:	.000
Total:	1.292

In Table 5.3 you will observe that all fit measures are shown for three different models:

1. The model at hand—called the *default model.*
2. The saturated model (with the maximum number of parameters), and
3. The independence model (with zero correlation among the manifest variables).

For models estimated by other methods than maximum likelihood AMOS will also state fit measures for the null model, where all parameters take on the value zero.

Table 5.4 Fit measures in AMOS

Absolute fit measures	Relative fit measures	Parsimony measures	Fit measures based on the non-central chi-square distribution	Information theoretic fit measures	Fit measures based on sample size
CMIN	NFI	PRATIO	NCP	AIC	HOELTER
CMIN/DF	RFI	PNFI	FMIN	BCC	
RMR	IFI	PCFI	F0	BIC	
GFI	TLI	(PGFI)	RMSEA	CAIC	
AGFI	CFI			ECVI	
PGFI				MECVI	

Fit measures are stated for several models in order to make a basis for comparison—in line with the above quotation by Fisher.

Absolute Fit Measures

In the first row beneath 'Summary of models' we first meet the number of parameters for the three models NPAR. Next to NPAR we find the minimum value of C, CMIN. As mentioned earlier C is defined as $C = (n - 1)F$, where F is the fit function to be minimized and CMIN is the minimum (the end result) of the minimization process. If ML or GLS estimation is used CMIN is asymptotically distributed as χ^2, and we have already met the CMIN or χ^2-value 341.863 in the output in Table 5.2. Next is the number of degrees of freedom DF, and last in the row CMIN divided by DF.

If the null hypothesis is true, $E(\chi^2) = DF$, so you could consider CMIN/DF to be a 'normalization' of χ^2. Usually a value of CMIN/DF near 1.00 is considered a sign of a good fit, and the value 341.863 for CMIN/DF confirms that our model fits extremely badly.

The fit is expressed in the residual covariance matrix. Analogous to the standard error of the estimate in traditional regression analysis, we could compute the *root mean-square residual*: the square root of the average of squared elements in the residual covariance matrix in its triangular form as printed in the output:

$$RMR = \sqrt{\frac{(sum)^2}{p(p+1)/2}} = \sqrt{\frac{2(sum)^2}{p(p+1)}} \tag{3}$$

Where '*sum*' represents the sum of all elements in the residual covariance matrix in triangular form.

Now, the size of this expression depends on the units of measurement for the various variables, so that it is more relevant to make an analogous calculation based on the residual correlation matrix. Unfortunately, this is not part of the output in AMOS, but is easily calculated by hand—which I leave to the reader as an exercise. Usually a RMR (based on correlations) less than 0.05 is taken as a sign of a good fit.

Next to RMR we find GFI—the classical *Goodness of Fit Index* introduced in LISREL many years ago. This index is calculated as

$$\text{GFI} = \frac{(\text{weighted sum of the variances in } \hat{\Sigma})^2}{(\text{weighted sum of the variances in } \mathbf{S})^2} \tag{4}$$

where the weights depend on the estimation method. It has been proposed that GFI is analogous to R^2 in multiple regression, and just as R^2 GFI takes on values between 0 and 1.00.

If GFI is adjusted for the number of degrees of freedom compared to the number of parameters, you get AGFI (Adjusted Goodness of Fit Index), which rewards models with fewer parameters.

In this case AGFI is negative, which should mean that not only is the model bad, but it is worse than no model at all! This of course is nonsense. Negative values of AGFI are rare, but the fact that they can occur is a weakness of this index.

A better way to take care of parsimony is to adjust GFI using James et al.'s (1982) index of parsimony (more on this below). This latter fit index is shown as PGFI.

Relative Fit Measures

As the saturated model has maximum fit and the independence model has the maximum number of constraints and consequently has minimum fit, these two models indicate the limits between which 'your' model is placed.

You can therefore evaluate a model by looking at its 'location' between these two extremes.

You could e.g. calculate how large a part of the way from the independence model to the perfect fitting model 'your' model—the *default model*—has 'traveled':

$$\text{NFI} = \frac{\text{CMIN}_{indp} - \text{CMIN}_{deflt}}{\text{CMIN}_{indp}} = \frac{1563.944 - 341.863}{1563.944} = 0.781 \tag{5}$$

This is the so-called NFI (Normed Fit Index) (Bentler and Bonnett, 1980), which is bounded within the interval 0 to 1.00.

RFI (Relative Fit Index) and IFI (Incremental Fit Index) also include the degrees of freedom: RFI is derived from NFI by dividing each variable in NFI with its degrees of freedom, and IFI by subtracting the degrees of freedom for the independence model in the denominator.

Like GFI, NFI has been used as a standard for many years, but as it has shown a tendency to underestimate the fit in small samples, it has been modified into CFI (Comparative Fit Index), (Bentler, 1990), which also takes the degrees of freedom into consideration:

$$CFI = \frac{(CMIN_{indp} - DF_{indp}) - (CMIN_{deflt} - DF_{deflt})}{(CMIN_{indp} - DF_{indp})}$$

$$= \frac{(1563.944 - 6) - (341.863 - 1)}{1563.944 - 6} = 0.781 \qquad (6)$$

NFI- and CFI-values larger than 0.95 are usually taken as an indication of a good fit.

It is worth noting that if $CMIN_{deflt} < DF_{deflt}$ then CFI > 1.000, but CFI is reported as 1.000 in the output. Therefore CFI $= 1.000$ is not an indication of a perfect fit, but only indicates that $CMIN_{deflt} < DF_{deflt}$.

The TLI (Tucker-Lewis Index) (Tucker and Lewis 1973):

$$TLI = \frac{\dfrac{C_{indp}}{DF_{indp}} - \dfrac{C_{deftt}}{DF_{deflt}}}{\dfrac{C_{indp}}{DF_{indp}} - 1} \qquad (7)$$

is another index, which (usually!) takes on values in the 0–1.00 interval, values near 1.00 as usual being seen as a sign of good fit.

Parsimony-Based Fit Measures

It is always possible to increase the fit by adding more parameters to a model—the full model has the maximum number of parameters, thus the maximum fit: the residual covariance matrix is a 0-matrix, i.e. it contains only zeroes.

By uncritically adding parameters to the model you run the risk of profiting on peculiarities in the sample at hand, and thus end up with a model that will not fit any comparable sample from the same population. This is one of the main reasons for preferring simple models with relatively few parameters: they are more generalizable.

PRATIO (Parsimony Ratio), defined as

$$PRATIO = \frac{DF_{deflt}}{DF_{indp}} \qquad (8)$$

is proposed by James et al. (1982) as a factor by which you can modify fit indices to take parsimony into consideration. In other words you can introduce a penalty for complicating the model. In this way PNFI and PCFI result from NFI and CFI by multiplication with PRATIO. Analogously, PGFI is defined as:

$$PGFI = GFI \frac{DF_{deflt}}{DF_{sat}} \qquad (9)$$

GFI is an 'absolute' measure, so the basis model is not the independence model, but the saturated model, i.e. no model at all.

Usually parsimony based fit indices are much lower than other normed fit measures. Values larger than 0.60 are generally considered satisfying.

Fit Indices Based on the Non-central χ^2-distribution

As mentioned at the beginning of this section, the main reason for the introduction of the many fit measures is that the global χ^2-test is a test of a null hypothesis that we *a priori* know is false: That our model is 100% correct.

As any model is only 'approximately true,' $C = (n - 1)F$ is actually distributed according to *the non-central χ^2-distribution with non-centrality parameter*

$$\delta = \chi^2 - DF \tag{10a}$$

The ordinary χ^2-distribution (the central) is thus a special variant of the non-central with $\delta = 0$. The more 'wrong' our model is, the larger δ is. Consequently, small values of δ are to be preferred.

δ is estimated as:

$$NCP = \max[CMIN - DF, 0] \tag{10b}$$

therefore $NCP = 0$ does not indicate a perfect fit, but only that CMIN $<$ DF (cf. the remarks in connection with equation (5)). This has similar consequences for the fit measures F0 and RMSEA mentioned below.

LO 90 and HI 90 are lower and upper 90% confidence limits for NCP.

FMIN is the minimum value of the minimization function F, while $F0 = NCP/n$ and thus a 'normalization' of NCP. The lower F0, the better. Next to F0 are lower and upper 90% confidence limits. F0 will, however, never encourage parsimony, as it will never favor a simpler model with fewer parameters.

RMSEA (Root Mean Square Error of Approximation) (Steiger and Lind, 1980) takes care of this problem by introducing the number of degrees of freedom:

$$RMSEA = \frac{F0}{DF} \tag{11}$$

As usual in this group of fit measures—which could also be called 'population based' fit indices—lower and upper 90% confidence limits are also shown. Usually a RMSEA around 0.05 is considered a sign of good fit and models with values larger than 0.10 should not be accepted. Last in this line is shown P-values (PCLOSE) for a test of the null hypothesis that RMSEA (in the population) is less than 0.05.

Information-Theoretic Fit Measures

This group of fit measures is based on the idea of expressing the extent to which the present model will cross-validate in future samples of the same size from the same population. Also they all reward parsimony. Another common feature is that small values are to be preferred, but that the measures have no upper limit and therefore these fit measures are primarily used as a basis for choosing among several substantive meaningful models.

I will not show formulas for these measures, of which further information can be found in the references mentioned in Table 5.5.

Table 5.5   Information-theoretic fit measures

AIC	Akaike Information Criterion	(Akaike, 1973, 1987)	Has only a penalty for degrees of freedom, but not for sample size
BCC	Browne-Cudeck Criterion	(Browne and Cudeck, 1989)	As AIC, but carries a slightly harder penalty for introducing additional parameters
BIC	Bayes Information Criterion	(Raftery, 1993, 1995; Schwarz, 1978)	Assigns a greater penalty for introducing additional parameters than any of the other indices shown in this table
CAIC	Consistent AIC	(Bozdogan, 1987)	Reformulation of AIC, carrying a greater penalty for model complexity than AIC and BCC
ECVI	Expected cross-validation index	(Browne and Cudeck, 1989)	Proportional to AIC
MECVI	Maximum likelihood ECVI	(Browne and Cudeck, 1989, 1993)	Proportional to BCC

The last fit index is CN (Critical N) (Hoelter, 1983), indicating the largest sample size for which the actual model will be accepted as 'true' based on the traditional χ^2-test and the actual data.

In this case our model will be accepted as 'true' with a sample size of 11, if we set $\alpha = 0.05$ and it would be rejected if the sample size were 12. For $\alpha = 0.01$ the corresponding sample sizes are 19 and 20.

What Indices Shall I Report?

With so many fit indices to choose from, this question is not irrelevant!

As indices that are placed in the same group in Table 5.4 measure about the same aspect of model fit, the question boils down to choosing the best fit index from each group. My suggestion is that you report the χ^2 with degrees of freedom and P-value, RMSEA with confidence interval and PCLOSE. If you compare *non-nested models* (see Example 6.1 for a definition of *nested* models) these indices can be supplemented with one of the information theoretic fit measures—the most used is perhaps AIC. (Browne and Cudeck, 1989, 1993) recommend reporting ECVI or in case of ML estimation MECVI.

If you want to report a relative fit measure I would suggest the use of CFI, but these measures have the common weakness that the baseline model is the very unrealistic independence model.

A common problem with most indices is that their sampling distribution is unknown. This means that decisions on whether the size of a fit index is 'satisfying' is based on rules of thumb obtained through experience and by computer simulations.

Also, always remember that fit measures are measures of the *average* fit of the model to the data. Even if this 'general' fit seems to be OK, the model could still have a bad fit in local places. Therefore, be careful in checking standard errors of the various parameters, and coefficients of determination.

In that connection I should like to point out that in covariance based SEM we are *not* predicting the dependent variables—we are predicting the covariance matrix. Therefore, covariance based SEM does not minimize the error variances. If you are more interested in making predictions than in explaining covariances, you should use another SEM methodology called *Partial Least squares* invented by Wold (1975). For an introduction see Fornell and Cha (1994).

3. The Identification Problem in Cyclic Models

In cyclic models identification problems arise more often than in acyclic models, and it is generally more difficult to judge whether a model is identified or not by inspection or the use of simple rules.

This is easily demonstrated using the Bass example we met in Figure 1.5c, which is repeated in Figure 5.3 below. From the figure we see that sales of filter cigarettes

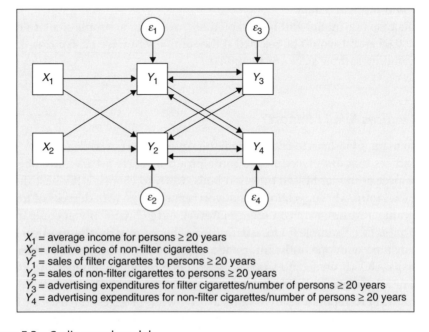

X_1 = average income for persons $\geq$ 20 years
X_2 = relative price of non-filter cigarettes
Y_1 = sales of filter cigarettes to persons $\geq$ 20 years
Y_2 = sales of non-filter cigarettes to persons $\geq$ 20 years
Y_3 = advertising expenditures for filter cigarettes/number of persons $\geq$ 20 years
Y_4 = advertising expenditures for non-filter cigarettes/number of persons $\geq$ 20 years

Figure 5.3 Cyclic causal model

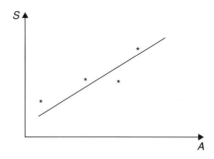

Figure 5.4   Example 3: Scattergram of sales revenue S and advertising budget A

(Y_1) depends on advertising for filter cigarettes (Y_3)—which is of course the very purpose of advertising—but at the same time (Y_3) could also depend on (Y_1) through advertising budgeting routines. How is it at all possible to map such relationships? Can we analytically separate the two functions—can we identify them?

Example 3

Let the problem be to map sales as a function of advertising:

$$S = f(A) \tag{12}$$

where S = sales and A = advertising budget.

The time series data can be graphed as shown in Figure 5.4. The observations form a nearly straight line, thus indicating a strong relationship between the two variables (for simplicity only four points are shown). The question is, however: Is it the sales function or the budget function that is depicted in the figure?

Now, any observation in Figure 5.4 must lie on both the sales curve and the advertising curve, which means that, except for 'noise,' the observations must be placed in the intersection of the two curves.

Figure 5.5 shows four possible situations with the 'true' functions marked. In reality, of course, we never know the exact position of the 'true' curves, because then there would be no need to estimate them!

In Figure 5.5a both functions have been stable during the period covered by our data. Consequently, our observations are all clustered around the intersection of the curves, and they do not give us any information on the location of the two curves.

In part (b) of the figure the budget function has been stable in the period, while the sales function has moved around, influenced by variables other than advertising. As a result of this the budget function can be identified. If instead the budget function had moved while the sales function had been stable, the sales function would have been identified.

In panel (c) both curves have moved, and consequently the points depict only the intersection points of the two functions, and say nothing about the location of them.

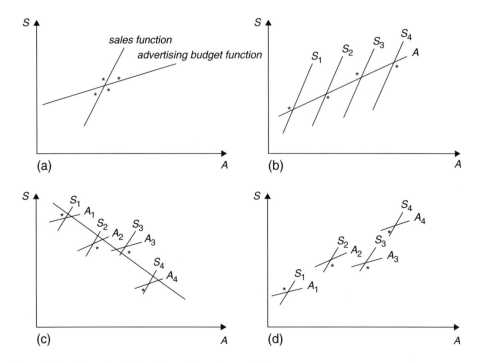

Figure 5.5 Example 3: The identification problem

However, the points are placed from northwest to southeast, so the analyst could hardly believe that he has located the sales function—if that was his purpose.

In panel (d), however, such a misinterpretation is more likely, but as you will by now know, if there is a two-way-causation, the points will only mirror the intersection of the curves and say nothing about their slopes.

To identify the functions in the model we must add to our model variables that can cause changes in the position of the functions, such as those shown in Figure 5.5b–d.

A Necessary Condition for Identification: The Order Condition

Writing the sales function and the advertising budget function as

$$S = \beta_{S0} + \beta_{S1}A + \varepsilon_S \tag{13a}$$
$$A = \beta_{A0} + \beta_{A1}S + \varepsilon_A \tag{13b}$$

it is easy to see that the problem is that we have two linear functions with exactly the same variables. Two such functions are impossible to separate (identify) empirically.

To identify a function we must add to our model one or more variables, the value of which is not determined within the model—i.e. we must add exogenous variables.

If we add income, I, to equation (13a), we get

$$S = \beta_{S0} + \beta_{S1}A + \beta_{S2}I + \varepsilon_S \tag{14a}$$
$$A = \beta_{A0} + \beta_{A1}S + \varepsilon_A \tag{14b}$$

As variations in I will cause the function (13a) to move, it is natural to assume that including I in (14a) will lead to identification of (14b). This is actually the case (cf. Figure 5.5b).

Model (14) comprises three variables: two endogenous variables (S and A) and one exogenous variable (I). If the number of exogenous variables not included in an equation is one less than the number of endogenous variables in that equation, the equation is *just-identified*. If there are fewer, the equation is *under-identified* (*unidentified*), and if there are more, it is *over-identified*. This is the so-called *order condition*, which is necessary, but not sufficient.

A sufficient condition for (13b) to be identified is that the coefficient β_{S2} is different from zero. This is the so-called rank condition, which for the two-equation model can be stated as follows:

A necessary and sufficient condition for identification of an equation in a two-equation model is that the other equation contains at least one exogenous variable with a non-zero coefficient that is excluded from the equation in question. So identification depends not only on the structure of the model, but (unfortunately) also on parameter values.

Now, the sales function is probably of greater interest than the budget function, and to identify the former it is necessary to include in (14b) one or more exogenous variables that do not affect sales. This, however, is not as easy as it sounds, because most variables you could take into consideration when deciding how much to spend on advertising would also influence sales: price of the product; degree of distribution etc.

A possible solution is to include the price of advertising.

The General Order Condition

If we have more than two equations in our model, the order condition is a little more complicated and can be stated as follows: A *necessary* condition for an equation to be identified is that the number of excluded *exogenous* variables is at least as large as the number of right-hand side *endogenous* variables.

Let us use this rule on the model in Figure 5.3 and we see that only the budget functions are identified.

	Left hand variable	Right hand endogenous variables		Excluded exogenous variables		
Equation No. 1	Y_1	Y_3	Y_4	none		under-identified
Equation No. 2	Y_2	Y_3	Y_4	none		under-identified
Equation No. 3	Y_3	Y_1	Y_2	X_1	X_2	just-identified
Equation No. 4	Y_4	Y_1	Y_2	X_1	X_2	just-identified

If these are the functions you are interested in, and equations 1 and 2 are only there to identify them, then of course that is OK and you can estimate functions 3 and 4—but not using AMOS. Unfortunately, AMOS will not estimate part of a model: If just one parameter in a model is unidentified AMOS will give a warning and stop calculations. Bass (partly) solved the identification problems by using two-stage least squares estimation—a limited information method not currently available in AMOS.

A Warning

Remember the formulation of the error message in the output in Table 4.2:

> The model is (probably) unidentified.

This formulation indicates that AMOS' identification check is not one hundred percent safe.

When I estimated the Bass model in Figure 5.3 using Bass's data I got no error message and AMOS estimated the total model even though it was only partially identified.

I must admit that this result was obtained using version 4.01, and repeating the calculations using version 16 gave the appropriate error message. However, as the formulation of the error message is still the same, it is only fair to warn the reader that he/she could run into the same problem.

If at all possible, you should examine the identification status of your model before you collect data, so that you can add the number of exogenous variables required to obtain identification.

It is possible to circumvent the warning and let AMOS try to fit a model that appears to be under-identified. However, this is usually not to be recommended— and for that reason I will not state the command!

A Sufficient Condition: The Rank Condition

As mentioned, the order condition is necessary but not sufficient. The reason is that the variables introduced in order to obtain identification must be independent of each other: If we introduce a variable, which co-varies with another already in the model, the new one will, to a larger or smaller degree, repeat information that we already have.

An exact formulation of the (general) rank condition is outside the scope of this book—but see e.g. Brown (1991)—because it is based on matrix algebra, but fortunately it is rather seldom in practice to find a model meeting the order condition that does not also meet the rank condition.

4.   What Does Two-Way Causation Really Mean?

In a model based on experimental data there is no doubt about the direction of the arrows: They depart from the manipulated variables—and it is absurd to

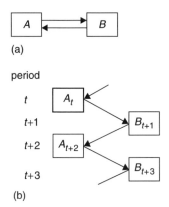

(a)

period

(b)

Figure 5.6 Cyclic and acyclic models

think about letting them point in the opposite direction. In models based on non-experimental data you may sometimes have your doubts as to the causal direction. Unfortunately, this subject is rather poorly treated in the literature—but have a look at Davis (1985). However, some guidance can be found in the following two 'rules':

1. Cause is prior to effect.
2. Causes are often variables whose values are more stable than effects.

Nevertheless, you may often feel tempted to draw the arrows in both directions, and then end up with a cyclic model with all its complications.

But: What does a two-way causation really mean? Is it not absurd to think of letting A have an effect on B, and at the same time letting B have an effect on A? At the very least you should expect some delay, so that A 'now' effects B 'a little later' and then B effects A again 'a bit later,' because, as Hume formulated it: Cause precedes effect.

If we accept this premise, the model in Figure 5.6b should be substituted for the model in 5.6a: all cyclical causal models are absurd and all realistic models are—or should be—acyclic!

Formally this is correct, but if the time period in Figure 5.6b is measured in months and we only have quarterly data, then both cause and effect will take place within one (data) time period. In other words: The length of the data time period compared to the reaction time will determine whether we will end up with a cyclic or a acyclic model.

Example 4

(Continuation of Example 3) If advertising affects sales in the same year while the budget is based on sales in the previous year, and we have yearly data, then equations (13) can be written:

$$S_t = \beta_{S0} + \beta_{S1}A_t + \varepsilon_S \tag{15a}$$
$$A_t = \beta_{A0} + \beta_{A1}S_{t-1} + \varepsilon_A \tag{15b}$$

If you assume the error-terms to be uncorrelated across the two equations, you have a recursive system: S_{t-1} is pre-determined in equation (15b), and A_t is pre-determined in equation (15a), where S_t is the only post-determined variable.

If you have only data for two-year periods, you have to fall back on a cyclic model.

A Final Advice

In the large majority of cases you will build your model on cross-section data, and then of course a cyclical model is the only possible choice if you have reciprocal causation.

Now, it is clear from Figure 5.6b that a two-way causation is a *dynamic* process, and we can think of the each of the two effects in Figure 5.6a as the sum of an infinite series of loops. Only in cases where the two sums are defined, i.e. where the corresponding series converge, is it possible to estimate the two effects.

However, such estimates only make sense if the process has, in reality, gone through the whole process, and brought it to the end. This is a rather hard assumption that is difficult (if not impossible) to judge.

As you can see, cyclical models are much more complicated than non-cyclical models. This is true, both as far as identification and estimation are concerned and when it comes to the substantive interpretation and recommendations based on the model.

Therefore, final advice would be: If at all possible, avoid cyclical models.

I will, however, show a single example of a cyclical model with only manifest variables in Chapter 8.

☞ In this chapter you have met the following concepts:

the zero B-rule and the	a wide range of fit indices:
recursive rule for	absolute fit measures
identification in acyclic	relative fit measures
models	parsimony-based fit measures
the order condition and the	fit measures based on the non-central
rank condition for	χ^2-distribution
identification in cyclic models	information-theoretic fit measures

Besides you have learned the following AMOS statement:
Sem.ResidualMoments

Questions

1. Explain the identification rules in your own words.
2. What characterizes each of the six groups of fit indices?

3. What are the numerical requirements usually used as rules of thumb in connection with the various indices?
4. State the various problems raised by using cyclic models.

Reference List

Aaker, D. A. and D. A. Day (1971) 'A recursive model of communication processes,' in D. A. Aaker (ed.), *Multivariate Analysis in Marketing*, Belmont, Calif.: Wadsworth.

Akaike, H. (1973) 'Information theory and an extension of the maximum likelihood principle,' in *Proceedings of the 2nd International Symposium on Information Theory*, B. N. Petrow and F. Csaki (eds), Budapest: Akademiai.

Akaike, H. (1987) 'Factor analysis and AIC,' *Psychometrika*, 52: 317–32.

Bentler, P. M. (1990) 'Comparative fit indexes in structural models,' *Psychological Bulletin*, 107: 238–46.

Bentler, P. M. (1995) *EQS Structural Equations Manual*, Encino, CA: Multivariate Software Inc.

Bentler, P. M. and D. G. Bonnett (1980) 'Significance tests and goodness of fit the analysis of covariance structures,' *Psychological Bulletin*, 88: 588–606.

Bozdogan, H. (1987) 'Model selection and Akaike's information criterion (AIC): The general theory and its analytical extensions,' *Psychometrika*, 52: 345–70.

Brown, W. S. (1991) *Introducing Econometrics*, St. Paul, MN: West Publishing Company.

Browne, M. W. and R. Cudeck (1989) 'Single sample cross-validation indices for covariance structures,' *Multivariate Behavioral Research*, 24: 445–55.

Browne, M. W. and R. Cudeck (1993) 'Alternative ways of assessing model fit,' in K. A. Bollen and J. S. Long (eds), *Testing Structural Equation Models*, Newbury Park CA: Sage.

Browne, M. W. and M. Mels (2002), 'Parth analysis (RAMONA),' in *SYSTAT 10.2— Statistics* II. Richmond, CA: SYSTAT Software Inc.

Davis, J. A. (1985) *The logic of Causal Order*, Beverly Hills, CA: Sage Publications.

Fornell, C. and J. Cha (1994) 'Partial least squares,' in P. Bagozzi (ed.), *Advanced Methods of Marketing Research*, Oxford: Blackwell.

Holter, J. W. (1983) 'The analysis of covariance structures: Goodness-of-fit-indices,' *Sociological Methods and Research*, 11: 325–44.

James, L. R., S. A. Mulaik, and J. M. Brett (1982) *Causal Analysis: Assumptions, Models and Data*, Beverly Hills: Sage.

Jöreskog, K. G. and D. Sörbom (1984) *LISREL 7 A Guide to Programs and Applications*, 3rd edition, Chicago: SPSS Inc.

Raftery, A.(1993) 'Bayesian model selection in structural equation models,' in K. Bollen and J. Long (eds), *Testing Structural Equation Models*, Newbury Park, CA: Sage.

Raftery, A. (1995) 'Bayesian model selection in social research,' in P. Marsden (ed.), *Sociological Methodology*, San Francisco: Jossey-Bass.

Schwarz, G. (1978) 'Estimating the dimension of a model,' *The Annals of Statistics*, 6: 461–64.

Steiger, J. H. and J. C. Lind (1980) 'Statistically based tests for the number of common factors,' in *Paper presented at the annual meeting of the Psychometric Society*, Iowa City, IA.

Tucker, L. R. and C. Lewis (1973) 'A reliability coefficient for maximum likelihood factor analysis,' *Psychometrika*, 38: 1–10.

Wheaton, B., B. Muthén, D. F. Alwin, and G. F. Summers (1977) 'Assessing reliability and stability in panel models,' in D. R. Heise (ed.), *Sociological Methodology*, San Francisco: Jossey Bass.

Wold, H. (1975) 'Path models with latent variables: The NIPALS approach,' in H. M. Blalock et al. (eds), *Quantitative Sociology: International Perspectives on Mathematical and Statistical modeling*, NY: Academic.

6

The Measurement Model in SEM: Confirmatory Factor Analysis

start the chapter by examining the differences between the three models, which are usually put under the common designation of factor analysis; namely component analysis, exploratory factor analysis and confirmatory factor analysis—the last-mentioned being in fact the measurement model of SEM.

Next, two rules for identification in confirmatory factor models are mentioned and estimation of confirmatory factor models are treated based on a classic example. You also learn how AMOS can help you in simplifying a model in order to obtain parsimony.

Then you will learn how confirmatory factor analysis can be used to construct summated scales and how to use SEM to measure reliability and validity in ways that are more in accordance with the theoretical definition of these concepts than those presented in Chapter 2.

The chapter ends with a short discussion of reflective and formative indicators—and points to a problem in scale construction that has often led researchers astray.

1. The Three Factor Models

In component analysis the components are linear functions of the original variables, whereas in factor analysis—whether exploratory or confirmatory—the roles are reversed: The variables are considered functions of latent variables called factors.

In exploratory factor analysis:

1. Every manifest variable is connected with every latent variable (as in component analysis).
2. Error terms are uncorrelated.
3. All parameters are estimated from the data.

In confirmatory factor analysis some or all of the above rules are violated:

1. Manifest variables are only connected with some pre-specified latent variables—the ideal being that every manifest variable is an indicator for one and only one factor.
2. Some error terms may be allowed to correlate.
3. Some of the parameters may be constrained to certain values or may be constrained to have same values as other parameters.

The differences among the three factor models are depicted in Figure 6.1 (it deserves mentioning that the component model and the exploratory factor models are shown prior to a possible rotation that could bring in correlations among the components or factors).

Comparing Figure 6.1 with Figure 1.6 it is obvious that the measurement models in SEM are confirmatory factor models, and that it is this model that was the

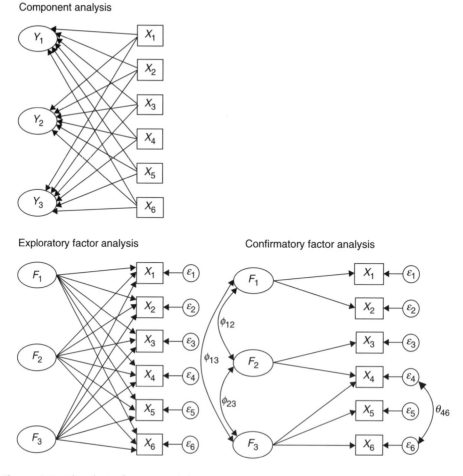

Figure 6.1   The three factor models

basis for the arguments against the classical methods of measuring validity in Chapter 2.

Remember that an indicator X_i can be:

1. A single item in a many-item scale,
2. A simple sum of several items, i.e. a summated scale, or
3. A weighted sum of several items, e.g. a principal component.

2. Identification and Estimation of Confirmatory Factor Models

In order to obtain identification every factor must have assigned a scale, either by fixing its variance or by fixing one of its regression weights and the same goes for the error terms. Further, the *t*-rule must be fulfilled, but as you have learned, this rule is only necessary, not sufficient.

Identification in Confirmatory Factor Models

Two rules—both of which are sufficient, but not necessary—deserve mentioning (compare Figure 4.1):

The three-indicator rule:
A confirmatory factor model is identified, if

1. Every factor has at least three indicators.
2. No manifest variable is indicator for more than one factor.
3. The error terms are not correlated.

The two-indicator rule:
A confirmatory factor model with at least two factors is identified if:

1. Every factor has at least two indicators.
2. No manifest variable is indicator for more than one factor.
3. The error terms are not correlated.
4. The covariance matrix for the latent variables does not contain zeros.

The main advantage of confirmatory models is that prior knowledge can be taken into account when formulating the model. Besides, confirmatory models open up for various methods for testing the models.

Example 1

Bollen has published several studies of the determinants of democratic development (e.g. Bollen, 1979, 1980). In this example I use data from Bollen (1989). In Table 6.1 a covariance matrix for eight variables is shown. The first four are

Table 6.1 Example 1: Covariance matrix

	X_1	X_2	X_3	X_4	X_5	X_6	X_7	X_8
X_1	6.89							
X_2	6.25	15.58						
X_3	5.84	5.84	10.76					
X_4	6.09	9.51	6.69	11.22				
X_5	5.06	5.60	4.94	5.70	6.83			
X_6	5.75	9.39	4.73	7.44	4.98	11.38		
X_7	5.81	7.54	7.01	7.49	5.82	6.75	10.80	
X_8	5.67	7.76	5.64	8.01	5.34	8.25	7.59	10.53

indications of degree of democracy in 75 developing countries in 1960, the four variables being:

$$X_1 = \text{freedom of the press}$$
$$X_2 = \text{freedom of group opposition}$$
$$X_3 = \text{fairness of election}$$
$$X_4 = \text{elective nature of the legislative body}$$

The next four variables are the same variables measured the same way in 1965.

A component analysis of the covariance matrix gives the first three eigen-values as:

$$57.17$$
$$8.47 \tag{1}$$
$$5.26$$

and shows a strong case for a one-component solution, although we know that in fact there are two sets of measurements: one for 1960 and one for 1965.

If we insist on a two-component solution, the component loadings (covariances) are (after a Varimax rotation):

$$
\begin{array}{ccc}
 & F_1 & F_2 \\
X_1 & 1.28 & 1.86 \\
X_2 & 3.53 & 0.96 \\
X_3 & 0.53 & 2.94 \\
X_4 & 2.23 & 1.94 \\
X_5 & 1.14 & 1.78 \\
X_6 & 2.79 & 1.09 \\
X_7 & 1.49 & 2.47 \\
X_8 & 2.12 & 1.80 \\
\end{array}
\tag{2}
$$

and we see that the two components in no way represent the two time periods.

Of course you can try an oblique rotation (which will show a correlation of 0.63 between the two components) or use exploratory factor analysis instead of component analysis—but none of these techniques will separate the two time periods.

This shows the dangers of letting automatic use of exploratory methods lead you astray instead of basing your decisions on theoretical considerations.

Now, let us see how such considerations can guide us:

1. We must maintain two factors: One expressing the degree of democracy in 1960 and the other the degree of democracy in 1965.
2. It is reasonable to assume that error terms in the same (manifest) measurement in the two years will correlate.
3. In the same way we will assume that the error terms for X_2 and X_4 (and X_6 and X_8) correlate, as these measurements are based on the same written source.

A model along these lines is shown in Figure 6.2. In order to estimate the model two conditions must be satisfied:

1. We must create scales for the latent variables.
2. The model must be identified.

As mentioned earlier the first condition can be met in two ways. The simplest is to fix one of the λs for each factor to 1.00. This will transfer the scale of the indicator in question to its latent variable. Another possibility is to standardize the factors by fixing their variances to 1.00. I have chosen the first possibility, hence the two 1s in Figure 6.2.

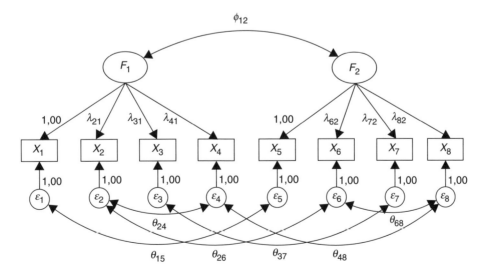

Figure 6.2 Example 1: Model

Regarding point 2 above, we have 23 parameters

6	coefficients
7	covariances
10	variances

to estimate. As input we have 8 variances and 28 covariances. We have thus 13 'pieces of information' or degrees of freedom left over for testing. The t-rule is satisfied. However, the 3-indicator rule cannot be used because of the correlated error terms. So the model is *possibly* identified.

A program for estimation of the model is shown in Table 6.2.

I use *generalized least squares* (Sem.Gls), and ask for *standardized parameters* (Sem.Standardized) and the *residual covariance matrix* (Sem.ResidualMoments),

Table 6.2   Example 1: AMOS-program

```
Sub Main
  Dim Sem As New AmosEngine
  Try
    Sem.Title ("Example 6.1")
    'Data from Bollen 1989
    Sem.TextOutput
    Sem.Gls
    Sem.Standardized
    Sem.ResidualMoments
    Sem.Crdiff

    Sem.BeginGroup ("Bollen.xls","sheet2")
    Sem.AStructure ("press60 = (1) F60 + (1) e_p60")
    Sem.AStructure ("opp60   =     F60 + (1) e_o60")
    Sem.AStructure ("fair60  =     F60 + (1) e_f60")
    Sem.AStructure ("elect60 =     F60 + (1) e_e60")

    Sem.AStructure ("press65 = (1) F65 + (1) e_p65")
    Sem.AStructure ("opp65   =     F65 + (1) e_o65")
    Sem.AStructure ("fair65  =     F65 + (1) e_f65")
    Sem.AStructure ("elect65 =     F65 + (1) e_e65")

    Sem.AStructure ("e_p60 <-> e_p65")
    Sem.AStructure ("e_o60 <-> e_o65")
    Sem.AStructure ("e_f60 <-> e_f65")
    Sem.AStructure ("e_e60 <-> e_e65")
    Sem.AStructure ("e_o60 <-> e_e60")
    Sem.AStructure ("e_o65 <-> e_e65")
    Sem.FitModel
  Finally
    Sem.Dispose
  End Try
End Sub
```

mentioned in Section 1.5. Furthermore, I ask for *Critical Ratios for Differences between Parameters* (Sem.Crdiff). This last command will be explained when I comment on the output.

The next line states that data are to be found in the Excel file 'Bollen1.xls' in 'sheet2.' Last in the program the model is formulated in a series of equations, which the reader is recommended to compare with the model in Figure 6.2.

Note that the correlation between the two factors is not specified in the program, as such correlations are default in AMOS when the programming interface is used. However, in the graphic interface you must specify the correlation, because here 'what you see is what you get.'

Table 6.3 shows the output.

1. First we find an account on the degrees of freedom as set out above.
2. We see that a χ^2-test of the model has a *P*-value of 0.509. This means that there is a probability of 0.509 to get this result or one that is more against our model, if the model is correct. A *P*-value near 50 pct. does not seem unsatisfying. We are, however, not interested in too large *P*-values, as this could be a sign of over-fitting, and therefore suggest that the model could be simplified.
3. The parameter estimates, their standard errors and C.R. values are next. AMOS labels each parameter for use later in the output.

   The only parameters that are not significant by traditional standards are e_f60 <--> e_f65 and e_e60 <--> e_e65 (one-sided tests, $\alpha = 0.05$). Remember that the *P*-values are for two-sided tests, but here one-sided tests seem more appropriate.
4. The residual covariance matrix in raw and standardized form follows. The standardized residual covariances are the raw covariances divided by their standard errors. Under the usual assumptions they are standard normal distributed, and we observe that none of them are very large. So there is not much to gain by introducing more parameters. On the contrary, it is perhaps possible to simplify the model by placing restrictions on parameters values.
5. Such restrictions could e.g. be that some parameters are fixed to take on the same values. As a help to judge whether the data are in accordance with such restrictions, 'critical ratios for differences between parameters' are shown next. These critical ratios are the differences between parameter estimates divided by the standard errors of the differences. Subject to the usual conditions these are standard normal distributed.

   However, you are strongly advised not to just fish for small differences that are not theoretically defendable.
6. Of the many fit indices only the first few are shown. Be assured, however, that all fit measures show extremely good fit.

As the fit is so good, it should perhaps be possible to simplify the model. Generally, we want a parsimonious model with as few free parameters as possible. Not only will a simple model be easier to interpret, it will also be easier to generalize.

Table 6.3   Example 1: Output from AMOS (extract)

Computation of degrees of freedom (Model 1)   (1)

```
            Number of distinct sample moments:   36
Number of distinct parameters to be estimated:   23
                Degrees of freedom (36–23):   13
```

Result (Model 1)   (2)

```
Minimum was achieved
Chi-square = 12.232
Degrees of freedom = 13
Probability level = .509
```

Group number 1 (Group number 1—Model 1)

Estimates (Group number 1—Model 1)   (3)

Scalar Estimates (Group number 1—Model 1)

```
Generalized Least Squares Estimates
```

Regression Weights: (Group number 1—Model 1)

			Estimate	S.E.	C.R.	P	Label
press60	<---	F60	1.000				
opp60	<---	F60	1.247	.182	6.836	***	par_1
fair60	<---	F60	1.081	.142	7.634	***	par_2
elect60	<---	F60	1.250	.147	8.502	***	par_3
press65	<---	F65	1.000				
opp65	<---	F65	1.236	.188	6.576	***	par_4
fair65	<---	F65	1.342	.170	7.904	***	par_5
elect65	<---	F65	1.305	.176	7.397	***	par_6

Covariances: (Group number 1—Model 1)

			Estimate	S.E.	C.R.	P	Label
F60	<-->	F65	4.419	.969	4.563	***	par_14
e_p60	<-->	e_p65	.593	.356	1.665	.096	par_7
e_o60	<-->	e_o65	1.575	.709	2.220	.026	par_8
e_f60	<-->	e_f65	.700	.590	1.187	.235	par_9
e_e60	<-->	e_e65	.480	.449	1.068	.286	par_10
e_o60	<-->	e_e60	1.252	.710	1.764	.078	par_11
e_o65	<-->	e_e65	.945	.560	1.690	.091	par_12

Table 6.3   Cont'd

Variances: (Group number 1—Model 1)

	Estimate	S.E.	C.R.	P	Label
F60	5.002	1.119	4.472	***	par_13
F65	4.174	1.067	3.911	***	par_15
e_p60	1.605	.420	3.821	***	par_16
e_o60	6.919	1.390	4.979	***	par_17
e_f60	4.006	.897	4.467	***	par_18
e_e60	3.048	.733	4.159	***	par_19
e_p65	2.505	.515	4.862	***	par_20
e_o65	3.852	.872	4.415	***	par_21
e_f65	3.031	.704	4.306	***	par_22
e_e65	2.984	.713	4.185	***	par_23

Matrices (Group number 1—Model 1)

Residual Covariances (Group number 1—Model 1) (4)

	elect65	fair65	opp65	press65	elect60	fair60	opp60	press60
elect65	.300							
fair65	.179	.105						
opp65	.464	-.264	1.001					
press65	-.177	.140	-.245	.060				
elect60	.213	-.028	.511	.098	.201			
fair60	-.670	-.197	-1.239	.095	-.163	.762		
opp60	.465	.042	.879	.014	.330	-.984	.673	
press60	-.172	-.199	.212	-.020	-.246	.353	-.072	.191

Standardized Residual Covariances (Group number 1—Model 1)

	elect65	fair65	opp65	press65	elect60	fair60	opp60	press60
elect65	.181							
fair65	.122	.061						
opp65	.313	-.182	.595					
press65	-.155	.119	-.216	.054				
elect60	.141	-.018	.350	.083	.112			
fair60	-.490	-.136	-.915	.087	-.113	.470		
opp60	.283	.025	.509	.010	.183	-.613	.278	
press60	-.148	-.167	.184	-.021	-.201	.313	-.053	.176

(Continued)

Table 6.3   Cont'd

Pairwise Parameter Comparisons (Model 1)

Critical Ratios for Differences between Parameters (Model 1)   (5)

	par_1	par_2	par_3	par_4	par_5	par_6	par_7	par_8
par_1	.000							
par_2	-.783	.000						
par_3	.022	1.021	.000					
par_4	-.052	.634	-.066	.000				
par_5	.415	1.356	.446	.593	.000			
par_6	.250	1.012	.272	.488	-.241	.000		
par_7	-1.716	-1.348	-1.798	-1.708	-2.061	-1.921	.000	
par_8	.438	.679	.449	.456	.317	.371	1.221	.000
par_9	-.879	-.602	-.903	-.855	-1.002	-.977	.142	-.979
par_10	-1.592	-1.286	-1.578	-1.553	-1.811	-1.645	-.197	-1.170
par_11	.006	.236	.002	.022	-.123	-.072	.805	-.338
par_12	-.512	-.235	-.525	-.471	-.678	-.587	.509	-.697
par_13	3.134	3.336	3.132	3.270	3.146	3.182	3.639	2.606
par_14	3.077	3.296	3.087	3.025	2.917	2.944	3.525	2.379
par_15	2.653	2.829	2.668	2.492	2.411	2.431	3.055	2.033
par_16	.833	1.278	.852	.827	.603	.680	2.623	.035
par_17	3.969	4.176	4.040	4.038	3.976	4.012	4.354	4.447
par_18	2.993	3.110	3.016	3.008	2.875	2.943	3.347	2.148
par_19	2.345	2.646	2.316	2.392	2.267	2.287	2.924	1.366
par_20	2.341	2.719	2.384	2.434	2.284	2.327	4.235	1.057
par_21	2.897	3.130	2.942	2.841	2.816	2.832	3.353	2.710
par_22	2.442	2.667	2.474	2.451	2.222	2.380	2.931	1.483
par_23	2.364	2.623	2.359	2.329	2.251	2.191	2.934	1.324

	par_9	par_10	par_11	par_12	par_13	par_14	par_15	par_16
par_9	.000							
par_10	-.280	.000						
par_11	.586	.904	.000					
par_12	.308	.680	-.318	.000				
par_13	3.488	3.773	2.841	3.262	.000			
par_14	3.369	3.708	2.697	3.171	-1.043	.000		
par_15	2.917	3.210	2.285	2.704	-.833	-.522	.000	
par_16	1.150	1.824	.430	.915	-2.676	-2.547	-2.184	.000
par_17	4.135	4.240	4.843	3.884	1.079	1.495	1.569	3.638
par_18	4.041	3.439	2.374	2.920	-.717	-.322	-.123	2.230
par_19	2.377	3.646	2.554	2.222	-1.472	-1.156	-.875	1.718
par_20	2.168	2.923	1.427	2.037	-1.983	-1.665	-1.326	1.500
par_21	3.087	3.264	2.237	3.955	-.816	-.443	-.236	2.242
par_22	3.388	2.883	1.788	2.261	-1.514	-1.190	-.913	1.687
par_23	2.404	3.809	1.658	3.423	-1.532	-1.214	-.936	1.648

Table 6.3 Cont'd

	par_17	par_18	par_19	par_20	par_21	par_22	par_23
par_17	.000						
par_18	-1.763	.000					
par_19	-2.595	-.797	.000				
par_20	-2.977	-1.402	-.600	.000			
par_21	-1.948	-.124	.675	1.323	.000		
par_22	-2.514	-.913	-.016	.572	-.739	.000	
par_23	-2.443	-.886	-.064	.541	-.828	-.044	.000

Model Fit Summary   (6)

CMIN

Model	NPAR	CMIN	DF	P	CMIN/DF
Default model	23	12.232	13	.509	.941
Saturated model	36	.000	0		
Independence model	8	70.002	28	.000	2.500
Zero model	0	296.000	36	.000	8.222

For example, you could argue that the connection between a latent variable and its indicator is the same for the two years, i.e. that the measuring instrument itself does not change between the two measurements. If so, you could stipulate the conditions:

$$\lambda_{12} = \lambda_{25}$$
$$\lambda_{13} = \lambda_{26} \qquad\qquad (3)$$
$$\lambda_{14} = \lambda_{27}$$

and in the program in Table 6.2 the following lines

```
Sem.AStructure ("press60 = (1) F60 + (1) e_p60")
Sem.AStructure ("opp60   = (a) F60 + (1) e_o60")
Sem.AStructure ("fair60  = (b) F60 + (1) e_f60")
Sem.AStructure ("elect60 = (c) F60 + (1) e_e60")


Sem.AStructure ("press65 = (1) F65 + (1) e_p65")
Sem.AStructure ("opp65   = (a) F65 + (1) e_o65")
Sem.AStructure ("fair65  = (b) F65 + (1) e_f65")
Sem.AStructure ("elect65 = (c) F65 + (1) e_e65")
```

are substituted for the corresponding ones. Placing the same letters in parentheses next to two variable forces, the two variables to have the same regression weight.

From point (5) in the output we see that these restrictions are not inconsistent with the data. The main results of this second run are shown in the model in Figure 6.3, and the fit figures are:

$$\chi^2 = 14.247 \quad df = 16 \quad \text{P-value} = 0.580$$
$$\chi^2/df = 0.890 \quad (0.941)$$
$$\text{RMSEA} = 0.000 \quad (0.000) \tag{4}$$
$$\text{PCLOSE} = 0.746 \quad (0.671)$$

the corresponding values from the first model being shown in parentheses. We compare the two models as follows:

	χ^2	f
New model	14.247	16
Old model	12.232	13
Difference	2.015	3

(5)

The difference is asymptotically distributed as χ^2 with 3 degrees of freedom. As a value of 2.015 with 3 degrees of freedom is not statistically significant according to traditional criteria, we prefer the new and simpler model.

This so-called χ^2-difference test is restricted to cases where one of the two models is nested under the other—i.e. one model can be obtained by placing restrictions on the other.

In introducing these restrictions I had an eye to point (5) in the output in Table 6.3, but my choice of restrictions was based on substantive reasoning. I was not fishing in the output. You can find a lot of very small differences in the this section of the output, but to restrict the corresponding parameters to be equal will in most cases be without meaning.

The revision of the original model was theory-driven; but if model revision is more or less driven by empirical evidence the 'testing' is not meaningful, as you test on the same data that have formed the hypotheses. For example, if you drop insignificant parameters from a model you can be almost sure that the χ^2-difference test will also be insignificant.

3. Confirmatory Factor Analysis and the Construction of Summated Scales

Very often confirmatory factor analysis will give a more differentiated picture of a scale's characteristics than traditional item analysis or exploratory factor analysis.

In Example 2.1 an item analysis in SPSS reduced the scale with 3 items and increased Cronbach's alpha from 0.831 to 0.866. In Example 3.3 we reached the same conclusion using principal component analysis.

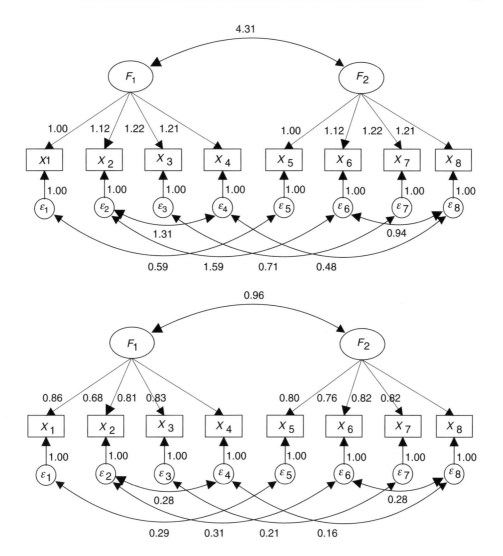

Figure 6.3 Example 1: The final model—raw and standardized parameters

These are the two 'classical' techniques for item analysis, but they are not without drawbacks:

1. A large Cronbach's alpha and/or large item-rest correlations is no guarantee for uni-dimensionality.
2. In component analysis (and exploratory factor analysis) every manifest variable is connected with every latent variable, whereas in the ideal scale, every manifest variable is only connected to one factor. This blurs the picture (c.f. Figure 6.1).
3. In both cases the possibilities for statistical testing are limited.

Example 2

Childers et al. (1985) constructed a scale for measuring 'Style of Processing' (SOP), i.e. a person's preference to engage in a verbal and/or visual modality of processing information about one's environment.

The SOP scale is a 22-item 4-point scale, of which 11 items are assumed to reflect a verbal processing style, and 11 a visual processing style. Childers et al. proposed the two sub-scales to be used either separately or in combination as one scale—although they preferred using the combined scale.

The items are shown in Table 6.4.

Table 6.4   Example 2: Style of processing scale: SOP

1. I enjoy work that requires the use of words.
2. There are some special times in my life that I like to relive by mentally 'picturing just how everything looked.'*
3. I can never seem to find the right word when I need it.*
4. I do a lot of reading.
5. When I'm trying to learn something new, I'd rather watch a demonstration than read how to do it.*
6. I think I often use words in the wrong way.*
7. I enjoy learning new words.
8. I like to picture how I could fix up my apartment or a room if I could buy anything I wanted.*
9. I often make written notes to myself.
10. I like to daydream.*
11. I generally prefer to use a diagram rather than a written set of instructions.*
12. I like to 'doodle.'*
13. I find it helps to think in terms of mental pictures when doing many things.*
14. After I meet someone for the first time, I can usually remember what they look like, but not much about them.*
15. I like to think in synonyms of words.
16. When I have forgotten something I frequently try to form a mental 'picture' to remember it.*
17. I like learning new words.
18. I prefer to read instructions about how to do something rather than have someone show me.
19. I prefer activities that don't require a lot of reading.*
20. I seldom daydream.
21. I spend very little time trying to increase my vocabulary.*
22. My thinking often consists of mental 'pictures' or images.*

NOTES: *Denotes items that are reverse scored. Items 1, 3, 4, 6, 7, 9, 15, 17, 18, 19, and 21 compose the verbal component. Items 2, 5, 8, 10 through 14, 16, 20, and 22 compose the visual component.

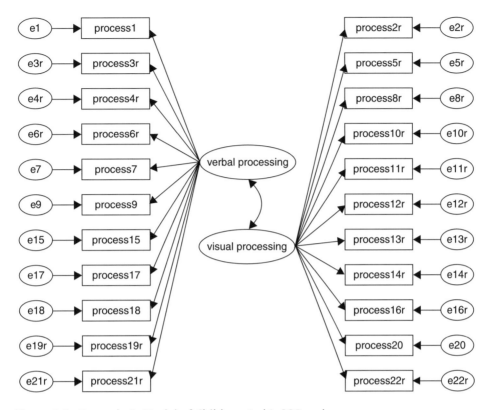

Figure 6.4   Example 2: Model of Childers et al.'s SOP scale

The scale was used by Sørensen (2001) in a project on consumer behavior, the respondents being 88 randomly selected Danish housewives. The scale used was a seven-point scale and not a four-point scale as the original one. You can find Sørensen's data on the book's website.

Cronbach's alpha was 0.76 for the verbal sub-scale and 0.71 for the visual sub-scale, while the alpha for the combined scale was 0.74. In Childers et al.'s (1985) original paper they stated the same alphas were 0.81, 0.86 and 0.88 respectively. In most circumstances alphas of this size will lead to acceptance of the scales as reliable and *uni-dimensional*.

Here I will use Sørensen's data in order to evaluate the scale, the measurement model being shown in Figure 6.4.

Program and output are shown in Table 6.5.

Note that I ask for *modification indices larger than 5* (Sem.Mods 5). A modification index is attached to a fixed parameter, and states by how much the χ^2-value will be reduced if the parameter is set free. In the output you will see that there are two covariances (e11r<--> e13r and e6r<-->e8r) and two regression weights (process13r<---process11r and process8r<---process6r) that can be expected to reduce χ^2 with at least 5.00 if they are set free.

Next to the modification indices (M.I.) you will see the expected change in parameter values (Par Change). At present these parameters are not in the model,

Table 6.5   Example 2: Program and output of first run (extract)

```
Sub Main
  Dim Sem As New AmosEngine
  Try
    SemTitle ("Example 6.3")
    'SOP scale, 1st run. Data from Sørensen (2001)
    Sem.TextOutput
    Sem.Gls
    Sem.Standardized
    Sem.Mods 5
    Sem.BeginGroup ("SOP","SOP")

    Sem.AStructure ("process1   = verbal + (1) e1")
    Sem.AStructure ("process3r  = verbal + (1) e3r")
    Sem.AStructure ("process4   = verbal + (1) e4")
    Sem.AStructure ("process6r  = verbal + (1) e6r")
    Sem.AStructure ("process7   = verbal + (1) e7")
    Sem.AStructure ("process9   = verbal + (1) e9")
    Sem.AStructure ("process15  = verbal + (1) e15")
    Sem.AStructure ("process17  = verbal + (1) e17")
    Sem.AStructure ("process18  = verbal + (1) e18")
    Sem.AStructure ("process19r = verbal + (1) e19r")
    Sem.AStructure ("process21r = verbal + (1) e21r")

    Sem.AStructure ("process2r  = visual + (1) e2r")
    Sem.AStructure ("process5r  = visual + (1) e5r")
    Sem.AStructure ("process8r  = visual + (1) e8r")
    Sem.AStructure ("process10r = visual + (1) e10r")
    Sem.AStructure ("process11r = visual + (1) e11r")
    Sem.AStructure ("process12r = visual + (1) e12r")
    Sem.AStructure ("process13r = visual + (1) e13r")
    Sem.AStructure ("process14r = visual + (1) e14r)
    Sem.AStructure ("process16r = visual + (1) e16r")
    Sem.AStructure ("process20  = visual + (1) e20")
    Sem.AStructure ("process22r = visual + (1) e22r")

    Sem.AStructure ("verbal (1)")
    Sem.AStructure ("visual (1)")
    Sem.FitModel
  Finally
    Sem.Dispose
  End Try
End Sub
```

Table 6.5 Cont'd

Result (Model 1)

```
Minimum was achieved
Chi-square = 242.238
Degrees of freedom = 208
Probability level = .052
```

Scalar Estimates (Group number 1—Model 1)

Generalized Least Squares Estimates

Regression Weights: (Group number 1—Model 1)

			Estimate	S.E.	C.R.	P	Label
process1	<---	verbal	.817	.150	5.453	***	
process3r	<---	verbal	-.379	.198	-1.908	.056	
process4	<---	verbal	.366	.209	1.749	.080	
process6r	<---	verbal	.150	.166	.902	.367	
process7	<---	verbal	.949	.114	8.293	***	
process9	<---	verbal	.129	.256	.504	.614	
process15	<---	verbal	.570	.222	2.566	.010	
process17	<---	verbal	.994	.112	8.890	***	
process18	<---	verbal	.059	.167	.353	.724	
process19r	<---	verbal	.292	.187	1.559	.119	
process21r	<---	verbal	.580	.198	2.936	.003	
process2r	<---	visual	.871	.185	4.704	***	
process5r	<---	visual	.151	.182	.827	.408	
process8r	<---	visual	.462	.146	3.170	.002	
process10r	<---	visual	1.513	.181	8.380	***	
process11r	<---	visual	-.070	.198	-.352	.725	
process12r	<---	visual	-.224	.234	-.957	.339	
process13r	<---	visual	.414	.224	1.847	.065	
process14r	<---	visual	.224	.225	.999	.318	
process16r	<---	visual	.178	.207	.861	.390	
process20	<---	visual	1.747	.194	8.990	***	
process22r	<---	visual	.428	.203	2.105	.035	

Covariances: (Group number 1—Model 1)

			Estimate	S.E.	C.R.	P	Label
verbal	<-->	visual	-.366	.117	-3.117	.002	

(Continued)

Table 6.5   Cont'd

Modification Indices (Group number 1–Model 1)

Covariances: (Group number 1–Model 1)

			M.I.	Par Change
e11r	<-->	e13r	6.103	.541
e6r	<-->	e8r	5.757	-.294

Variances: (Group number 1–Model 1)

	M.I.	Par Change

Regression Weights: (Group number 1–Model 1)

			M.I.	Par Change
process13r	<---	process11r	6.088	.278
process8r	<---	process6r	5.471	-.413

i.e. they are fixed at zero. Consequently the expected parameter changes are the expected parameter values.

However, always remember that these figures are indications of marginal changes, and do not say anything about what would happen if more than one parameter were set free simultaneously.

The two last Structure-lines in the program fixes the variances of the two factors to 1.00 in order to identify the model.

A Chi-square of 242.236 with 208 degrees of freedom giving a P-value of 0.052 is a little on the low side. What is more serious is that the fit indices are not quite satisfactory:

CMIN/DF	CFI	RMSEA	LO 90	HI 90	PCLOSE
1.165	0.531	0.043	0.000	0.065	0.665

CFI-indices below 0.80 should be taken seriously. So let us have a look at the modification indices.

Causal paths between items in a summated scale are of course meaningless, and so are the suggested covariances (although the covariance between e11r and e13r could be taken as a sign that the two items are a little too close).

As I have advocated earlier, it is usually a good idea to base suggestions for modifications in a model on substantive rather than pure empirical evidence, so let us have a look at the items in Table 6.4. A few items catch the eye:

1. Item 10 and item 20 say nearly the same and serve as mutual controls on the consistency of the answers, so they should correlate more than caused by their common cause: 'visual.'

2. The same can be said of items 7 and 17.
3. Items 3 and 6 are also very close: If you cannot find a special word when you need it and therefore use another word, I think you would find that other word less suitable in the situation.

At least you should consider introducing these correlations in the model.

4. You should also expect correlations among items 5, 11 and 18. Whereas the other items only mention one of the processing styles, these three explicitly mention both, and compare them.

According to their wording these three items could be placed in both sub-scales. You should therefore consider letting them load on both factors.

A program along these lines is shown in Table 6.6 together with output.

With a chi-square of 216.288 with 202 degrees of freedom giving a P-value of 0.233, the model seems satisfactory, and a look at the fit-indices confirms this:

CMIN/DF	CFI	RMSEA	LO 90	HI 90	PCLOSE
1.071	0.804	0.029	0.000	0.055	0.895

Although CFI are not quite up to standard (>0.90–0.95), it is considerably larger than in the first run, and the other indices are fine.

Studying the parameters of the model, you observe the following:

1. Item 18 has significant loadings on both factors whereas items 5 and 11, which were supposed to measure visual processing style, actually both have significant loadings on 'verbal' and insignificant loadings on 'visual.' However, all coefficients have the expected signs.
2. The following regression weights are insignificant (one-sided test, $\alpha = 0.05$): 15, 17, 21r, 5r, 11r and 12r.
3. All the covariances are significant, and the correlation between the two factors is 0.680 (as the two factors are standardized, the correlation equals the covariance).

What, then, can we conclude?

1. The SOP scale has two dimensions as suggested by Childers et al.—in fact it has *more* than two dimensions showing up as highly significant correlations between items in the same 'main dimension.'
2. Some of the items have very little loading on the factor they are supposed to measure. A reformulation or exclusion should be considered.
3. Although the two sub-scales correlate, there are in fact *two* dimensions, and treating them as one scale could—depending on the research question—cause problems, as it assumes that the two ways of processing are alternatives.

Table 6.6   Example 2: Program and output for the second run

```
Sub Main
  Dim Sem As New AmosEngine
  Try
    SemTitle ("Example 6.3")
    'SOP scale, 2st run. Data from Sørensen (2001)
    Sem.TextOutput
    Sem.Gls
    Sem.Standardized
    Sem.Mods 5
    Sem.BeginGroup ("Elin2.xls","Elin2")

    Sem.AStructure ("process1    = verbal + (1) e1")
    Sem.AStructure ("process3r   = verbal + (1) e3r")
    Sem.AStructure ("process4    = verbal + (1) e4")
    Sem.AStructure ("process6r   = verbal + (1) e6r")
    Sem.AStructure ("process7    = verbal + (1) e7")
    Sem.AStructure ("process9    = verbal + (1) e9")
    Sem.AStructure ("process15   = verbal + (1) e15")
    Sem.AStructure ("process17   = verbal + (1) e17")
    Sem.AStructure ("process18   = verbal +visual + (1) e18")
    Sem.AStructure ("process19r = verbal + (1) e19r")
    Sem.AStructure ("process21r = verbal + (1) e21r")
    Sem.AStructure ("process2r   = visual + (1) e2r")
    Sem.AStructure ("process5r   = visual + verbal + (1) e5r")
    Sem.Structure  ("process8r   = visual + (1) e8r")
    Sem.AStructure ("process10r = visual + (1) c10r")
    Sem.AStructure ("process11r = visual + verbal + (1) e11r")
    Sem.AStructure ("process12r = visual + (1) e12r")
    Sem.AStructure ("process13r = visual + (1) e13r")
    Sem.AStructure ("process14r = visual + (1) e14r")
    Sem.AStructure ("process16r = visual + (1) e16r")
    Sem.AStructure ("process20   = visual + (1) e20")
    Sem.AStructure ("process22r = visual + (1) e22r")

    Sem.AStructure ("verbal (1)")
    Sem.AStructure ("visual (1)")

    Sem.AStructure ("e10r<-->e20")
    Sem.AStructure ("e7 <-->e17")
    Sem.AStructure ("e3r<-->e6r")
    Sem.AFitModel
  Finally
    Sem.Dispose
  End Try
End Sub
```

Table 6.6 Cont'd

Result (Model 1)

```
Minimum was achieved
Chi-square = 216.288
Degrees of freedom = 202
Probability level = .233
```

Scalar Estimates (Group number 1—Model 1)

Generalized Least Squares Estimates

Regression Weights: (Group number 1—Model 1)

			Estimate	S.E.	C.R.	P	Label
process1	<---	verbal	.505	.177	2.858	.004	
process3r	<---	verbal	.760	.202	3.756	***	
process4	<---	verbal	.262	.218	1.204	.229	
process6r	<---	verbal	.529	.169	3.131	.002	
process7	<---	verbal	.225	.137	1.646	.100	
process9	<---	verbal	.768	.265	2.892	.004	
process15	<---	verbal	.314	.235	1.335	.182	
process17	<---	verbal	.198	.136	1.456	.145	
process18	<---	verbal	1.858	.386	4.808	***	
process18	<---	visual	-.996	.425	-2.343	.019	
process19r	<---	verbal	1.247	.203	6.155	***	
process21r	<---	verbal	.085	.209	.405	.685	
process2r	<---	visual	.802	.197	4.065	***	
process5r	<---	visual	-.430	.380	-1.131	.258	
process5r	<---	verbal	1.745	.355	4.915	***	
process8r	<---	visual	.874	.160	5.474	***	
process10r	<---	visual	.571	.210	2.718	.007	
process11r	<---	visual	-.212	.343	-.620	.535	
process11r	<---	verbal	1.232	.321	3.834	***	
process12r	<---	visual	.318	.243	1.310	.190	
process13r	<---	visual	1.282	.216	5.930	***	
process14r	<---	visual	.701	.231	3.035	.002	
process16r	<---	visual	.684	.212	3.225	.001	
process20	<---	visual	.649	.228	2.848	.004	
process22r	<---	visual	1.285	.197	6.524	***	

Covariances: (Group number 1—Model 1)

			Estimate	S.E.	C.R.	P	Label
verbal	<-->	visual	.680	.124	5.469	***	
e10r	<-->	e20	1.409	.355	3.968	***	
e7	<-->	e17	.349	.105	3.335	***	
e3r	<-->	e6r	.456	.211	2.161	.031	

(Continued)

Table 6.6   Cont'd

Modification Indices (Group number 1–Model 1)

Covariances: (Group number 1–Model 1)

			M.I.	Par Change
e3r	<-->	e2r	6.299	−.474

Variances: (Group number 1–Model 1)

	M.I.	Par Change

Regression Weights: (Group number 1–Model 1)

			M.I.	Par Change
process2r	<---	process3r	5.834	−.276

4. In fact it has long been known that verbal and visual processes take place in functionally separate cognitive systems and thus are not alternatives (Paivio, 1971).

From the last point above we learn that it is of the utmost importance to spend a good deal of time making clear the nature of the concepts you intend to measure. This preliminary step is, all too often, not given the necessary care.

This line of reasoning immediately gives birth to another question: The SOP scale is intended to measure preference—but do all items really measure preference? It seems to me that items 3, 6 and 14 measure ability rather than preference. Of course preference and ability must be expected to correlate, because you generally prefer activities where you feel you have the largest potential—but is ability not exogenous, and should the arrows connecting items 3, 6 and 14 to their latent variables not point in the opposite direction?

Also observe that the modifications to the original model were *not* based on the modification indices, but on substantive reasoning. The last two points have taught us an important lesson—that serious thinking on the subject area is much to be preferred to thoughtless dependence on computer output.

Now, in the light of point 4 above, you may wonder why the two factors correlate at all? A possible explanation is that the correlation is caused by item 18 loading on both factors, and that the correlation would disappear if this item (together with items 5 and 11) were removed. If we do so we get the output in Table 6.7.

The fit of this model is not too bad:

CMIN/DF	CFI	RMSEA	LO 90	HI 90	PCLOSE
1.096	0.801	0.033	0.000	0.062	0.807

Table 6.7   Example 2: Output from 3rd run

Result (Model 1)

```
Minimum was achieved
Chi-square = 162.176
Degrees of freedom = 148
Probability level = .201
```

Group number 1 (Group number 1—Model 1)

Estimates (Group number 1—Model 1)

Scalar Estimates (Group number 1—Model 1)

Generalized Least Squares Estimates

Regression Weights: (Group number 1—Model 1)

			Estimate	S.E.	C.R.	P	Label
process1	<---	verbal	.932	.167	5.579	***	
process3r	<---	verbal	.292	.218	1.341	.180	
process4	<---	verbal	.828	.224	3.705	***	
process6r	<---	verbal	.860	.171	5.037	***	
process7	<---	verbal	.730	.133	5.493	***	
process9	<---	verbal	.350	.285	1.229	.219	
process15	<---	verbal	.654	.233	2.805	.005	
process17	<---	verbal	.682	.133	5.125	***	
process19r	<---	verbal	.781	.218	3.581	***	
process21r	<---	verbal	.930	.201	4.623	***	
process2r	<---	visual	1.053	.202	5.218	***	
process8r	<---	visual	.596	.156	3.829	***	
process10r	<---	visual	.570	.216	2.641	.008	
process12r	<---	visual	.151	.251	.599	.549	
process13r	<---	visual	1.198	.220	5.454	***	
process14r	<---	visual	.462	.241	1.922	.055	
process16r	<---	visual	.633	.218	2.910	.004	
process20	<---	visual	.922	.227	4.065	***	
process22r	<---	visual	1.070	.195	5.484	***	

Covariances: (Group number 1—Model 1)

			Estimate	S.E.	C.R.	P	Label
verbal	<-->	visual	-.030	.161	-.187	.852	
e10r	<-->	e20	1.421	.371	3.832	***	
e7	<-->	e17	.323	.117	2.772	.006	
e3r	<-->	e6r	.396	.220	1.800	.072	

(Continued)

Table 6.7 Cont'd

Correlations: (Group number 1—Model 1)

			Estimate
verbal	<-->	visual	-.030
e10r	<-->	e20	.724
e7	<-->	e17	.553
e3r	<-->	e6r	.346

Modification Indices (Group number 1—Model 1)

Covariances: (Group number 1—Model 1)

	M.I.	Par Change

Variances: (Group number 1—Model 1)

	M.I.	Par Change

Regression Weights (Group number 1—Model 1)

	M.I.	Par Change

and as the three models are not significantly different (output not shown), there is no reason not to prefer the third and most simple model. However, the most striking support for this model is found using the decision theoretic measures:

	Model 1	Model 2	Model 3
AIC	332	318	246
BCC	365	355	271
BIC	444	445	350
CAIC	489	496	392

Looking at the parameter estimates, we see that:

1. The correlation between the two factors disappeared, as it should according to theory.
2. The other three correlations are all significant.
3. Items 3r, 9 and 12 are not significant.

The purist would remove items 3, 7 and 20 in order to get rid of the remaining correlations. However, as these correlations would probably be (nearly) constant and repeat themselves in future uses of the scale, they will not reduce its reliability. You could also consider removing or re-phrasing the insignificant items—and perhaps also exclude the three 'ability items.'

4. Reliability and Validity

The classical methods of judging the reliability and the validity of a measuring instrument all have their shortcomings from the fact that none of them take the latent variables explicitly into account as part of the measurement model.

Therefore, the theoretical definitions of reliability and validity as coefficients of determination when regressing the measurement on the theoretical constructs could not be used as a basis for calculations. However, using a SEM model as the basis for judging reliability and validity should open up this possibility.

Reliability

In equation (2.3a) the reliability coefficient was defined as the coefficient of determination, when a measurement (an indicator, a manifest variable) is regressed on its latent variable(s). Using SEM, you can use this definition to calculate reliability coefficients.

Example 2

(continued) If you include the statement

Sem.Smc

(Smc = squared multiple correlation) in the program in Table 6.7, the output will include the estimates in Table 6.8.

It comes as no surprise that the four items with the smallest reliabilities are the ones that have non-significant regression weights. However, a few of the highly significant items have rather small reliabilities and should be discarded or reformulated.

Anyway, if apart from measuring SOP you also want to measure several other concepts in order to construct a causal model, 22 is quite a lot of items. If the other latent variables require a similar number of items your questionnaire can easily grow to a length that could cause messy data, because respondents refuse to participate, they do not answer all the questions, or they fill out the questionnaire more or less at random in order to get the job done as quickly as possible.

Very often scale constructors, in their efforts to obtain perfection, end up with scales that are too long for practical (commercial) use. The SOP scale is perhaps an example of that.

This way of calculating a reliability coefficient has at least five advantages:

1. It is based on the very definition of reliability.
2. It is possible to calculate the reliability of every single item and not just a (weighted) sum of them.
3. It can be used whether the measurements are parallel, tau-equivalent or congeneric.

Table 6.8 Example 2: Calculation of reliabilities

Squared multiple correlations:
(Group number 1 - Model 1)

	Estimate
process22r	.475
process20	.306
process16r	.159
process14r	.061
process13r	.537
process12r	.008
process10r	.140
process8r	.334
process2r	.527
process21r	.367
process19r	.262
process17	.435
process15	.159
process9	.036
process7	.485
process6r	.445
process4	.257
process3r	.057
process1	.499

4. It does not assume errors to be uncorrelated across items.
5. It can be used when an item is an indicator for more than just one latent variable.

If you have only cross-sectional data it is in general not possible to estimate the specific variance, which is then absorbed into the error variance. In this case you must either assume that the specific variance is zero or you may consider the estimated reliabilities to be lower bounds.

Validity

Calculation of a suitable measure for the validity is more complicated.

Let us assume that we have a manifest variable X, which is an indicator for more than one latent variable in our model. If we take as our starting point that the validity of X is the extent to which X is connected to the concepts it is assumed to measure, then the most straightforward measures of validity are the coefficients λ in raw or standardized form. Each of these measures has the same advantages and drawbacks, as we know from traditional regression analysis. One advantage of the standardized coefficients is that they are independent of the measurement units. This is very important in the case of SEM, where the measurement scales of the variables and especially those of the latent variables, are often more or less arbitrary. On the other hand standardized coefficients depend on the variances in the populations, and if you wish to compare several groups from different populations this could be a problem.

Another way is to start with the reliability coefficient as the coefficient of determination when regressing the variable X on all variables that have a direct effect on it. This is of course the Smc as defined in the section above on reliability.

If we want the validity coefficient to measure that part of the variance in X attributable to, e.g. F_1, we must deduce from the squared multiple correlation coefficient the variation caused by all other factors influencing X.

We can then define the validity coefficient of X with regard to F_1 as

$$U_{XF_1} = R_X^2 - R_{X(F_1)}^2 \tag{6}$$

where R_X^2 is the coefficient of determination obtained by regressing X on all variables that have a direct influence on X, while $R_{X(F_1)}^2$ is the coefficient of determination obtained by regressing X on the same variables except F_1. The symbols in (6) are taken from Bollen (1989), who proposed the measure, which he called *Unique Validity Variance*.

Example 2

(continued) Let us estimate the unique validity variance of *process18* with regard to *verbal*.

We have

$$U_{process\ 18\ verbal_1} = R_{process\ 18}^2 - R_{process\ 18\ (verbal)}^2 \tag{7}$$

$R_{process\ 18}^2$ is estimated including the statement Sem.Smc in the program in Table 6.9, and $R_{process\ 18\ (verbal)}^2$ by regressing process18 only on 'visual':

$$U_{process\ 18\ verbal_1} = 0.728 - 0.095 = 0.633 \tag{8}$$

As pointed out several times the concept of validity is much more problematic both to define and to measure than reliability. The reader is referred to Bollen (1989) for further reading.

5. Reflexive and Formative Indicators

In a confirmatory factor model (and also in an exploratory factor model), the arrows point *from* the latent variable *to* its manifest indicators. As a consequence, indicators of the same latent variable must correlate—cf. Figure 6.5a.

It is a very common mistake among newcomers to SEM to overlook this simple fact, and use indicators that are not *necessarily* correlated.

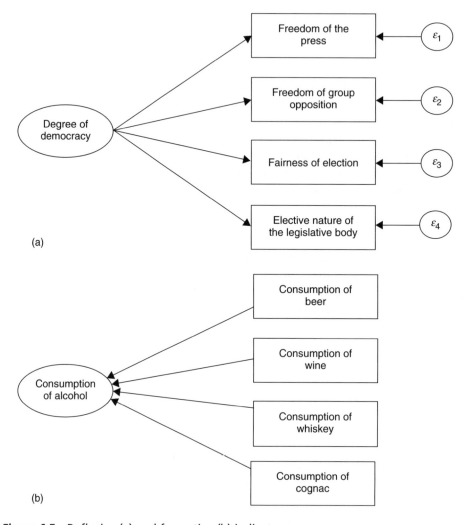

Figure 6.5   Reflexive (a) and formative (b) indicators

The classical example is that you want to measure a person's consumption of alcoholic beverages, and to that end use a series of questions each measuring the consumption of one single beverage; i.e. use indicators such as:

> Consumption of beer
> Consumption of wine
> Consumption of whiskey
> Consumption of cognac
> etc.

While a (weighted) sum of these variables is a measure of total consumption of alcohol, there is no reason to believe that all these indicators should be correlated.

In a graphic illustration of this situation, the arrows should point *from* the indicators and *to* the latent variable c.f. Figure 6.5b.

The indicators in panel (a) of the figure are called *reflexive*: They reflect the underlying latent variable. In contrast the indicators in panel (b) are called *formative*: They *form* or define the latent variable—which in this case is not at all latent: Being a weighted sum of manifest variables is itself manifest. Following the tradition I have, however, depicted it as an ellipse.

While a certain amount of correlation should exist among reflexive indicators for the same latent variable, inter-item correlations for formative indicators should—if possible—be avoided.

It is important to be aware that classical test theory and concepts like reliability and validity assume items to be reflexive. Also, programs like AMOS do not accept formative indicators. Instead you can use a single item, a summated scale or a principal component.

In fact, you have already met examples of formative indicators, namely the three problematic items forb38, forb39 and forb41 in the fish example (Example 2.1).

In many applications of SEM, socio-economic variables are used to characterize a person. The various indicators used are most realistically seen as formative, but it is not at all seldom to see them treated as reflexive.

If your model includes several 'latent' variables with formative indicators, you should try using another SEM technique, *partial least squares* (PLS), invented by Herman Wold (1975). An introduction to this technique can be found in Fornell and Cha (1994).

You could say that PLS relates to covariance based SEM as component analysis to factor analysis (see Figure 6.1).

☞ In this chapter you have met the following concepts:
confirmatory factor analysis   smc as a measure of reliability
three-indicator rule   unique variance as a measure of validity
two-indicator rule χ^2-difference test

Besides, you have been introduced to the AMOS statements:
Sem.Crdiff   Sem.Mods (−)

Questions

1. State the differences among the three (main) factor models, and discuss their virtues and vices.
2. Could you suggest further modifications to the model in Figure 3?
3. Comment on the various instruments AMOS offers for helping you with model modifications. Discuss their virtues and vices.
4. Comment on the differences between reflective and formative indicators. Why is this distinction important?

Reference List

Bollen, K. A. (1979) 'Political Democracy and the timing of development,' *American Sociological Review*, 44: 572–87.

Bollen, K. A. (1980) 'Issues in the comparative measurement of political democracy,' *American Sociological Review*, 45: 370–90.

Bollen, K. A. (1989) *Structural Equations with Latent Variables*, N.Y.: Wiley.

Childers, T. L., M. J. Houston, and S. Heckler (1985), 'Measurement of Individual Differences in Visual versus Verbal Information Processing,' *Journal of Consumer Research*, 12: 124–34.

Fornell, C. and J. Cha (1994) 'Partial least squares,' in *Advanced Methods of Marketing Research*, P. Bagozzi (ed), Oxford: Blackwell.

Paivio, A. (1971) *Imagery and Verbal Processes*, New York: Holt, Rinehart & Winston.

Sørensen, E. (2001) 'Means-end chains og laddering i et kognitivt perspektiv,' PhD thesis, Aarhus School of Business, Denmark.

Wold, H. (1975) 'Path models with latent variables: The NIPALS approach,' in H. M. Blalock et al. (ed), *Quantitative Sociology: International Perspectives on Mathematical and Statistical Modelling*, N.Y.: Academic.

CHAPTER

7

The General Causal Model

I n this chapter the structural model (Chapter 5) and the measurement model (Chapter 6) are brought together to form the general causal model.

This model is introduced by way of Example 4.1, which is modified by letting the structural variables be latent instead of manifest. After this simple example has demonstrated the advantages of basing your analyzes on latent variable models, we move on to a larger example.

This example will demonstrate the two-step strategy: separate analysis of the measurement and structural models. Among other things you will learn how to analyze indirect effects, i.e. effects that are mediated by other variables.

Next we look at a time series model, which has one real advantage compared to cross-section models: There is no doubt about the causal directions.

1. Combining Structural and Measurement Model

As you will probably have guessed, the combination of the structural and the measurement model into one model complicates the analysis. Among the questions to be answered are:

1. If I have problems with model fit, is the problem then with the measurement model or the structural model?
2. The combination of the two models into one makes them dependent on each other. Therefore the parameter estimates in one sub-model could depend on the parameter estimates in the other. What are the consequences for the substantive interpretation if that should happen?

Before I try to answer these questions, let us examine what happens when we transform a model with only manifest variables into one with latent variables.

Example 1

In Example 4.1 you were introduced to AMOS programming by way of a simple multiple regression example (which you are welcome to re-read!) using only manifest variables—in this case summated scales. This pre-supposes that measurement error is absent—that the measurements are 100% reliable. This is of course a very unrealistic assumption, and we can loosen it by introducing latent variables. In Figure 7.1 you can compare the original regression model in panel

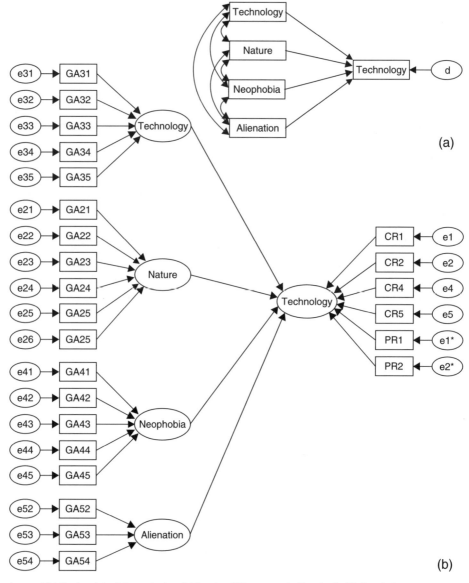

In panel (b) the four latent dependent variables should be connected by six double-headed arrows, but these are not shown in order to make the illustration clearer.

Figure 7.1   Example 1: A regression model (a) without and (b) with latent variables

(a) with the model in panel (b), obtained by splitting the various summated scales into their separate items.

Identification: The Two-Step Rule

As already mentioned there is no general necessary and sufficient condition for identification, and often you have to rely on the computer's messages about 'probably non-identified' parameters.

As the general model consists of two sub-models, intuitively the total model must be identified if its two parts are identified if considered separately. This can in fact be proved to be the case, and can be formulated in the so-called *two-step rule*.

First you look at the model in Figure 7.1b is as a confirmatory factor analysis model (i.e. you let the arrows in the structural model be substituted by two-headed arrows depicting covariances) and make sure that it is identified. Then you regard the structural part of the model as consisting of only manifest variables, and you make sure that this model is identified too. If both conditions are fulfilled this is *sufficient* (but not necessary) to secure identification of the original model.

The first condition is met according to the three-indicator rule (mentioned in Section 6.2), and the second follows from the zero-B rule (mentioned in Section 5.1).

Estimation

A program for estimation of the model is shown in Table 7.1 and part of the output in Table 7.2. The data can be found on the book's website.

The main results from the analysis in Example 4.1 and the present analysis is most easily compared in Table 7.3.

What first strikes the eye is the increase in the coefficient of determination caused by introducing latent variables: from 0.387 to 0.584—an increase of no less than 50%. So part of the reason for the apparently low over-all explanatory power in the original regression model is the low reliability of the measurements.

Also observe that rather dramatic changes in regression weights have taken place, and that neglecting the measurement errors underestimates most of the standard errors.

The Effects of Introducing Latent Variables

From the above example, you will see that neglecting the inevitable measurement error ε has the following consequences:

1. Unreliable measurement of the dependent variable deflates the coefficient of determination and increases the standard error of the estimated regression weights.
2. Unreliable measurements of independent variables bias the estimated regression weights and the coefficient of determination.

Both problems can be taken care of by regarding the variables in question as latent.

Table 7.1 Example 1: Program

```
Sub Main
    Dim Sem As New AmosEngine
    Sem.TextOutput
    Sem.Standardized
    Sem.Smc

    Sem.BeginGroup "F:\Bredahl.xls","Latent"
    Sem.GroupName "Germany"

    Sem.AStructure "GA31 = (1)Technology + (1)e31"
    Sem.AStructure "GA32 =    Technology + (1)e32"
    Sem.AStructure "GA33 =    Technology + (1)e33"
    Sem.AStructure "GA34 =    Technology + (1)e34"
    Sem.AStructure "GA35 =    Technology + (1)e35"

    Sem.AStructure "GA21 = (1)Nature + (1)e21"
    Sem.AStructure "GA22 =    Nature + (1)e22"
    Sem.AStructure "GA23 =    Nature + (1)e23"
    Sem.AStructure "GA24 =    Nature + (1)e24"
    Sem.AStructure "GA25 =    Nature + (1)e25"
    Sem.AStructure "GA26 =    Nature + (1)e26"

    Sem.AStructure "GA41 = (1)Neophobia + (1)e41"
    Sem.AStructure "GA42 =    Neophobia + (1)e42"
    Sem.AStructure "GA43 =    Neophobia + (1)e43"
    Sem.AStructure "GA44 =    Neophobia + (1)e44"
    Sem.AStructure "GA45 =    Neophobia + (1)e45"

    Sem.AStructure "GA52 = (1)Alienation + (1)e52"
    Sem.AStructure "GA53 =    Alienation + (1)e53"
    Sem.AStructure "GA54 =    Alienation + (1)e54"

    Sem.AStructure "CR1 = (1)Risks + (1)e1"
    Sem.AStructure "CR2 =    Risks + (1)e2"
    Sem.AStructure "CR4 =    Risks + (1)e4"
    Sem.AStructure "CR5 =    Risks + (1)e5"
    Sem.AStructure "PR1 =    Risks + (1)e1*"
    Sem.AStructure "PR2 =    Risks + (1)e2*"

    Sem.AStructure "Risks = Technology + Nature + Neophobia
    + Alienation + (1)d_1
End Sub
```

Table 7.2 Example 1: Output

Regression Weights: (Germany - Model 1)

			Estimate	S.E.	C.R.	P
Risks	<---	Technology	−.327	.067	−4.878	***
Risks	<---	Nature	.617	.090	6.824	***
Risks	<---	Neophobia	.378	.080	4.712	***
Risks	<---	Alienation	.341	.079	4.329	***
GA31	<---	Technology	1.000			
GA32	<---	Technology	.979	.080	12.212	***
GA33	<---	Technology	.933	.077	12.064	***
GA34	<---	Technology	.880	.079	11.192	***
GA35	<---	Technology	.888	.078	11.373	***
GA21	<---	Nature	1.000			
GA22	<---	Nature	.830	.089	9.322	***
GA23	<---	Nature	.658	.090	7.331	***
GA24	<---	Nature	.736	.102	7.226	***
GA25	<---	Nature	.554	.097	5.696	***
GA26	<---	Nature	.690	.093	7.412	***
GA41	<---	Neophobia	1.000			
GA42	<---	Neophobia	1.306	.132	9.902	***
GA43	<---	Neophobia	1.319	.138	9.567	***
GA44	<---	Neophobia	1.505	.143	10.510	***
GA45	<---	Neophobia	1.308	.137	9.570	***
GA52	<---	Alienation	1.000			
GA53	<---	Alienation	1.097	.085	12.971	***
GA54	<---	Alienation	.899	.082	10.988	***
CR1	<---	Risks	1.000			
CR2	<---	Risks	.696	.059	11.881	***
CR4	<---	Risks	.662	.051	13.058	***
CR5	<---	Risks	.851	.059	14.467	***
PR1	<---	Risks	.815	.063	12.986	***
PR2	<---	Risks	1.073	.066	16.203	***

Squared Multiple Correlations: (Germany–Model 1)

	Estimate
Risks	.584

2. Analysis of the General Model

In the above example the measurement model is over-identified and the structural model is just-identified (cf. Table 4.2). This means that the χ^2-test is a test of the measurement model only and that all the fit indices only measure the fit of the measurement part of the model! If you substitute unexplained covariances for the one-headed arrows in the structural part of the model, you end up with exactly the same fit measures: The two models are equivalent.

Table 7.3 Example 1: Comparing the results of the two analyzes. Estimated regression weights (standard errors in parentheses) and coefficients of determination

	Manifest variables	Latent variables
Technology	−.240	−.327
	(.052)	(.067)
Nature	.371	.617
	(.048)	(.090)
Neophobia	.274	.378
	(.043)	(.080)
Alienation	.684	.341
	(.082)	(.079)
R^2	.387	.584

Therefore the only measure of the fit for the structural part of the model is R squared.

Often the measurement model and the structural model are estimated in one go—the so-called *one-step strategy*. However, this could raise problems, one of which is that if the (complete) model does not fit the data, it can sometimes be complicated to find out whether the structural model depicting your theory is wrong, or the bad fit is due to unreliable measurements.

Therefore, a two-step rule should also be applied to the analysis of the model: First analyze the model as a confirmatory factor analysis model and then put in the one-headed arrows and analyze the full model. This is the so-called *two-step strategy*—anyway, it is meaningless to analyze the structural part of the model if the measurement model does not show satisfactory reliabilities.

Another problem is this: If the model fits the data, and a measurement model shows a satisfactory reliability, can we then be sure that it will show the same excellent qualities if used in connection with another structural model? In other words: A measuring instrument should ideally work in the same way whenever used, irrespective of the structural model. Therefore, the regression weights in the measurement model should not change significantly when making modifications to the structural part of the model.

The two-step strategy could therefore easily be expanded to a many-step procedure. Mulaik and Millsap (2000) have proposed a four-step strategy starting with an exploratory factor analysis. However, using an exploratory technique as the first step could be a bit dangerous if at least two samples are not used for cross-validation—and if you forego substantive thinking.

Another point to consider is whether the measuring instruments also generalize to other populations, other points in time, etc.—a subject I shall take up in the next chapter.

Example 2

Using Danish data Thomsen et al. (2004) have mapped the relationships between rumination (negative recurrent thoughts), immune parameters and health care utilization for two samples: one of young and one of elderly people. I will use only the elderly sample. The data can be found on the books website.

The model that seems to be the basis of their analysis is shown in Figure 7.2.

Rumination was measured using the rehearsal subscale from the *Emotional Control Questionnaire* version 2 (Roger and Narajian, 1989), sadness by the depression-dejection subscale from the short version of the *Profile of Moods Scale* (McNair et al., 1981; Shacham, 1983) and sleep quality by the one item on subjective sleep quality from the *Pittsburgh Sleep Quality Index* (Buysse et al., 1989). The items used are shown in Table 7.4.

The following immune parameters were measured: number of leukocytes, number of lymphocytes, number of CD19+ lymphocytes and PHA-stimulated T-cell profileration. Data on health care utilization was extracted from the country's central register where the following two variables were used: number of personal consultations with G.P. during follow-up period and number of telephone consultations during the same period. In the following analysis both these variables are divided by five in order to bring their variances on level with the other manifest variables.

Thomsen et al., 2004, analyzed the various effects on immune parameters and on health care utilization in two separate sets of stepwise regressions—one with immune parameters as dependent variables, the other with health care utilization as dependent variables.

I will re-analyze their data using SEM, taking as my point of departure the model sketched in Figure 7.2.

There is a rather large number of missing values in the data, which means that only two of the four immune parameters will be used. Furthermore, I will use only respondents who have no missing values on any measurement.

This limits the sample to 247 respondents and is, of course, not the most efficient use of the data. However, this choice is taken for pedagogical reasons, which should be clear when you have read Chapter 9 on the 'missing value problem.'

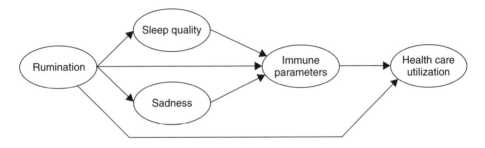

Figure 7.2   Example 2: Structural model

Table 7.4   Example 2: Scales used for measuring the psychological constructs

Rumination	
ecq 1	I remember things that upset me or make me angry for a long time afterwards
ecq 2	I generally don't bear a grudge—when something is over, it's over, and I don't think about it again
ecq 3	I get 'worked up' just thinking about things that have upset me in the past
ecq 4	I often find myself thinking over and over about things that have made me angry
ecq 5	I can usually settle things quickly and be friendly again after an argument
ecq 6	If I see or hear about an accident, I find myself thinking about something similar happening to me or to people close to me
ecq 7	I think about ways of getting back on people who have made me angry along time after the event have happened
ecq 8	I never forget people making me angry or upset, even about small things
ecq 9	I find it hard to get thoughts about things that have upset me out of my mind
ecq 10	I often daydream about situations where I'm getting my own back at people
ecq 11	If I see something that frightens or upsets me, the image of it stays in my mind for a long time afterwards
ecq 12	Thinking about upsetting things just seems to keep them going, so I try to put them out of my mind
ecq 13	If I lose out on something, I get over it quickly
ecq 14	If I have to confront someone, I try not to think too much about it beforehand
Sadness	(5-point scale, scaled 'not at all' to 'extremely')
poms4d	Unhappy
poms8d	Sad
poms12d	Blue
poms14d	Hopeless
poms20d	Discouraged
poms23d	Miserable
poms28d	Helpless
poms33d	worthless
Subjective sleep quality: psqik1	During the past month, how would you rate your sleep quality overall (scaled 0–4, the smaller, the better)?

As a first step, I will analyze the model as a confirmatory factor model. The program and part of the output is shown in Table 7.5. In this preliminary analysis I fix the error variance of psqik1 at 0.00 in order to solve the 'one-indicator problem'—the same procedure used with X_5 in Figure 1.3.

Observe that although stipulated in the program, the path from 'Sleep Quality' to 'psqik1' is *not* estimated. Consequently the R *squared* of 'psqik1' cannot be interpreted as a measure of reliability.

Table 7.5 Example 2: Program and output, first run

```
Public Sub Main()
    Dim Sem As New AmosEngine
    Try
        Sem.TextOutput
        Sem.Smc
        Sem.Mods(20)
        Sem.Standardized
    End Sub
    End Module
    Sem.BeginGroup("Thomsen1.xls","Elder")
    Sem.AStructure("ecq1    = (1)Rumination + (1) e_ecq1")
    Sem.AStructure("ecq2    =    Rumination + (1) e_ecq2")
    Sem.AStructure("ecq3    =    Rumination + (1) e_ecq3")
    Sem.AStructure("ecq4    =    Rumination + (1) e_ecq4")
    Sem.AStructure("ecq5    =    Rumination + (1) e_ecq5")
    Sem.AStructure("ecq6    =    Rumination + (1) e_ecq6")
    Sem.AStructure("ecq7    =    Rumination + (1) e_ecq7")
    Sem.AStructure("ecq8    =    Rumination + (1) e_ecq8")
    Sem.AStructure("ecq9    =    Rumination + (1) e_ecq9")
    Sem.AStructure("ecq10   =    Rumination + (1) e_ecq10")
    Sem.AStructure("ecq11   =    Rumination + (1) e_ecq11")
    Sem.AStructure("ecq12   =    Rumination + (1) e_ecq12")
    Sem.AStructure("ecq13   =    Rumination + (1) e_ecq13")
    Sem.AStructure("ecq14   =    Rumination + (1) e_ecq14")

    Sem.AStructure("poms4d  = (1)Sadness + (1) e_poms4d")
    Sem.AStructure("poms8d  =    Sadness + (1) e_poms8d")
    Sem.AStructure("poms12d =    Sadness + (1) e_poms12d"
    Sem.AStructure("poms14d =    Sadness + (1) e_poms14d")
    Sem.AStructure("poms20d =    Sadness + (1) e_poms20d")
    Sem.AStructure("poms23d =    Sadness + (1) e_poms23d")
    Sem.AStructure("poms28d =    Sadness + (1) e_poms28d")
    Sem.AStructure("poms33d =    Sadness + (1) e_poms33d")

    Sem.AStructure("psqik1 = (1)Sleep Quality + (1) e_psqik1")

    Sem.AStructure("leukocyt = (1)Immunity + (1) e_Imm1")
    Sem.AStructure("lymphocy =    Immunity + (1) e_Imm2")
```

(Continued)

Table 7.5 Cont'd

```
    Sem.AStructure ("consult = (1)Health care + (1) e_health1")
    Sem.AStructure ("telephone =    Health care + (1) e_health2")


    Sem.AStructure("Sleep Quality <--> Rumination")
    Sem.AStructure("Sleep Quality <--> Sadness")
    Sem.AStructure("Sleep Quality <--> Immunity")
    Sem.AStructure("Sleep Quality <--> Health care")


    Sem.AStructure("e_psqik1 (0)")


    Sem.FitModel
  Finally
    Sem.Dispose
  End Try
End Sub
End Module
```

Result (Model 1)

```
Minimum was achieved
Chi-square = 847.989
Degrees of freedom = 315
Probability level = .000
```
Maximum Likelihood Estimates

Regression Weights: (Group number 1—Model 1)

			Estimate	S.E.	C.R.	P	Label
ecq1	<---	Rumination	1.000				
ecq2	<---	Rumination	.358	.099	3.607	***	
ecq3	<---	Rumination	.807	.075	10.715	***	
ecq4	<---	Rumination	.786	.071	11.057	***	
ecq5	<---	Rumination	.426	.088	4.833	***	
ecq6	<---	Rumination	.493	.086	5.762	***	
ecq7	<---	Rumination	.350	.050	6.989	***	
ecq8	<---	Rumination	.583	.067	8.752	***	
ecq9	<---	Rumination	.866	.078	11.100	***	
ecq10	<---	Rumination	.215	.034	6.236	***	
ecq11	<---	Rumination	.608	.075	8.057	***	
ecq12	<---	Rumination	.136	.093	1.467	.142	
ecq13	<---	Rumination	.372	.096	3.866	***	
ecq14	<---	Rumination	-.006	.088	-.070	.944	
poms4d	<---	Sadness	1.000				
poms8d	<---	Sadness	.934	.068	13.704	***	
poms12d	<---	Sadness	.859	.066	13.008	***	

Table 7.5 Cont'd

			Estimate	S.E.	C.R.	P	Label
poms14d	<---	Sadness	.656	.070	9.304	***	
poms20d	<---	Sadness	.941	.069	13.679	***	
poms23d	<---	Sadness	.598	.057	10.452	***	
poms28d	<---	Sadness	.530	.058	9.096	***	
poms33d	<---	Sadness	.596	.065	9.166	***	
psqik1	<---	e_psqik1	1.000				
leukocyt	<---	Immunity	1.000				
lymphocy	<---	Immunity	.331	.104	3.201	.001	
consult	<---	Health care	1.000				
telephone	<---	Health care	1.580	.494	3.198	.001	

Covariances: (Group number 1—Model 1)

			Estimate	S.E.	C.R.	P	Label
Rumination	<-->	Sadness	.212	.041	5.156	***	
Rumination	<-->	Immunity	.287	.102	2.816	.005	
Sadness	<-->	Immunity	-.007	.062	-.111	.912	
Rumination	<-->	Health care	.098	.046	2.147	.032	
Sadness	<-->	Health care	.101	.037	2.716	.007	
Immunity	<-->	Health care	.048	.067	.712	.477	
Sleep Quality	<-->	Rumination	.156	.044	3.578	***	
Sleep Quality	<-->	Sadness	.188	.032	5.824	***	
Sleep Quality	<-->	Immunity	.164	.077	2.136	.033	
Sleep Quality	<-->	Health care	.115	.042	2.724	.006	

Variances: (Group number 1—Model 1)

	Estimate	S.E.	C.R.	P	Label
e_psqik1	.000				
Rumination	.704	.106	6.631	***	
Sadness	.352	.047	7.509	***	
Immunity	1.429	.503	2.841	.004	
Health care	.282	.106	2.659	.008	
e_ecq1	.522	.059	8.842	***	
e_ecq2	1.411	.128	10.985	***	
e_ecq3	.462	.049	9.440	***	
e_ecq4	.388	.042	9.221	***	
e_ecq5	1.063	.098	10.893	***	
e_ecq6	.960	.089	10.797	***	
e_ecq7	.306	.029	10.625	***	
e_ecq8	.467	.046	10.242	***	
e_ecq9	.463	.050	9.191	***	
e_ecq10	.152	.014	10.738	***	
e_ecq11	.639	.061	10.418	***	
e_ecq12	1.294	.117	11.074	***	
e_ecq13	1.315	.120	10.969	***	

(Continued)

Table 7.5 Cont'd

	Estimate	S.E.	C.R.	P	Label
e_ecq14	1.158	.104	11.090	***	
e_poms4d	.179	.021	8.688	***	
e_poms8d	.185	.020	9.064	***	
e_poms12d	.191	.020	9.434	***	
e_poms14d	.302	.029	10.485	***	
e_poms20d	.189	.021	9.078	***	
e_poms23d	.184	.018	10.262	***	
e_poms28d	.209	.020	10.519	***	
e_poms33d	.259	.025	10.508	***	
Sleep Quality	.524	.047	11.091	***	
e_Imm1	1.892	.471	4.021	***	
e_Imm2	.241	.053	4.556	***	
e_health1	.724	.108	6.733	***	
e_health2	.474	.218	2.176	.030	

Squared Multiple Correlations: (Group number 1 - Model 1)

	Estimate
telephone	.598
consult	.280
lymphocy	.395
leukocyt	.430
psqik1	.000
poms33d	.325
poms28d	.321
poms23d	.406
poms20d	.622
poms14d	.334
poms12d	.576
poms8d	.624
poms4d	.663
ecq14	.000
ecq13	.069
ecq12	.010
ecq11	.290
ecq10	.176
ecq9	.533
ecq8	.339
ecq7	.220
ecq6	.151
ecq5	.107
ecq4	.529
ecq3	.498
ecq2	.060
ecq1	.574

Table 7.5   Cont'd

`Modification Indices (Group number 1—Model 1)`

`Covariances: (Group number 1—Model 1)`

			M.I.	Par Change
e_poms14d	<-->	e_poms33d	31.205	.105
e_poms14d	<-->	e_poms28d	21.353	.078
e_ecq13	<-->	e_ecq14	25.352	.398
e_ecq12	<-->	e_ecq14	25.881	.397
e_ecq12	<-->	e_ecq13	75.091	.725
e_ecq7	<-->	e_ecq10	45.334	.096
e_ecq7	<-->	e_ecq9	26.585	−.136
e_ecq5	<-->	e_ecq13	55.339	.568
e_ecq5	<-->	e_ecq12	35.068	.447
e_ecq2	<-->	e_ecq13	22.666	.417
e_ecq2	<-->	e_ecq5	49.506	.556

`Variances: (Group number 1—Model 1)`

	M.I.	Par Change

`Regression Weights: (Group number 1—Model 1)`

			M.I.	Par Change
poms14d	<---	poms33d	20.111	.260
ecq14	<---	ecq13	23.377	.279
ecq14	<---	ecq12	25.588	.303
ecq13	<---	ecq14	25.351	.344
ecq13	<---	ecq12	74.242	.554
ecq13	<---	ecq5	48.652	.470
ecq13	<---	ecq2	21.128	.276
ecq12	<---	ecq14	25.880	.343
ecq12	<---	ecq13	69.242	.508
ecq12	<---	ecq5	30.826	.369
ecq10	<---	ecq7	34.104	.235
ecq9	<---	ecq7	20.109	−.336
ecq7	<---	ecq10	36.340	.505
ecq5	<---	ecq13	51.036	.398
ecq5	<---	ecq12	34.672	.341
ecq5	<---	ecq2	46.151	.367
ecq2	<---	ecq13	20.902	.292
ecq2	<---	ecq5	43.522	.460

Although all but two regression weights are significant, the fit is not very good (CMIN/DF = 2.692, CFI = 0.756, RMSEA = 0.083, LO 90 = 1.831, HI 90 = 0.090, PCLOSE = 0.000). A look at the squared multiple correlations shows that some of the indicators have very small reliabilities—and what is more eye-catching: The five items with the lowest reliabilities (items 2, 5, 12, 13 and 14) are exactly the five items that are worded in opposite direction to the rest.

A preliminary component analysis of the ecq scale would have shown the scale to be two-dimensional, the two dimensions being made up of items worded positively and negatively respectively (and an item analysis on the complete scale would have eliminated the dimension with fewest items). It is obvious that, by splitting the latent variable into two, larger reliabilities would come out. However, I decided to skip the smaller of the two dimensions and re-run the analysis.

A look at the modification indices shows quite a few suggestions of letting items 2, 5, 12, 13 and 14 inter-correlate. This is no surprise, since the inter-correlations signal that these items have something in common that they do not share with the other items—and we know what it is: They are oppositely worded.

However, I decided to skip the smaller of the two dimensions and re-run the analysis.

On the other hand, a look at the wording of the items 7, 10, 14 and 33 shows that introduction of the correlations

e_poms14d<-->e_poms33d and e_ecq7<-->e_ecq10

is defendable.

Output is shown in Table 7.6.

The fit is considerably better (CMIN/DF = 1.929, CFI = 0.902, RMSEA = 0.061, LO 90 = 0.052, HI 90 = 0.074, PCLOSE = 0.022), and even if some of the reliabilities are rather low, I will keep them for now. All regression weights and covariances but two are significant.

The fit could be increased by including the suggested correlation between e_ecq7 and e_ecq9, but I am reluctant to follow this advice until the correlation has been confirmed in other applications of the ecq scale.

It is now time to move on to the analysis of the hypothesized causal model.

Table 7.6   Example 2: Output, second run

Result (Model 1)

Minimum was achieved
Chi-square = 382.009
Degrees of freedom = 198
Probability level = .000

Maximum Likelihood Estimates

Table 7.6 Cont'd

```
Regression Weights: (Group number 1—Model 1)
```

			Estimate	S.E.	C.R.	P	Label
ecq1	<---	Rumination	1.000				
ecq3	<---	Rumination	.810	.074	10.923	***	
ecq4	<---	Rumination	.793	.070	11.313	***	
ecq6	<---	Rumination	.503	.085	5.938	***	
ecq7	<---	Rumination	.329	.050	6.607	***	
ecq8	<---	Rumination	.576	.066	8.742	***	
ecq9	<---	Rumination	.872	.077	11.347	***	
ecq10	<---	Rumination	.189	.034	5.510	***	
ecq11	<---	Rumination	.582	.075	7.791	***	
poms4d	<---	Sadness	1.000				
poms8d	<---	Sadness	.932	.067	13.958	***	
poms12d	<---	Sadness	.857	.065	13.238	***	
poms14d	<---	Sadness	.619	.070	8.809	***	
poms20d	<---	Sadness	.933	.068	13.810	***	
poms23d	<---	Sadness	.594	.056	10.552	***	
poms28d	<---	Sadness	.513	.058	8.870	***	
poms33d	<---	Sadness	.562	.065	8.670	***	
psqik1	<---	e_psqik1	1.000				
leukocyt	<---	Immunity	1.000				
lymphocy	<---	Immunity	.322	.104	3.098	.002	
consult	<---	Health care	1.000				
telephone	<---	Health care	1.638	.521	3.146	.002	

```
Covariances: (Group number 1—Model 1)
```

			Estimate	S.E.	C.R.	P	Label
Rumination	<-->	Sadness	.214	.042	5.121	***	
Rumination	<-->	Immunity	.278	.103	2.701	.007	
Sadness	<-->	Immunity	−.007	.064	−.106	.915	
Rumination	<-->	Health care	.101	.046	2.179	.029	
Sadness	<-->	Health care	.098	.037	2.656	.008	
Immunity	<-->	Health care	.051	.066	.763	.445	
Sleep Quality	<-->	Rumination	.147	.044	3.352	***	
Sleep Quality	<-->	Sadness	.189	.033	5.800	***	
Sleep Quality	<-->	Immunity	.167	.078	2.152	.031	
Sleep Quality	<-->	Health care	.111	.042	2.661	.008	
e_poms14d	<-->	e_poms33d	.108	.021	5.111	***	
e_ecq7	<-->	e_ecq10	.098	.016	6.061	***	

```
Squared Multiple Correlations: (Group number 1—Model 1)
```

	Estimate
telephone	.620
consult	.271
lymphocy	.384
leukocyt	.443

(Continued)

Table 7.6 Cont'd

	Estimate
psqik1	.000
poms33d	.294
poms28d	.306
poms23d	.409
poms20d	.623
poms14d	.303
poms12d	.584
poms8d	.633
poms4d	.675
ecq11	.271
ecq10	.139
ecq9	.551
ecq8	.337
ecq7	.197
ecq6	.160
ecq4	.548
ecq3	.513
ecq1	.586

Modification Indices (Group number 1—Model 1)

Covariances: (Group number 1—Model 1)

	M.I.	Par Change
e_ecq7 <--> e_ecq9	24.326	−.116

Variances: (Group number 1—Model 1)

	M.I.	Par Change

Regression Weights: (Group number 1—Model 1)

	M.I.	Par Change

Now, however, I must decide how to handle the sleep quality factor. The 'one-indicator problem' is most often dealt with by fixing the error variance at 0.00. In most cases it is of course unrealistic to assume that measurement error is 100% absent, and I will deal with the problem in another way.

The average reliability of the (kept) items from the ecq scale is about 0.40 and the average reliability of the poms items is about 0.50. As the psqik1 question seems rather unproblematic, I will assume that the reliability of psqik1 is 0.50, and consequently fix the error variance of psqik1 at 50% of the variance of psqik1. This is done by substituting the line

```
Sem.AStructure("e_psqik1(0.263)")
```

for

```
Sem.AStructure("e_psqik1(0)")
```

Of course this is a 'guesstimate,' but it is more realistic than 0.

Program and output is shown in Table 7.7.

The model is not too bad, but could be better (CMIN/DF = 2.080, CFI = 0.886, RMSEA = 0.066, LO 90 = 0.057, HI 90 = 0.075, PCLOSE = 0.002); also observe that now the reliability of psqik1 is correctly reported as 0.498. Sadness and low sleeping quality go together, but it is obvious that this could be due to causes other than rumination. Introducing the correlation between d_1 and d_2 as suggested by the output would be expected to reduce χ^2 by 27.849. I will leave it to the experts to consider the suggestions about causal links between 'Sleep Quality' and 'Sadness.'

After this change, the parameters are estimated as shown in Table 7.8.

The fit is not too bad (CMIN/DF = 1.929, CFI = 0.902, RMSEA = 0.061, LO 90 = 0.052, HI 90 = 0.071, PCLOSE = 0.022) but, as mentioned several times, it takes more to accept a model: It must also be substantively meaningful.

In short the model says that rumination raises the defense system of your body, both through direct effect and by reducing sleep quality and causing depression. However, rumination and the increase in the measurement of the immune parameters do not seem to have direct effects on the health care utilization.

On the other hand rumination could still have indirect effects on health care utilization—and what is more, we can measure that effect:

The effect of rumination on sleep quality is measured by the regression weight 0.205 and the effect of sleep quality on immunity is measured by the regression weight 0.967. So, of the rumination 'carried' to sleep quality (0.205), a share of 0.967, i.e. $0.205 \times 0.967 = 0.198$, is 'carried' through to immunity.

In the same way the indirect effect of rumination on immunity via sadness can be calculated to $0.298 \times (-0.781) = -0.233$. So the indirect effect of rumination on immunity is $0.198 - 0.233 = -0.035$, which, added to the direct effect (0.422), gives a total effect of 0.387.

If you add the order

```
Sem.TotalEffects
```

to the program AMOS will calculate direct, indirect and total effects for all regression functions—whether the calculations are relevant or not. As you may have guessed, this takes up a lot of space in the output and for space considerations I show only a small part of the output in Table 7.9.

From Table 7.9 you can see e.g. that the indirect effect of rumination on health care is nearly one and a half times the size of the direct effect (which is not significant). So, it is possible that a significant total effect of rumination on health care utilization could be present.

Table 7.7   Example 2: Program and Output for First causal model

```
Sub Main()
  Dim Sem As New AmosEngine
  Try
    Sem.TextOutput
    Sem.Smc
    Sem.Standardized
    Sem.Mods(20)
    Sem.BeginGroup("Thomsen1.xls","Elder")

    Sem.AStructure("ecq1   = (1)  Rumination + (1) e_ecq1")
    Sem.AStructure("ecq3   =      Rumination + (1) e_ecq3")
    Sem.AStructure("ecq4   =      Rumination + (1) e_ecq4")
    Sem.AStructure("ecq6   =      Rumination + (1) e_ecq6")
    Sem.AStructure("ecq7   =      Rumination + (1) e_ecq7")
    Sem.AStructure("ecq8   =      Rumination + (1) e_ecq8")
    Sem.AStructure("ecq9   =      Rumination + (1) e_ecq9")
    Sem.AStructure("ecq10  =      Rumination + (1) e_ecq10")
    Sem.AStructure("ecq11  =      Rumination + (1) e_ecq11")

    Sem.AStructure("poms4d  = (1)  Sadness + (1) e_poms4d")
    Sem.AStructure("poms8d  =      Sadness + (1) e_poms8d")
    Sem.AStructure("poms12d =      Sadness + (1) e_poms12d")
    Sem.AStructure("poms14d =      Sadness + (1) e_poms14d")
    Sem.AStructure("poms20d =      Sadness + (1) e_poms20d")
    Sem.AStructure("poms23d =      Sadness + (1) e_poms23d")
    Sem.AStructure("poms28d =      Sadness + (1) e_poms28d")
    Sem.AStructure("poms33d =      Sadness + (1) e_poms33d")

    Sem.AStructure("psqik1 = (1) Sleep Quality + (1) e_psqik1")

    Sem.AStructure("leukocyt = (1) Immunity + (1) e_Imm1")
    Sem.AStructure("lymphocy = Immunity + (1) e_Imm2")

    Sem.AStructure ("consult = (1) Health care + (1) e_health1")
    Sem.AStructure ("telephone = Health care + (1) e_health2")

    Sem.AStructure("e_psqik1 (0.263)")

    Sem.AStructure("e_ecq7 <-> e_ecq10")
    Sem.AStructure("e_poms14d <-> e_poms33d")

    Sem.AStructure("Sleep Quality = Rumination + (1) d_1")
    Sem.AStructure("Sadness = Rumination + (1) d_2")
```

Table 7.7 Cont'd

```
Sem.AStructure("Immunity = Rumination + Sleep Quality
    + Sadness +(1)d_3")
    Sem.AStructure("Health care = Rumination + Sleep Quality
    + Sadness+Immunity+ (1) d_4")

    Sem.FitModel
  Finally
    Sem.Dispose
  End Try
    End Sub
End Module
```

Minimum was achieved
Chi-square = 413.825
Degrees of freedom = 199
Probability level = .000

Regression weights: (Group number 1—Model 1)

			Estimate	S.E.	C.R.	P	Label
Sleep Quality	<---	Rumination	.226	.058	3.905	***	
Sadness	<---	Rumination	.310	.052	5.970	***	
Immunity	<---	Rumination	.375	.170	2.201	.028	
Immunity	<---	Sleep Quality	.716	.327	2.190	.029	
Immunity	<---	Sadness	−.477	.206	−2.315	.021	
Health care	<---	Rumination	.031	.067	.452	.651	
Health care	<---	Sleep Quality	.313	.163	1.921	.055	
Health care	<---	Sadness	.155	.093	1.656	.098	
Health care	<---	Immunity	−.013	.051	−.246	.806	
ecq1	<---	Rumination	1.000				
ecq3	<---	Rumination	.806	.074	10.948	***	
ecq4	<---	Rumination	.783	.070	11.258	***	
ecq6	<---	Rumination	.497	.084	5.895	***	
ecq7	<---	Rumination	.325	.050	6.564	***	
ecq8	<---	Rumination	.570	.065	8.707	***	
ecq9	<---	Rumination	.873	.076	11.442	***	
ecq10	<---	Rumination	.189	.034	5.541	***	
ecq11	<---	Rumination	.582	.074	7.838	***	
poms4d	<---	Sadness	1.000				
poms8d	<---	Sadness	.929	.066	14.115	***	
poms12d	<---	Sadness	.862	.064	13.530	***	
poms14d	<---	Sadness	.607	.070	8.708	***	
poms20d	<---	Sadness	.915	.067	13.642	***	
poms23d	<---	Sadness	.592	.056	10.614	***	

(Continued)

Table 7.7 Cont'd

			Estimate	S.E.	C.R.	P	Label
poms28d	<---	Sadness	.497	.057	8.650	***	
poms33d	<---	Sadness	.556	.064	8.653	***	
psqik1	<---	Sleep Quality	1.000				
leukocyt	<---	Immunity	1.000				
lymphocy	<---	Immunity	.323	.094	3.442	***	
consult	<---	Health care	1.000				
telephone	<---	Health care	1.641	.565	2.904	.004	

Covariances: (Group number 1—Model 1)

			Estimate	S.E.	C.R.	P	Label
e_ecq7	<-->	e_ecq10	.098	.016	6.068	***	
e_poms14d	<-->	e_poms33d	.110	.021	5.162	***	

Squared multiple correlations: (Group number 1—Model 1)

	Estimate
Sleep Quality	.142
Sadness	.192
Immunity	.194
Health care	.164
telephone	.616
consult	.266
lymphocy	.391
leukocyt	.447
psqik1	.498
poms33d	.292
poms28d	.292
poms23d	.411
poms20d	.606
poms14d	.296
poms12d	.599
poms8d	.638
poms4d	.684
ecq11	.273
ecq10	.140
ecq9	.555
ecq8	.333
ecq7	.194
ecq6	.158
ecq4	.539
ecq3	.511
ecq1	.589

Table 7.7 Cont'd

Modification Indices (Group number 1—Model 1)

Covariances: (Group number 1—Model 1)

			M.I.	Par Change
d_2	<-->	d_1	27.849	.134
e_psqik1	<-->	d_2	28.117	.136
e_ecq7	<-->	e_ecq9	23.730	−.115

Variances: (Group number 1—Model 1)

	M.I.	Par Change

Regression Weights: (Group number 1—Model 1)

			M.I.	Par Change
Sleep Quality	<---	Sadness	21.345	.351
Sadness	<---	Sleep Quality	20.688	.445
psqik1	<---	Sadness	21.546	.354
psqik1	<---	poms28d	28.232	.417
psqik1	<---	poms20d	32.091	.349

Table 7.8 Example 2: Output from 2nd run of causal model

```
Minimum was achieved
Chi-square = 382.009
Degrees of freedom = 198
Probability level = .000
```

Regression Weights: (Group number 1—Model 1)

			Estimate	S.E.	C.R.	P	Label
Sleep Quality	<---	Rumination	.205	.058	3.510	***	
Sadness	<---	Rumination	.298	.052	5.746	***	
Immunity	<---	Rumination	.422	.160	2.629	.009	
Immunity	<---	Sleep Quality	.967	.452	2.139	.032	
Immunity	<---	Sadness	−.781	.323	−2.416	.016	
Health care	<---	Rumination	.058	.065	.903	.366	
Health care	<---	Sleep Quality	.377	.215	1.758	.079	
Health care	<---	Sadness	.040	.135	.296	.767	
Health care	<---	Immunity	−.019	.054	−.354	.723	
ecq1	<---	Rumination	1.000				
ecq3	<---	Rumination	.810	.074	10.923	***	
ecq4	<---	Rumination	.793	.070	11.313	***	
ecq6	<---	Rumination	.503	.085	5.938	***	
ecq7	<---	Rumination	.329	.050	6.607	***	
ecq8	<---	Rumination	.576	.066	8.742	***	
ecq9	<---	Rumination	.872	.077	11.347	***	

(Continued)

Table 7.8 Cont'd

			Estimate	S.E.	C.R.	P	Label
ecq10	<---	Rumination	.189	.034	5.510	***	
ecq11	<---	Rumination	.582	.075	7.791	***	
poms4d	<---	Sadness	1.000				
poms8d	<---	Sadness	.932	.067	13.958	***	
poms12d	<---	Sadness	.857	.065	13.238	***	
poms14d	<---	Sadness	.619	.070	8.809	***	
poms20d	<---	Sadness	.933	.068	13.810	***	
poms23d	<---	Sadness	.594	.056	10.552	***	
poms28d	<---	Sadness	.513	.058	8.870	***	
poms33d	<---	Sadness	.562	.065	8.670	***	
psqik1	<---	Sleep Quality	1.000				
leukocyt	<---	Immunity	1.000				
lymphocy	<---	Immunity	.322	.104	3.098	.002	
consult	<---	Health care	1.000				
telephone	<---	Health care	1.638	.521	3.146	.002	

Covariances: (Group number 1—Model 1)

			Estimate	S.E.	C.R.	P	Label
d_1	<-->	d_2	.145	.029	5.023	***	
e_ecq7	<-->	e_ecq10	.098	.016	6.061	***	
e_poms14d	<-->	e_poms33d	.108	.021	5.111	***	

Squared Multiple Correlations: (Group number 1—Model 1)

	Estimate
Sleep Quality	.115
Sadness	.178
Immunity	.193
Health care	.187
telephone	.620
consult	.271
lymphocy	.384
leukocyt	.443
psqik1	.498
poms33d	.294
poms28d	.306
poms23d	.409
poms20d	.623
poms14d	.303
poms12d	.584
poms8d	.633
poms4d	.675
ecq11	.271
ecq10	.139
ecq9	.551
ecq8	.337

Table 7.8 Cont'd

	Estimate
ecq7	.197
ecq6	.160
ecq4	.548
ecq3	.513
ecq1	.586

Modification indices (Group number 1 - Model 1)

Covariances: (Group number 1 - Model 1)

			M.I.	Par Change
e_ecq7	<-->	e_ecq9	24.326	-.116

Variances: (Group number 1 - Model 1)

	M.I.	Par Change

Regression Weights: (Group number 1 - Model 1)

	M.I.	Par Change

Table 7.9 Example 2: Total, direct and indirect effects

Total Effects

	Rumination	Sleep quality	Sadness	Immunity	Health care
Immunity	.387	.967	-.781		
lymphocy	.125	.312	-.252	.322	
leutocyt	.387	.967	-.781	1.000	
Health care	.140	.359	.055	-.019	
telephone	.229	.587	.090	-.032	1.638
consult	.140	.359	.055	-.019	1.000

Direct Effects

	Rumination	Sleep quality	Sadness	Immunity	Health care
Immunity	.422	.967	-.781		
lymphocy				.322	
leutocyt				1.000	
Health care	.058	.377	.040	-.019	
telephone				.000	1.638
consult				.000	1.000

(Continued)

Table 7.9 Cont'd

Indirect Effects

	Rumination	Sleep quality	Sadness	Immunity	Health care
Immunity	−.035				
lymphocy	.140	.359	.055		
leutocyt	.125	.312	−.252		
Health care	.082	−.019	.015		
telephone	.229	.587	.090	−.032	
consult	.140	.359	.055	−.019	

However, two things about AMOS must be kept in mind:

1. AMOS does not calculate standard errors on the indirect and total 'regression weights,' but these can be estimated by bootstrapping—a subject to be taken up in Chapter 9.
2. AMOS does not calculate separate indirect effects via each of the mediating factors—they must be calculated by hand if you need them.

I will leave it to the specialists to defend the direction of the arrows. However, let an amateur to the field speculate: Is it not possible that depression—as measured by 'sadness'—influences rumination and not the other way round?

3. Time Series Models

Models where the measurements are taken at various points in time have at least two characteristics that differentiate them from models based on cross-section data:

1. The question of direction as far as causal influences are concerned is less problematic because future events cannot affect the present, and
2. Such models will often include correlations among error terms in measurement models across latent variables describing the same concept at different points in time (cf. Example 6.1).

Example 3

(Example 5.2 continued) The structure of the model in Figure 5.2 is very similar to the model in Figure 6.2: In both cases the same variables are measured at two points in time. A reformulation of the model in Figure 5.2 incorporating latent variables, as in the model in Figure 6.2, is shown in Figure 7.3 below.

A quick look will show that the model is not identified:

The model has 11 parameters to be estimated—3 regression weights, 2 covariances and 6 variances—but we have only 10 observations. Consequently the model must be simplified. If we assume that the two covariances are of the same magnitude, and that the same apply to the four ε-variances, we have 3 degrees of freedom left over for testing. The program is shown in Table 7.10.

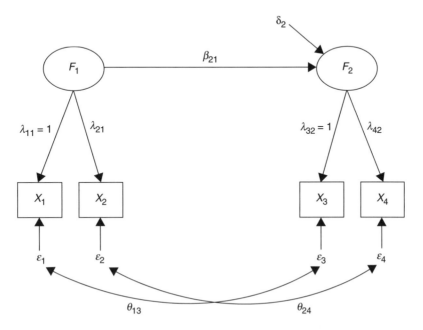

Figure 7.3   Example 2: Model

Table 7.10   Example 3: Program

```
Public Sub Main()
    Dim Sem As New AmosEngine
    Try
        Sem.TextOutput
        Sem.Standardized
        Sem.ResidualMoments
        Sem.BeginGroup ("Wheaton.xls","sheet1")

        Sem.AStructure ("F71              =      F67 + (1) d2")
        Sem.AStructure ("anomia67         = (1) F67 + (1) e1")
        Sem.AStructure ("powerlessness67 =      F67 + (1) e2")
        Sem.AStructure ("anomia71         = (1) F71 + (1) e3")
        Sem.AStructure ("powerlessness71 =      F71 + (1) e4")

        Sem.AStructure ("e1 <-> e3 (alpha)")
        Sem.AStructure ("e2 <-> e4 (alpha)")
```

(Continued)

Table 7.10 Cont'd

```
        Sem.AStructure ("e1      (beta)")
        Sem.AStructure ("e2      (beta)")
        Sem.AStructure ("e3      (beta)")
        Sem.AStructure ("e4      (beta)")

        Sem.FitModel
    Finally
        Sem.Dispose
    End Try
End Sub
End Module
```

As usual the regression weights of the error terms are fixed to have the value 1. In addition, labeling the covariances and variances, 'alpha' and 'beta,' forces the parameters with the same label to take on the same estimated value.

With these restrictions we get the output in Table 7.11, from which we see that the model fits the data extremely well.

Table 7.11 Example 3: Output

Computation of degrees of freedom (Model 1)

```
          Number of distinct sample moments:    10
Number of distinct parameters to be estimated:   7
                  Degrees of freedom (10–7):     3
```

Result (Model 1)

Minimum was achieved
Chi-square = 1.436
Degrees of freedom = 3
Probability level = .697

Maximum Likelihood Estimates

Regression Weights: (Group number 1–Model 1)

			Estimate	S.E.	C.R.	P	Label
F71	<---	F67	.716	.038	18.834	***	
anomia67	<---	F67	1.000				
powerlessness67	<---	F67	.845	.031	27.075	***	
anomia71	<---	F71	1.000				
powerlessness71	<---	F71	.839	.030	28.369	***	

Standardized Regression Weights: (Group number 1–Model 1)

			Estimate
F71	<---	F67	.685
anomia67	<---	F67	.834

Table 7.11 Cont'd

			Estimate
powerlessness67	<---	F67	.787
anomia71	<---	F71	.845
powerlessness71	<---	F71	.798

Covariances: (Group number 1—Model 1)

			Estimate	S.E.	C.R.	P	Label
e1	<-->	e3	.905	.122	7.449	***	alfa
e2	<-->	e4	.905	.122	7.449	***	alfa

Correlations: (Group number 1—Model 1)

			Estimate
e1	<-->	e3	.252
e2	<-->	e4	.252

Variances: (Group number 1—Model 1)

	Estimate	S.E.	C.R.	P	Label
F67	8.192	.544	15.056	***	
d2	4.746	.376	12.627	***	
e1	3.596	.122	29.589	***	beta
e2	3.596	.122	29.589	***	beta
e3	3.596	.122	29.589	***	beta
e4	3.596	.122	29.589	***	beta

Matrices (Group number 1—Model 1)

Residual Covariances (Group number 1—Model 1)

	powerlessness71	anomia71	powerlessness67	anomia67
powerlessness71	.079			
anomia71	-.020	-.023		
powerlessness67	-.041	.130	-.090	
anomia67	-.144	.041	.018	.033

Standardized Residual Covariances (Group number 1—Model 1)

	powerlessness71	anomia71	powerlessness67	anomia67
powerlessness71	.173			
anomia71	-.045	-.039		
powerlessness67	-.116	.331	-.206	
anomia67	-.371	.090	.044	.060

(Continued)

Table 7.11 Cont'd

Model Fit Summary

CMIN

Model	NPAR	CMIN	DF	P	CMIN/DF
Default model	7	1.436	3	.697	.479
Saturated model	10	.000	0		
Independence model	4	1563.944	6	.000	260.657

Baseline Comparisons

Model	NFI Delta1	RFI rho1	IFI Delta2	TLI rho2	CFI
Default model	.999	.998	1.001	1.002	1.000
Saturated model	1.000		1.000		1.000
Independence model	.000	.000	.000	.000	.000

RMSEA

Model	RMSEA	LO 90	HI 90	PCLOSE
Default model	.000	.000	.041	.979
Independence model	.528	.506	.550	.000

☞ In this chapter you have met the following concepts:

The two-step rule	Direct, indirect and total effects
The two- and four-step strategy	

Besides, you have been introduced to the AMOS statement
Sem.TotalEffects

Questions

1. State the consequences of measurement error in the dependent and independent variables in (traditional) regression analysis.
2. Comment on the various strategies for analyzing structural (causal) models.
3. Go through the various outputs in Example 2 and comment on the changes in the measurement part of the model.
4. Define direct, indirect and total effects, and explain how to (hand)calculate the two latter.
5. Comment on the fit of the model in Example 3. Can you suggest modifications?

Reference List

Buysse, D. J., C. F. Reynolds, T. H. Monk, S. R. Berman, and D. J. Kupfer (1989) 'The Pittsburgh Sleep Quality Index: a new instrument for psychiatric practice and research,' *Psychiatry Res*, 28 (x): 305–06.

McNair, P. M., M. Lorr, and L. F. Dopplemann (1981) *POMS Manual* (2nd ed.), San Diego: Educational and Industrial Testing Service.

Mulaik, S. A. and R. E. Millsap (2000) 'Doing the four-step right,' *Structural Equation Modelling*, 7: 36–73.

Roger, D. and R. D. Narajian (1989) 'The construction and validation of a new scale for measuring emotion control,' *Pers. Indiv. Diff.*, 10: 845–53.

Shacham, S. (1983) 'A shortened version of the Profile of Moods Scale,' *Perss. Assess*, 47: 305–06.

Thomsen, D. K., Y. M. Mehlsen, M. Hokland, A. Viidik, F. Olesen, K. Avlund, and R. Zachariae (2004) 'Negative thoughts and health: associations among rumination, immunity and health care utilization in a young and elderly sample,' *Psychosomatic Medicine*, 66: 363–71.

8

Multi-group Analysis and Mean Structures

It is now time to have a look at how to estimate SEM in several groups at the same time and how to examine the degree to which the models are equivalent across groups.

A traditional regression model will serve as an introduction to multi-group analysis. Then you move on to a larger model also involving only manifest variables—although it has a complication: a two-way causation. As this is the first (and only!) worked example of a non-recursive model, I will add some comments—and a warning!—to the ones in Section 5.4.

We have hitherto analyzed only *relations* among variables, but not been very interested in the *values* of the variables. You will also learn how to estimate means of latent variables and compare means across groups.

As this necessitates estimation of intercepts in addition to regression weights, you will also learn how to analyze *mean structures*. Therefore your input covariance matrix must be supplemented by the means of the manifest variables.

You will also learn how to judge the equivalence of a model across several samples through a systematic sequence of tests.

1. Comparing Covariance Structures across Groups

You will often want to fit a model to more than one data set—e.g. for comparing two or more populations or for cross-validating within the same population.

Of course you can do separate analyzes of the various samples, but there are several advantages in doing a simultaneous analysis in which the parameters in the various samples are estimated in one go.

It is possible to test whether parameters in the models can be assumed equal across samples, and parameters that based on such tests are considered equal, are estimated on data from all samples.

Often such analyzes begin with a global test of equality of the covariance matrices for the various data sets. The argument is that if the same model describes the data equally well across groups, then the matrices are bound to be equal.

I cannot recommend the procedure. One problem is that the test does not build on a model of the data-generating process. With small or moderate sample sizes you run the risk that you accept the null hypothesis of equal covariance matrices even if it is not possible to find a meaningful model that describes the data. Anyway, the earlier mentioned problem of two-sided tests dependence on sample size is in itself a good reason for quitting this procedure altogether.

A traditional multiple regression model with only manifest variables will introduce you to multi-sample analysis.

Example 1

What determines if we find members of the opposite sex attractive? Felson and Bohrnstedt (1979) proposed the following hypotheses:

1. Height has a positive effect on attraction for boys, but a negative or no effect for girls.
2. Weight has a negative effect on attraction for both boys and girls.

It is only fair to mention that the two hypotheses were not the central issues in Felson and Bohrnstedt's study, which we shall have a closer look at in the next example. For space considerations description of measuring instruments and samples are postponed until then.

I will use their data (which are shown in Table 8.3) to estimate the parameters in a regression model:

$$attraction = height + weight + error$$

for both boys and girls. The program and output is shown in Table 8.1.

As was demonstrated in Example 4.1, a traditional regression model is just-identified, i.e. it has zero degrees of freedom, and the χ^2-value cannot be calculated—and for the same reason the fit indices are meaningless. The only fit measures are the two squared multiple correlations.

From the output we see that the data seems to support the two hypotheses: 'height' is not significant for girls, but is for boys, and 'weight' is significant for both groups. Note, however, that even if significant connections could be found, the coefficients and the squared multiple correlations are very small. Statistical significance is also a function of sample size!

A simpler model could be obtained by omitting 'height' from the girls' equation and letting the regression weights for 'weight' be equal across the two groups.

Table 8.1 Example 1: AMOS program and output, first run

```
Public Sub Main()
  Dim Sem As New AmosEngine
  Try
    Sem.TextOutput()
    Sem.Standardized()
    Sem.Smc
    Sem.BeginGroup( "Felson.xls","Fels_fem")
    Sem.GroupName ("girls")
    Sem.AStructure ("attract = height + weight + error (1)")

    Sem.BeginGroup ("Felson.xls","Fels_mal")
    Sem.GroupName( "boys")
    Sem.AStructure("attract = height + weight + error (1)")

    Sem.FitModel
  Finally
    Sem.Dispose
  End Try
End Sub
```

Maximum Likelihood Estimates

Regression Weights: (girls–Model 1)

	Estimate	S.E.	C.R.	P	Label
attract <--- height	.005	.012	.379	.705	
attract <--- weight	−.004	.002	−2.328	.020	

Standardized Regression Weights: (girls–Model 1)

	Estimate
attract <--- height	.028
attract <--- weight	−.169

Covariances: (girls–Model 1)

	Estimate	S.E.	C.R.	P	Label
attract <--> weight	19.024	4.098	4.642	***	

Correlations: (girls–Model 1)

	Estimate
height <--> weight	.340

Variances: (girls–Model 1)

	Estimate	S.E.	C.R.	P	Label
height	8.428	.826	10.198	***	
weight	371.476	36.427	10.198	***	
error	.233	.023	10.198	***	

Table 8.1 Cont'd

Squared multiple correlations: (girls–Model 1)

	Estimate
attract	.026

Maximum Likelihood Estimates

Regression Weights: (boys–Model 1)

	Estimate	S.E.	C.R.	P	Label
attract <--- height	.027	.011	2.358	.018	
attract <--- weight	−.006	.002	−3.624	***	

Standardized Regression Weights: (boys–Model 1)

	Estimate
attract <--- height	.185
attract <--- weight	−.284

Covariances: (boys–Model 1)

	Estimate	S.E.	C.R.	P	Label
height <--> weight	42.091	6.455	6.521	***	

Correlations: (boys–Model 1)

	Estimate
height <--> weight	.510

Variances: (boys–Model 1)

	Estimate	S.E.	C.R.	P	Label
height	11.572	1.140	10.149	***	
weight	588.605	57.996	10.149	***	
error	.224	.022	10.149	***	

Squared multiple correlations: (boys–Model 1)

	Estimate
attract	.061

The data seems not to conflict with such a model. The program and part of the output is seen in Table 8.2. You should, by now, be familiar with the way you restrict parameters to have the same value by letting them have the same label (if not, have another look at Example 6.1).

Table 8.2 Example 1: Program and output, second run

```
Sub Main()
  Dim Sem As New AmosEngine
  Try
    Sem.TextOutput
    Sem.Standardized
    Sem.Smc

    Sem.BeginGroup( "Felson.xls","Fels_fem")
    Sem.GroupName ("girls")
    Sem.AStructure ("attract = (a) weight + error (1)")

    Sem.BeginGroup ("Felson.xls","Fels_mal")
    Sem.GroupName( "boys")
    Sem.AStructure("attract = height + (a) weight + error (1)")

    Sem.FitModel
  Finally
    Sem.Dispose
  End Try
    End Sub
```

Computation of degrees of freedom (Model 1)

Number of distinct sample moments:	9
Number of distinct parameters to be estimated:	8
Degrees of freedom (9–8):	1

Result (Model 1)

```
Minimum was achieved
Chi-square = .506
Degrees of freedom = 1
Probability level = .477
```

Regression Weights: (girls–Model 1)

	Estimate	S.E.	C.R.	P	Label
attract <--- weight	−.005	.001	−4.251	***	a

Regression Weights: (boys–Model 1)

	Estimate	S.E.	C.R.	P	Label
attract <--- height	.024	.011	2.249	.025	
attract <--- weight	−.005	.001	−4.251	***	a

Observe that while the first model is just-identified, the second has one degree of freedom left over for testing. This is because the imposed restriction reduced the number of parameters to be freely estimated by one.

A χ^2-value of 0.506 with a P-value of 0.477 would (taking the sample sizes into consideration) lead to acceptance of the model, *if it were the only model under consideration* (and so would the fit indices, which are not shown for space considerations). However, one question still persists: Assuming the first model to be correct, is the second then significantly worse? Unfortunately we cannot answer this question using the χ^2-difference test—as in Example 6.1—because no χ^2 could be calculated for the first model.

You can go on testing for equal variances and covariances, but that does not seem very interesting in this case. Anyway, always remember that if your hypotheses are data-driven they should be tested on a new sample from the same population.

Example 2

It is generally agreed that a person's appearance affects other persons' impressions. A long line of evidence supports the assumption that physically attractive people are often attributed more positive qualities, and quite a few studies suggests that physically attractive people are more often seen as more intelligent than people that are less physically attractive (Byrne et al., 1968; Clifford and Walster, 1973; Landy and Sigall, 1974; Sarty, 1975). However, there also exist a few studies that point the other way: that persons with attractive personalities are perceived as more physically attractive (Gross and Crafton, 1977; Owens and Ford, 1978).

Felson and Bohrnstedt (1979) studied 209 girls and 207 boys from sixth to eight grade in order to find out the direction of a (possible) causal effect between physical attractiveness and perceived academic ability—or if there perhaps exists a two-way causation (Felson and Bohrnstedt, in a single passage in their article, write that the number of girls is 207 and the number of boys 209. However, the two figures are so close that, whatever is correct, it will not affect the conclusions.)

Felson and Bohrnstedt measured the following variables:

1. *academic*: Perceived academic ability, based on the item: Name who you think are the three smartest classmates.
2. *attract*: Perceived attractiveness based on the item: Name the three girls (boys) in the classroom who you think are the most good-looking (excluding yourself).
3. *GPA*: Grade point average.
4. *height*: Deviation of height from the mean for a subject's grade and sex.
5. *weight*: Weight, adjusted for height.
6. *rating*: Ratings of physical attractiveness obtained by having children from another city rate photographs of subjects.

Felson and Bohrnstedt's model is shown in Figure 8.1.

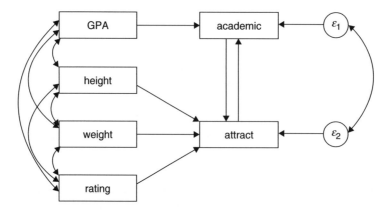

Figure 8.1   Example 2: Felson and Bohrnstedt's model

The reason why the model includes height and weight is that Felson and Bohrnstedt (as mentioned in the previous example) also wanted to test the following two hypotheses:

1. *Height* has a positive effect on *attract* for boys, but a negative or no effect for girls.
2. *Weight* has a negative effect on *attract* for both girls and boys.

Formulating the two regression equations as

$$academic = attract + GPA + \varepsilon_1$$
$$attract = academic + height + weight + rating + \varepsilon_2 \qquad (1)$$

it is evident that the model is identified as the two functions have no exogenous variables in common.

Observe the two opposed arrows that depict the hypothesized effects between *academic* and *attract*. While the possible correlations among the exogenous variables only express traditional multi-colinearity, the inclusion of a correlation between the error terms is more doubtful. The only reason Felson and Bohrnstedt give is that 'it is unrealistic in a simultaneous equation model to assume they are uncorrelated'—I would prefer a substantive argument.

We start by estimating the model separately for the two groups—from now on referred to as model A. A few points in the program in Table 8.3 deserve mentioning:

1. As no estimation method is stated AMOS uses maximum likelihood as default.
2. We have to state that the two error terms are possibly correlated (`Sem.Structure "error2 <--> error1"`), because otherwise AMOS will by default assume all error terms to be un-correlated.
3. It is recommendable to include comments in the program. Any line beginning with ', will not be read by AMOS during execution.

Table 8.3 Example 2: Program for model A and data files

```
' Example 8.2: Model A
' A reciprocal causation model of perceived academic ability, using
' both female and male samples of the Felson and Bohrnstedt (1979)
' dataset.
'
Sub Main()
  Dim Sem As New AmosEngine
  Try
    Sem.TextOutput
    Sem.Standardized
    Sem.ResidualMoments
    Sem.Smc

    Sem.BeginGroup ("Felson.xls","Fels_fem")
    Sem.GroupName ("Girls")
    Sem.AStructure ("academic = GPA + attract + (1) error1")
    Sem.AStructure ("attract = height + weight + rating + academic + (1) error2")
    Sem.AStructure ("error1 < -- > error2")

    Sem.BeginGroup ("Felson.xls","Fels_mal")
    Sem.GroupName ("Boys")
    Sem.AStructure ("academic = GPA + attract + (1) error1"
    Sem.AStructure ("attract = height + weight + rating + academic + (1) error2")
    Sem.AStructure ("error1 < -- > error2")
    Sem.FitModel
  Finally
    Sem.Dispose
  End Try
End Sub
```

Fels_fem

rowtype_	varname_	academic	athletic	attract	GPA	height	weight	rating
n		209	209	209	209	209	209	209
corr	academic	1.000						
corr	athletic	0.430	1.000					
corr	attract	0.500	0.180	1.000				
corr	GPA	0.490	0.220	0.320	1.000			
corr	height	0.100	−0.040	−0.030	0.180	1.000		
corr	weight	0.040	0.020	−0.160	−0.100	0.340	1.000	
corr	rating	0.090	0.140	0.430	0.150	−0.160	−0.270	1.000
stddev		0.160	0.070	0.490	3.490	2.910	19.320	1.010
mean		0.120	0.050	0.420	10.340	0.000	94.130	2.650

(Continued)

Note that as the input consists of correlation coefficients and not covariances, the standard deviations have been added, so that AMOS can calculate the covariance matrix as a basis for estimation of the model parameters. The means are also included in the data file but will not be used in this example.

Table 8.3 Cont'd

Fels_mal

rowtype_	varname_	academic	athletic	attract	GPA	height	weight	rating
n		207	207	207	207	207	207	207
corr	academic	1.000						
corr	athletic	0.470	1.000					
corr	attract	0.490	0.720	1.000				
corr	GPA	0.580	0.270	0.300	1.000			
corr	height	−0.020	0.150	0.040	−0.110	1.000		
corr	weight	−0.110	−0.010	−0.190	−0.160	0.510	1.000	
corr	rating	0.110	0.240	0.280	0.130	0.060	−0.180	1.000
stddev	stddev	0.160	0.210	0.490	4.040	3.410	24.320	0.970
mean	mean	0.100	0.170	0.440	8.630	0.000	101.910	2.590

The output is shown in Table 8.4. As is easily seen from the standardized residual covariances, the fit is extremely good, and the various fit indices, which are not shown in order to save space, confirm this.

The estimates of the coefficients seem to support Felson and Bohrnstedt's hypotheses (level of significance 0.05 one-sided test):

1. Perceived academic ability does not depend on attractiveness (C.R. = −0.039 for girls and C.R. = 1.071 for boys), whereas the opposite effect seems to exist (C.R. = 4.599 and 4.398).
2. Height has nearly no effect on attractiveness for girls (C.R. = 0.050), but has a positive effect for boys (C.R. = 1.967).
3. Attractiveness does not depend on weight for girls (C.R. = −1.321) but does for boys (C.R. = −2.484).
4. Error1 and error2 are not correlated (C.R. = −0.382 and −0.898, two-sided test). Felson and Bohrnstedt should have foreseen this result: It is difficult to imagine that *academic* and *attract* should have correlations that are not fully explained by their possible two-way causation.
5. Weight and GPA are not correlated (C.R. = −1.435).

Point 1 above made out the doubt that was the initial reason for performing the study, and point 2 supports hypothesis 1 and point 3 partly hypothesis 2.

However, just as in traditional regression analysis these are marginal tests, and you cannot use such tests to argue that several parameters should be removed at the same time.

We could of course exclude one parameter at a time, but due to colinearity this is perhaps not the most preferable procedure. Instead we can formulate a few reasonable models and compare them.

No doubt the effect from *attract* to *academic* and the correlations between the error terms should be excluded, while all correlations among exogenous variables should be maintained. These correlations are not given by the model but more or less by 'nature', and there would be no sense in restricting them to zero – even if they were not significant.

Table 8.4 Example 2: Output for Model A

Result (Model 1)
Minimum was achieved
Chi-square = 3.183
Degrees of freedom = 4
Probability level = .528
Maximum Likelihood Estimates

Regression Weights: (Girls–Model 1)

			Estimate	S.E.	C.R.	P	Label
academic	<---	GPA	.023	.004	6.241	***	
attract	<---	height	.000	.010	.050	.960	
attract	<---	weight	−.002	.001	−1.321	.186	
attract	<---	rating	.176	.027	6.444	***	
academic	<---	attract	−.002	.051	−.039	.969	
attract	<---	academic	1.607	.350	4.599	***	

Standardized Regression Weights: (Girls–Model 1)

			Estimate
academic	<---	GPA	.492
attract	<---	height	.003
attract	<---	weight	−.078
attract	<---	rating	.363
academic	<---	attract	−.006
attract	<---	academic	.525

Covariances: (Girls–Model 1)

			Estimate	S.E.	C.R.	P	Label
GPA	<-->	height	1.819	.712	2.555	.011	
GPA	<-->	weight	−6.710	4.676	−1.435	.151	
height	<-->	weight	19.024	4.098	4.642	***	
GPA	<-->	rating	.526	.246	2.139	.032	
height	<-->	rating	−.468	.205	−2.279	.023	
weight	<-->.	rating	−5.243	1.395	−3.759	***	
error1	<-->	error2	−.004	.010	−.382	.702	

Correlations: (Girls–Model 1)

			Estimate
GPA	<-->	height	.180
GPA	<-->	weight	−.100
height	<-->	weight	.340
GPA	<-->	rating	.150
height	<-->	rating	−.160
weight	<-->	rating	−.270
error1	<-->	error2	−.076

(Continued)

Table 8.4 Cont'd

Variances: (Girls—Model 1)

	Estimate	S.E.	C.R.	P	Label
GPA	12.122	1.189	10.198	***	
height	8.428	.826	10.198	***	
weight	371.476	36.427	10.198	***	
rating	1.015	.100	10.198	***	
error1	.019	.003	5.747	***	
error2	.143	.014	9.974	***	

Squared Multiple Correlations: (Girls—Model 1)

	Estimate
attract	.402
academic	.236

Residual Covariances (Girls—Model 1)

	rating	weight	height	GPA	attract	academic
rating	.000					
weight	.000	.000				
height	.000	.000	.000			
GPA	.000	.000	.000	.000		
attract	.004	.379	.007	.000	.000	
academic	.003	.271	.005	.000	.000	.000

Standardized Residual Covariances (Girls—Model 1)

	rating	weight	height	GPA	attract	academic
rating	.000					
weight	.000	.000				
height	.000	.000	.000			
GPA	.000	.000	.000	.000		
attract	.114	.569	.074	.000	.000	
academic	.270	1.264	.161	.000	.000	.000

Notes for Group/Model (Girls—Model 1)

Stability index for the following variables is .003
attract
academic

Table 8.4 Cont'd

Maximum Likelihood Estimates

Regression Weights: (Boys—Model 1)

			Estimate	S.E.	C.R.	P	Label
academic	<---	GPA	.021	.003	6.927	***	
attract	<---	height	.019	.010	1.967	.049	
attract	<---	weight	-.003	.001	-2.484	.013	
attract	<---	rating	.095	.030	3.150	.002	
academic	<---	attract	.063	.059	1.071	.284	
attract	<---	academic	1.386	.315	4.398	***	

Standardized Regression Weights: (Boys—Model 1)

			Estimate
academic	<---	GPA	.522
attract	<---	height	.132
attract	<---	weight	-.171
attract	<---	rating	.189
academic	<---	attract	.192
attract	<---	academic	.453

Covariances: (Boys—Model 1)

			Estimate	S.E.	C.R.	P	Label
GPA	<-->	height	-1.508	.961	-1.569	.117	
GPA	<-->	weight	-15.645	6.899	-2.268	.023	
height	<-->	weight	42.091	6.455	6.521	***	
GPA	<-->	rating	.507	.274	1.850	.064	
height	<-->	rating	.198	.230	.860	.390	
weight	<-->	rating	-4.226	1.662	-2.543	.011	
error1	<-->	error2	-.010	.011	-.898	.369	

Correlations: (Boys—Model 1)

			Estimate
GPA	<-->	height	-.110
GPA	<-->	weight	-.160
height	<-->	weight	.510
GPA	<-->	rating	.130
height	<-->	rating	.060
weight	<-->	rating	-.180
error1	<-->	error2	-.209

(Continued)

Table 8.4 Cont'd

Variances: (Boys–Model 1)

	Estimate	S.E.	C.R.	P	Label
GPA	16.243	1.600	10.149	***	
height	11.572	1.140	10.149	***	
weight	588.605	57.996	10.149	***	
rating	.936	.092	10.149	***	
error1	.015	.002	7.571	***	
error2	.164	.016	10.149	***	

Squared Multiple Correlations: (Boys–Model 1)

	Estimate
attract	.313
academic	.424

Residual Covariances (Boys–Model 1)

	rating	weight	height	GPA	attract	academic
rating	.000					
weight	.000	.000				
height	.000	.000	.000			
GPA	.000	.000	.000	.000		
attract	−.001	.021	.012	.000	.000	
academic	−.002	.049	.017	.000	.000	.000

Standardized Residual Covariances (Boys–Model 1)

	rating	weight	height	GPA	attract	academic
rating	.000					
weight	.000	.000				
height	.000	.000	.000			
GPA	.000	.000	.000	.000		
attract	−.040	.035	.105	.000	.000	
academic	−.174	.150	.147	.000	.000	.000

Notes for Group/Model (Boys–Model 1)

Stability index for the following variables is .087
attract
academic

So much said there are still quite a few models that could all be substantively grounded and also, to a certain extent, are supported by the data:

Model B: One of Felson and Bohrnstedt's hypotheses was that height had a positive effect on *attract* for boys but a negative or no effect for girls. As the effect for girls was not significant by traditional standards I will exclude this effect in model B.

Model C: Even if weight is not significant for the girls but is significant for the boys, you could argue that the two regression weights are so close (−0.02 and −0.03) that, for all practical purposes they could be considered equal. The same argument goes for the regression weights for GPA.

Model D: The regression weights attract<--academic are nearly identical, and could be restricted to be equal.

Model E: Even if you could argue that rating as a measure of *attract* is possibly more 'sex-dependent' than GPA is as a measure of *academic*, I will tentatively restrict attract<--rating to have the same value in the two groups.

Model F: Finally I will test a model where all regression weights are assumed equal across the two groups.

The program in Table 8.5 demonstrates how to estimate several models in the same run—a possibility that was already touched upon in

Table 8.5 Example 2: Program for estimating Models A–F

```
Sub Main
' A reciprocal causation model of perceived academic ability, using
' both female and male samples of the Felson and Bohrnstedt (1979) dataset.
'
  Dim Sem As New AmosEngine
  Try
    Sem.TextOutput
    Sem.BeginGroup ("Felson.xls","Fels_fem")
    Sem.GroupName ("girls")
    Sem.Structure ("academic = (g1)GPA + (g2)attract + error1 (1)")

    Sem.Structure ("attract = (g3)height + (g4)weight + (g5)rating + (g6)academic
      + error2 (1)")
    Sem.Structure ("(g7)error2 <--> error1")

    Sem.BeginGroup ("Felson","Fels_mal")
    Sem.GroupName ("boys")
    Sem.AStructure ("academic = (b1)GPA + (b2)attract + error1 (1)")
    Sem.AStructure ("attract = (b3)height + (b4)weight + (b5)rating+ (b6)academic
      + error2 (1)")
    Sem.AStructure ("(b7)error2 <--> error1")

    Sem.Model ("Model A)"
    Sem.Model ("Model B", "g2=0","g3=0", "g7=0","b2=0","b7=0")
    Sem.Model ("Model C", "g2=b2=0","g3=0", "g7=b7=0","g4=b4","g1=b1")
    Sem.Model ("Model D", "g2=b2=0","g3=0", "g7=b7=0","g4=b4","g1=b1","g6=b6")
    Sem.Model ("Model E","g2=b2=0","g3=0","g7=b7=0","g4=b4","g1=b1","g6=b6", "g5=b5")
    Sem.Model ("Model F", "g2=b2","g3=b3","g4=b4","g1=b1","g6=b6","g5=b5")
    Sem.FitAllModels
  Finally
    Sem.Dispose
  End Try
End Sub
```

Example 4.1:

1. All restricted parameters—in one model or another—are given a label in parentheses next to it.
2. The various restrictions are expressed in the lines Sem.Model ("Model A"), Sem.Model ("Model B"), etc.

Remember to use 'FitAllModels' instead of 'FitModel' when using the 'Model method'—otherwise AMOS will only estimate the first model.

As you can imagine there is a tremendous amount of output. Therefore I will show only a very small portion of it.

Towards the end of the output all the fit measures are shown for the various models. For space considerations only the first table is shown in Table 8.6. We see that *judged by themselves*, all six models are acceptable, and would have been accepted if only one model was under consideration. The various fit measures (not shown) exhibit the same picture: The six models all have acceptable fit, so how do we choose among them?

Table 8.6   Example 2: Fit measures for the various models

CMIN

Model	NPAR	CMIN	DF	P	CMIN/DF
Model A	38	3.183	4	.528	.796
Model B	33	4.503	9	.875	.500
Model C	31	4.996	11	.931	.454
Model D	30	5.039	12	.957	.420
Model E	29	8.618	13	.801	.663
Model F	32	9.493	10	.486	.949
Saturated model	42	.000	0		
Independence model	12	475.682	30	.000	15.856

One possibility is to use the χ^2-difference test for hierarchical models that you met in Example 6.1 and the very last part of the output shows the results of a series of such tests, as shown in Table 8.7.

The last four columns show changes in the fit indices relative to the basis model. None of the models are significantly different according to traditional norms, and changes in fit measures seem insignificant.

One could argue that, as the models are not significantly different, parsimony should lead us to accept model F, the most simple of the six. On the other hand the first table shows a rather dramatic drop in *P*-value at model F.

In a situation like this where one has to choose among several defendable models it is most reasonable to base the choice on information theoretic fit measures, as shown in Table 8.8. Note that BIC and CAIC are not stated in multi-sample analysis.

Based on the output in Table 8.8, it is evident that the initial model A as well as model F must be rejected. Model D seems most in accordance with the data with model E dose behind. Table 8.9 shows the regression weights of the two models.

Table 8.7 Example 2: Marginal χ^2-test for hierarchical models

Nested Model Comparisons

Assuming model Model_A to be correct:

Model	DF	CMIN	P	NFI Delta-1	IFI Delta-2	RFI rho-1	TLI rho2
Model B	5	1.320	.933	.003	.003	−.019	−.020
Model C	7	1.812	.970	.004	.004	−.022	−.023
Model D	8	1.856	.985	.004	.004	−.024	−.025
Model E	9	5.434	.795	.011	.012	−.008	−.009
Model F	6	6.310	.389	.013	.013	.010	.010

Assuming model Model_B to be correct:

Model	DF	CMIN	P	NFI Delta-1	IFI Delta-2	RFI rho-1	TLI rho2
Model C	2	.492	.782	.001	.001	−.003	−.003
Model D	3	.536	.911	.001	.001	−.005	−.005
Model E	4	4.114	.391	.009	.009	.010	.011

Assuming model Model_C to be correct:

Model	DF	CMIN	P	NFI Delta-1	IFI Delta-2	RFI rho-1	TLI rho2
Model D	1	.044	.834	.000	.000	−.002	−.002
Model E	2	3.622	.163	.008	.008	.013	.014

Assuming model Model_D to be correct:

Model	DF	CMIN	P	NFI Delta-1	IFI Delta-2	RFI rho-1	TLI rho2
Model E	1	3.578	.059	.008	.008	.015	.016

Table 8.8 Example 2: Information theoretic fit measures

AIC

Model	AIC	BCC	BIC	CAIC
Model A	79.183	81.843		
Model B	70.503	72.813		
Model C	66.996	69.166		
Model D	65.039	67.139		
Model E	66.618	68.648		
Model F	73.493	75.733		
Saturated model	84.000	86.940		
Independence model	499.682	500.522		

Table 8.9   Example 2: Regression weights for models D and E

REGRESSION WEIGHT FOR	MODEL D		MODEL E	
	Girls	Boys	Girls	Boys
GPA	0.023	0.023	0.023	0.023
Height	—	0.015	—	0.014
Weight	−0.003	−0.003	−0.003	−0.003
Rating	0.174	0.100	0.142	0.142
Attract	—	—	—	—
Academic	1.422	1.422	1.419	0.419

In model E the regression weight of *height* for boys (italicized) is *not* significant. All other regression weights in the table are significant, $P < 0.01$ (one-sided).

As the model formulations B–F were partly data-driven, the results of the analysis should be cross-validated on a new independent sample from the same population.

A Short Remark on Two-way-Causation

This is the first (and only!) worked example of a cyclic model, and a few remarks are appropriate.

Remember from the last paragraph of Chapter 5 that two conditions must be met in order to give a meaningful substantive interpretation of model parameters in a cyclic model:

1. As the regression weights in a loop are interpreted as the result of an infinite sum of loops, it is necessary that the sum is defined.
2. It is assumed that the whole process has come to an end.

AMOS calculates a *stability index* for each two-way causation. If this index is numerically less than 1.00, the first condition can be considered fulfilled. A stability index that is numerically larger than 1.00 is meaningless in the same sense as a negative variance. As you can see from Table 8.4 stability indices in Model A are 0.003 for girls and 0.087 for boys.

However, a stability index numerically larger than 1.00 could also indicate that the sample is too small to estimate the effects with any degree of precision.

It is a common misunderstanding that a stability index having a numerical value less than 1.00 guarantees that the second condition is met. It does NOT!

It takes time series data to judge the second condition—and if such data were at hand you would probably specify a time series model.

2.   Identifying and Estimating Mean Structures

Until now we have only estimated covariance structures: We were only interested in *relations* between variables—be they manifest or latent—but not in the *values* of the variables.

As long as we are only working with manifest variables, hypotheses about means can be tested by traditional statistical techniques: t-test, analysis of variance, multivariate analysis of variance and the like, but these techniques cannot treat means of *latent* variables.

Now, have a look at the simple measurement model:

$$X = \lambda_0 + \lambda_1 F + \varepsilon \tag{2a}$$

Taking the expectation you get

$$\mu_X = \lambda_0 + \lambda_1 \mu_F \tag{2b}$$

It is this decomposition of the means of dependent variables that has given birth to the name *analysis of mean structures*. As is evident from (2b) this necessitates the estimation of regression intercepts and consequently the input sample covariance matrix has to be supplemented by the sample means.

In one-group analysis means are, in most cases, of no interest, but nevertheless I will introduce mean structure analysis by estimating the intercept in the regression model from Example 4.1.

Example 3

(Example 4.1 continued). A program for estimation of the regression model without intercept (as in Example 4.1) is shown in Table 8.10a, and a program for estimation of the same model including an intercept term is shown in 8.10b. In both cases, based on the data from Figure 4.4, but this time the means in the input is used. The program in panel (b) differs from that in panel (a) in two respects:

1. The line 'Sem.ModelMeansAndIntercepts' tells AMOS that it should consider means and intercepts parameters in the model.
2. The empty bracket in the 'Sem.AStructure line' tells AMOS that the intercept will be freely estimated. If this bracket is not there, AMOS will fix the intercept at 0, even if you have ordered AMOS to 'ModelMeansAndIntercepts.'
3. The same goes for the four 'Sem.Mean' statements. If one of these statements is missing, the mean will be fixed at 0.

The output is the same as the output shown in Table 4.2, but for the addition of the estimates shown in Table 8.11.

In Example 4.1 we had 15 'pieces of information' (5 variances and 10 covariances) on which to estimate 15 parameters (4 regression weights, 6 covariances and 5 variances), which left us with 0 degrees of freedom. Now, we could add to our input information 5 means, but as the number of parameters to be estimated also grew by 5 (4 means and one intercept), we still have 0 degrees of freedom and a just-identified model.

Table 8.10 Example 3: Program for regression analysis (a) without and (b) with intercept

```
Sub Main()                                                              (a)
  Dim sem As New AmosEngine
  Try
    Sem.Title ("Example 8.3")
    'Data from Bredahl (2001)
    Sem.TextOutput()
    Sem.Standardized()
    Sem.Smc

    Sem.BeginGroup ("Bredahl.xls", "Manifest")
    Sem.GroupName ("Germany")
    Sem.AStructure ("Risk = Tech + Nature + Neophobia + Alienation + (1)d")
    Sem.FitModel()
  Finally
    Sem.Dispose()
    End Try
End Sub


Sub Main()                                                              (b)
  Dim sem As New AmosEngine
  Try
    Sem.Title ("Example 8.3")
    'Data from Bredahl (2001)
    Sem.TextOutput()
    Sem.Standardized()
    Sem.Smc
    Sem.ModelMeansAndIntercepts

    Sem.BeginGroup ("Bredahl.xls", "Manifest")
    Sem.GroupName ("Germany")
    Sem.AStructure ("Risk = ()+Technology + Nature + Neophobia + Alienation +(1)d")
    Sem.Mean ("Technology")
    Sem.Mean ("Nature")
    Sem.Mean ("Neophobia")
    Sem.Mean ("Alienation")

    Sem.FitModel()
  Finally
    Sem.Dispose()
  End Try
End Sub
```

Identification of Mean Structures

As you will have guessed from the above example, degrees of freedom is a rare 'good' in mean structure modelling. The problem is that the mean structure and the covariance structure must be identified *separately*—and it is obvious that identification of the mean structure is generally very problematic.

Table 8.11 Example 3: Additional output

`Means: (Germany–Model 1)`

	Estimate	S.E.	C.R.	P	Label
Technology	25.002	.252	99.106	***	
Nature	32.357	.276	117.118	***	
Neophobia	18.985	.303	62.562	***	
Alienation	16.578	.161	103.253	***	

`Intercepts: (Germany–Model 1)`

	Estimate	S.E.	C.R.	P	Label
Risk	7.289	2.388	3.052	.002	

3. Mean Structures in Multi-Group Studies

We easily run out of degrees of freedom when trying to estimate mean structures in single-group studies and the same is the case in multi-group studies. If such a study is done in order to compare means of latent variables across groups, it is not possible to estimate means in all groups. However, if we fix the means of the latent variables in one group at 0, it is possible to estimate the means in the other groups, and these means will then express the *differences* in means between the various groups and the reference group.

In Examples 4 and 5, you will need the input shown in Table 8.12.

Example 4

The Food-Related Lifestyle instrument (FRL) is a 69-item battery, measuring 23 dimensions in five major domains (ways of shopping, cooking methods, quality aspects, consumption situations and buying motives). Since its invention (Brunsø and Grunert, 1995), it has been widely used in several European countries. I use data from Scholderer et al. (2004).

In order to keep things simple I will use only data from the two-factor domain 'consumption situations,' the items of which are listed in Table 8.13.

I will test the hypothesis that the two factor means in this domain have not changed from 1994 to 1998 in France.

In order to do so, we must make sure that the measures are comparable, i.e. that the measuring instrument functions in the same way at the two points in time. Otherwise there is no sense in comparing the factor means.

So we must demand that regression weights and regression intercepts are equal across groups—and of course also that the same general two-factor structure exists in both groups.

Table 8.12   Input for Examples 4 and 5

F94

rowtype_	varname_	v10	v65	v23	v27	v45	v42
n		991	991	991	991	991	991
cov	v10	3.547					
cov	v65	1.707	4.038				
cov	v23	1.219	1.131	2.131			
cov	v27	0.149	0.426	0.541	3.837		
cov	v45	0.131	0.362	0.173	1.528	4.561	
cov	v42	0.118	0.072	0.071	1.183	0.959	4.793
mean		2.501	2.996	1.873	3.066	4.358	4.215

F98

rowtype_	varname_	v10	v65	v23	v27	v45	v42
n		995	995	995	995	995	995
cov	v10	2.751					
cov	v65	1.385	3.430				
cov	v23	1.178	1.195	2.301			
cov	v27	0.498	0.391	0.667	3.485		
cov	v45	0.359	0.348	0.356	1.429	3.932	
cov	v42	0.207	0.241	0.200	1.068	0.661	3.888
mean		2.366	3.039	2.005	3.119	4.378	4.520

UK98

rowtype_	varname_	v10	v65	v23	v27	v45	v42
n		1000	1000	1000	1000	1000	1000
cov	v10	3.370					
cov	v65	0.990	3.719				
cov	v23	0.881	1.155	3.368			
cov	v27	0.236	0.204	0.347	3.990		
cov	v45	0.167	−0.067	0.202	1.579	4.435	
cov	v42	−0.061	−0.029	0.154	1.205	0.787	4.988
mean		2.894	3.520	2.413	3.159	3.501	3.872

Table 8.13   Example 4: Items used in the analysis

How are meals spread over the day? (snacks versus meals)
  (v10) I eat before I get hungry, which means that I am never hungry at meal time
  (v65) I eat whenever I feel the slightest bit hungry
  (v23) In our house, nibbling has takien over and replaced set eating hours
How important is eating-out? (social event)
  (v27) Going out for dinner is a regular part of our eating habits
  (v45) We often get together with friends to enjoy an easy-to-cook, casual dinner
  (v42) I do not consider it a luxury to go out with my family to have dinner in a restaurant

Table 8.14 Example 4: Program

```
Sub Main()
  Dim sem As New AmosEngine
  Try
    Sem.Title ("Example 8.4")
    'Data from Scholderer et al. 2004
    Sem.TextOutput()
    Sem.Standardized()
    Sem.Smc
    Sem.ModelMeansAndIntercepts

    Sem.BeginGroup ("Scholderer.xls", "F94")
    Sem.GroupName ("France")
    Sem.GroupName ("France 1994")
    Sem.AStructure ("v10 = (a) + (1) snacks + (1) e_10")
    Sem.AStructure ("v65 = (b) + (g) snacks + (1) e_65")
    Sem.AStructure ("v23 = (c) + (h) snacks + (1) e_23")
    Sem.AStructure ("v27 = (d) + (1) social + (1) e_27")
    Sem.AStructure ("v45 = (e) + (i) social + (1) e_45")
    Sem.AStructure ("v42 = (f) + (j) social + (1) e_42")

    Sem.BeginGroup ("Scholderer.xls", "F98")
    Sem.GroupName ("France 1998")
    Sem.AStructure ("v10 = (a) + (1) snacks + (1) e_10")
    Sem.AStructure ("v65 = (b) + (g) snacks + (1) e_65")
    Sem.AStructure ("v23 = (c) + (h) snacks + (1) e_23")
    Sem.AStructure ("v27 = (d) + (1) social + (1) e_27")
    Sem.AStructure ("v45 = (e) + (i) social + (1) e_45")
    Sem.AStructure ("v42 = (f) + (j) social + (1) e_42")
    Sem.Mean ("snacks")
    Sem.Mean ("social")

    Sem.FitModel()
  Finally
    Sem.Dispose()
  End Try
End Sub
```

A program that constrains the regression weights and intercepts to be equal across groups and test the hypothesis of equal factor means is shown in Table 8.14.

By now, you should be familiar with the way regression weights are constrained, so I will not comment on that. Note that I ask for estimation of the two factor means in 1998, but not in 1994, because—as mentioned in Example 2—if not asked for, AMOS assumes zero means.

Part of the output is shown in Table 8.15. For space considerations regression weights and intercepts are shown for the year 1994 only.

Table 8.15 Example 4: Output

Result (Model 1)
Minimum was achieved
Chi-square = 76.490
Degrees of freedom = 24
Probability level = .000

Regression Weights: (France 1994—Model 1)

			Estimate	S.E.	C.R.	P	Label
v10	<---	snacks	1.000				
v65	<---	snacks	.992	.054	18.491	***	g
v23	<---	snacks	.800	.043	18.465	***	h
v27	<---	social	1.000				
v45	<---	social	.674	.070	9.640	***	i
v42	<---	social	.514	.056	9.138	***	j

Intercepts: (France 1994—Model 1)

	Estimate	S.E.	C.R.	P	Label
v10	2.413	.053	45.467	***	a
v65	3.012	.055	54.563	***	b
v23	1.931	.043	45.212	***	c
v27	3.045	.061	50.135	***	d
v45	4.335	.055	79.410	***	e
v42	4.358	.052	84.201	***	f

Covariances: (France 1994—Model 1)

			Estimate	S.E.	C.R.	P	Label
social	<-->	snacks	.389	.091	4.280	***	

Standardized Residual Covariances (France 1994—Model 1)

	v42	v45	v27	v23	v65	v10
v42	.011					
v45	1.107	.046				
v27	.048	−.110	−.077			
v23	−.864	−.368	2.467	−.648		
v65	−.909	.750	.316	−.955	.222	
v10	−.632	−1.037	−2.050	−.197	1.345	.373

Standardized Residual Means (France 1994—Model 1)

v42	v45	v27	v23	v65	v10
−2.057	.335	.330	−1.234	−.256	1.476

Table 8.15 Cont'd

Means: (France 1998—Model 1)

	Estimate	S.E.	C.R.	P	Label
snacks	.014	.066	.209	.834	
social	.091	.082	1.118	.264	

Covariances: (France 1998—Model 1)

	Estimate	S.E.	C.R.	P	Label
snacks <--> social	.554	.084	6.577	***	

Standardized Residual Covariances (France 1998—Model 1)

	v42	v45	v27	v23	v65	v10
v42	−.239					
v45	−.552	−.036				
v27	−.130	.049	.091			
v23	−.302	.600	2.492	.602		
v65	−.354	−.193	−1.435	.494	−.216	
v10	−.738	−.147	−.570	.240	−.451	−.382

Standardized Residual Means (France 1998—Model 1)

v42	v45	v27	v23	v65	v10
1.826	−.305	−.302	.330	.226	−1.147

CMIN

Model	NPAR	CMIN	DF	P	CMIN/DF
Default model	30	76.490	24	.000	3.187
Saturated model	54	.000	0		
Independence model	24	1644.099	30	.000	54.803

Baseline Comparisons

Model	NFI Delta1	RFI rho1	IFI Delta2	TLI rho2	CFI
Default model	.953	.942	.968	.959	.967
Saturated model	1.000		1.000		1.000
Independence model	.000	.000	.000	.000	.000

RMSEA

Model	RMSEA	LO 90	HI 90	PCLOSE
Default model	.033	.025	.042	1.000
Independence model	.165	.158	.171	.000

With a χ^2 of 76.490 with 24 degrees of freedom giving a P-value of 0.000, the model does not seem to hold. However, such a conclusion is perhaps a little too hasty, because with a sample size of about 2×1000 the dependence of χ^2 on sample size becomes a problem.

Therefore I will (as did Scholderer et al.) fall back on RMSEA as my main measure of model fit.

In this case RMSEA is 0.033, and the hypotheses of *configural invariance*, equal regression weights and equal intercepts are accepted.

As the factor means in the F94 data are fixed at zero, the F98 means should estimate the *differences* between the F94 and the F98 factor means.

From the output we see that none of factor means are significantly different across the two measurements.

These, however are marginal tests. In order to test the hypothesis that the two factor means *taken together* are equal, we must fix the F94 factor means to be equal to the F98, i.e. fix them both to zero. This can be done by excluding the two Sem.Mean statements form the program in Table 8.14, or by just placing a single opening quote at the beginning of the two lines. Then the models can be compared using χ^2-difference test or—better—by comparing the various fit measures.

Another possibility is to use the 'model method' as in Example 2. I will illustrate this method in the next example.

Testing a Measuring Instrument for Cross-group Equivalence

In the example we were very lucky in that the FRL scale showed intra-country stability to a degree that made it possible for us to compare the factor means. We are not always that lucky.

In order to compare research results across groups it is of course important to make sure that the measurements are comparable.

Cross-group validity of a measuring instrument is usually done by going through a series of tests, where the demands to the equivalence of the measuring instrument are increased step by step, as we ask the following questions:

1. *Configural invariance*: Are the model structure the same across groups? I.e. is the graphical picture of the measurement model the same across groups?
2. *Metric invariance*: Are the regression weights $(X \leftarrow F)$ equal across groups? If so, the manifest variables are measured in the same scale units across groups.
3. *Scale invariance*: Are the item intercepts equal across groups? If so, the manifest variables are measured on common interval scales.
4. *Factor covariance invariance*: Are the factors inter-related in the same way across groups?
5. *Factor variance invariance*: Does the factors exhibit the same variation across groups?

6. *Error variance (and covariance) invariance*: Are the error variances (and covariances) equal across groups? The last two points secure equal reliabilities for the items and the complete measuring instrument across groups.

Example 5

Let us test the inter-cultural validity of the FRL across UK and French consumers with data from Scholderer et al. (2004). Again I will (in order to save space) only use the 'Consumption Situation Domain.'

The program is shown in Table 8.16.

Table 8.16   Example 5: Program

```
Public Sub Main()
  Dim Sem As New AmosEngine
  Try
    Sem.TextOutput
    Sem.Standardized
    Sem.ResidualMoments
    Sem.Smc
    Sem.ModelMeansAndIntercepts

    Sem.BeginGroup ("Scholderer.xls", "UK98")
    Sem.GroupName ("UK 1998")
    Sem.AStructure ("v10 = (a1) + (1) snacks + (1) e_10")
    Sem.AStructure ("v65 = (b1) + (g1) snacks + (1) e_65")
    Sem.AStructure ("v23 = (c1) + (h1) snacks + (1) e_23")
    Sem.AStructure ("v27 = (d1) + (1) social + (1) e_27")
    Sem.AStructure ("v45 = (e1) + (i1) social + (1) e_45")
    Sem.AStructure ("v42 = (f1) + (j1) social + (1) e_42")
    Sem.AStructure ("snacks<->social (k1)")
    Sem.AStructure ("snacks (m1)")
    Sem.AStructure ("social (n1)")
    Sem.AStructure ("e_10 (o1)")
    Sem.AStructure ("e_65 (p1)")
    Sem.AStructure ("e_23 (q1)")
    Sem.AStructure ("e_27 (r1)")
    Sem.AStructure ("e_45 (s1)")
    Sem.AStructure ("e_42 (t1)")

    Sem.BeginGroup ("Scholderer.xls", "F98")
    Sem.GroupName ("France 1998")
    Sem.AStructure ("v10 = (a2) + (1) snacks + (1) e_10")
    Sem.AStructure ("v65 = (b2) + (g2) snacks + (1) e_65")
    Sem.AStructure ("v23 = (c2) + (h2) snacks + (1) e_23")
    Sem.AStructure ("v27 = (d2) + (1) social + (1) e_27")
    Sem.AStructure ("v45 = (e2) + (i2) social + (1) e_45")
```

(Continued)

Table 8.16   Cont'd

```
Sem.AStructure ("snacks<->social (k2)")
Sem.AStructure ("snacks (m2)")
Sem.AStructure ("social (n2)")
Sem.AStructure ("e_10 (o2)")
Sem.AStructure ("e_65 (p2)")
Sem.AStructure ("e_23 (q2)")
Sem.AStructure ("e_27 (r2)")
Sem.AStructure ("e_45 (s2)")
Sem.AStructure ("e_42 (t2)")

Sem.Model ("Model A")
Sem.Model ("Model B", "g1=g2","h1=h2","i1=i2","j1=j2")
Sem.Model ("Model C", "g1=g2","h1=h2","i1=i2","j1=j2",
        "a1=a2","b1=b2","c1=c2","d1=d2","e1=e2","f1=f2")
Sem.Model ("Model D", "g1=g2","h1=h2","i1=i2","j1=j2",
        "a1=a2","b1=b2","c1=c2","d1=d2","e1=e2","f1=f2","k1=k2")
Sem.Model ("Model E", "g1=g2","h1=h2","i1=i2","j1=j2",
       "a1=a2","b1=b2","c1=c2","d1=d2","e1=e2","f1=f2","k1=k2",
       "m1=m2","n1=n2")
Sem.Model ("Model F", "g1=g2","h1=h2","i1=i2","j1=j2",
        "a1=a2","b1=b2","c1=c2","d1=d2","e1=e2","f1=f2","k1=k2",
        "m1=m2","n1=n2","o1=o2","p1=p2","q1=q2","r1=r2","s1=s2",
        "t1=t2")

Sem.FitAllModels

   Finally
      Sem.Dispose
   End Try
End Sub
End Module
```

I have used the now familiar 'model method,' known from Example 1, to estimate six models placing increasing restrictions on the invariance of the measuring instrument in the two populations:

A. Configural invariance:	Basis model: The same structure is assumed
B. Metric invariance:	Regressions weights are assumed equal
C. Scale invariance:	As B + the intercepts are assumed equal
D. Factor covariance invariance:	As C + the factor covariances are assumed equal
E. Factor variance invariance:	As D + factor variances are assumed equal
F. Error variance invariance:	As E + error variances are assumed equal

Table 8.17 Example 5: Output

CMIN

Model	NPAR	CMIN	DF	P	CMIN/DF
Model A	38	22.994	16	.114	1.437
Model B	34	27.219	20	.129	1.361
Model C	28	249.464	26	.000	9.595
Model D	27	257.216	27	.000	9.527
Model E	25	261.057	29	.000	9.002
Model F	19	413.438	35	.000	11.813
Saturated model	54	.000	0		
Independence model	24	1344.395	30	.000	44.813

RMSEA

Model	RMSEA	LO 90	HI 90	PCLOSE
Model A	.015	.000	.027	1.000
Model B	.013	.000	.025	1.000
Model C	.066	.058	.073	.000
Model D	.065	.058	.073	.000
Model E	.063	.056	.071	.001
Model F	.074	.067	.080	.000
Independence model	.148	.142	.155	.000

AIC

Model	AIC	BCC	BIC	CAIC
Model A	98.994	99.532		
Model B	95.219	95.700		
Model C	305.464	305.861		
Model D	311.216	311.598		
Model E	311.057	311.411		
Model F	451.438	451.707		
Saturated model	108.000	108.764		
Independence model	1392.395	1392.735		

From Table 8.17 we see that Models A and B are accepted at any conventional significance level, while all other models are rejected, As the χ^2-test has excessive power in large samples, this is a very heavy argument for the measurement model having *at least* metric invariance.

As in Example 8.4—and for the same reasons—I will forego testing and use RMSEA as the main fit measure. From Table 8.17 you see that although RMSEA is generally rather small, it has a marked increase from model B to model C, which could cast doubt on the hypothesis of scale invariance across the two populations. Also observe that the null hypothesis 'that RMSEA in the population is less than

Table 8.18   Example 5: Output, marginal analysis

Assuming prior model to be correct:

Model	DF	CMIN	P	NFI Delta-1	IFI Delta-2	RFI rho-1	TLI rho2
Model B	4	4.225	.376	.003	.003	−.002	−.002
Model C	6	222.245	.000	.165	.168	.184	.188
Model D	1	7.752	.005	.006	.006	−.002	−.002
Model E	2	3.841	.147	.003	.003	−.012	−.012
Model F	6	152.381	.000	.113	.116	.063	.064

0.05' is rejected for all models except A and B. The information theoretic criteria points at Model B as the 'best.'

Another way to judge the fit of the various models is to look at the incrementel fit measures as shown in Table 8.18. The table is constructed from several tables of Marginal χ^2-test for Hierarchical Models of the type shown in Table 8.7.

As mentioned several times, the χ^2-square difference test is of little value in such large samples, but from the NFI column we see that the value of NFI (which for Model A is 0.983) only drops with 0.003 when we impose the restriction of metric invariance, whereas the (marginal) drop when we also impose scale invariance is no less than 0.165. Adding restrictions on factor covariances and factor variances (in that order) only makes NFI drop by 0.006 and 0.003 respectively, whereas adding the last restriction of equal errror variances once more causes NFI to drop by a a considerable amount. The other fit indices show the same tendencies, as do the RMSEA and the information theoretic fit measures in Table 8.17.

Our conclusion is: The measuring instrument shows configural, metric, factor covariance and factor variance invariances, whereas metric invariance and error variance invariance are not supported by the data.

It deserves mentioning that the two French datasets used in Example 4 went through the whole sequence of tests with the result mentioned in that example, that there was full equivalence of the measuring instrument at the two points in time.

Multi-group Analysis of Causal Models with Latent Variables

When doing multi-group analysis of causal models things become a little more complicated, because, in addition to analyzing the measurement model, you must also analyze the causal model.

As in all other cases, it is of utmost importance to make sure that that the measurement model is valid before trying to analyze the structural model. So, I would reccommend using the two-step strategy mentioned in Chapter 7 and start the analysis by going through the same sequence of steps as in Example 4.

Then you should go on with the structural model, first testing for the equivalence of the regression weights (and intercepts if this is relevant) and then the variances and covariances of the disturbances.

Usually error and disturbance variances (and covariances) are of the least interest and then you could put error variances (and covariances) last in the sequence together with the disturbance variances.

☞ In this chapter you have met the following concepts:

stability index   scale invariance
mean structure   factor covariance invariance
configural invariance   factor variance invariance
metric invariance   error variance invariance

Besides you have learned the following AMOS statements:

Sem.Model   Sem.ModelMeansAndIntercepts
Sem.FitAllModels   Sem.Mean

Questions

1. Comment on the problems of cyclical models.
2. List the various steps in testing a measuring instrument for cross-group equivalence. Comment on the rationale behind the procedure.

Reference List

Brunsø, K. and K. G. Grunert (1995) 'Development and testing of a cross-cultural valid instrument: Food-related lifestyle,' *Advances in Consumer Research*, 22: 475–80.

Byrne, D. O., O. London, and K. Reeves (1968) 'The effects of physical attractiveness, sex and attitude similarity on interpersonal attraction,' *Journal of Personality*, 36: 259–71.

Clifford, M. M. and E. Walster (1973) 'The affect of physical attractiveness on teacher expectations,' *Sociology of Education*, 46: 248–58.

Felson, R. B. and G. W. Bohrnstedt (1979), 'Are the good beautiful or the beautiful good?,' *Social Psychology Quarterly*, 42: 386–92.

Gross, A. E. and C. Crafton (1977) 'What is good is beautiful,' *Sociometry*, 40: 85–90.

Landy, D. and Sigall, H. (1974) 'Beauty is talent: Task evaluation is a function of the performer's physical attractiveness,' *Journal of Personality and Social Psychology*, 29: 229–304.

Owens, G. and J. G. Ford (1978) 'Further considerations of the "what is good is beautiful" finding,' *Social Psychology*, 41: 73–75.

Sarty, M. (1975) 'The "pretty girl" as a sexual and reproductive stereotype,' presented at Western Psychology Association; summary from Department of Human Behaviour, University of Southern California School of Medicine.

Scholderer, J., K. Brunsø, L. Bredahl, and K. G. Grunets (2004) 'Cross-cultural validity of the food-related lifestyle instrument (FRL) within Western Europe,' *Appetite*, 42: 197–211.

9

Incomplete and Non-Normal Data

Missing data is more the rule than the exception in empirical research, and several solutions to the problem have been suggested. As will be argued in the opening paragraphs of the chapter none of them are wholly satisfactory.

Then I turn to the special ML procedure invented in AMOS, that makes it possible to estimate a model using all data at hand even if some data are missing. However, it turns out that even this technique is not without its drawbacks—the most serious being that you easily run out of degrees of freedom, because it is necessary to estimate means and intercepts.

Another common problem is non-normality of data. No variable is strictly normal, and, more often than not, deviations from normality are so serious that they cannot be ignored. We take a look at the consequences of non-normality and the remedies most often used.

Then I move on to bootstrapping, which is an estimation procedure that makes no distributional demands at all.

Bootstrapping is some sort of Swiss army knife, capable of solving a lot of different problems inside and outside of SEM—but, like all statistical methods, it has its shortcomings.

1. Incomplete Data

It is very unlikely that you will do a large research project without meeting the problem of making out the heading. The most obvious consequence of incomplete data is that it could—depending on how you choose to handle the problem—reduce your sample. What is more serious is that it biases the estimation.

Of the many ways of coping with the missing data problem the following seem to be the most popular:

1. *Listwise Deletion* (LD): Delete all observations that have missing values on any variable.

2. *Pairwise Deletion* (PD): Use LD for all pairs of variables.
3. *Mean Imputation* (MI): Replace the missing value with the mean of the variable.
4. *Regression Imputation* (RI): Estimate the value of the missing observation by regressing the variable on other variables.

It is obvious that the first method, which is default in many computer programs (including SPSS) could easily reduce the sample size to an unacceptable size, and also bias your estimates, depending on the mechanism that produces the missing data.

If you use PD, calculation of variances and covariances in the input matrix are based on all observations where the one or two variables involved are not missing. One problem with this procedure is that the various sample moments are based on different sample sizes. What sample size should then go into calculation of test statistics and the like?

No doubt some rough rules of thumb could be put forward, but what is more serious: If separate parts of the covariance matrix are based on different observations you run the risk that the matrix will not be positive definite.

It is obvious that MI will reduce the sample variances and covariances, and as SEM is based on variances and covariances this too seems to be a bad solution to the problem.

RI also reduces estimates of variances and covariances, but to a lesser degree than MI.

In general the *full information maximum likelihood* (FIML) procedure as implemented in AMOS gives the best results, as it allows maximum likelihood estimation to be based on a data set with missing data and still make use of all available data without any form of imputation. Of course, it necessitates that analysis is based on the original data and not a data summary. Besides, model evaluation is a bit more complicated, as you have fewer global fit measures at your disposal.

There is, however, one situation in which none of the above-mentioned methods, including FIML, will give consistent estimates. That is, when the very fact that a value is missing conveys information on its value. An example is when the probability that a respondent will not report her income is larger for higher incomes. In this case an empty cell in the data matrix indicates that the respondent may belong to the higher income classes. Even in this situation, however, FIML is less biased than any of the methods mentioned above.

Example 1

I will use the Thomsen et al. data to illustrate FIML estimation with incomplete data, estimating the measurement model in Table 7.5 after having deleted 20 per cent of the measurements by simple random sampling. As usual, you can find the data on the website.

The program is shown in Table 9.1.

Table 9.1   Example 1: Program

```
Public Sub Main()
  Dim Sem As New AmosEngine
  Try
    Sem.TextOutput
    Sem.Smc
    Sem.Standardized
    Sem.ModelMeans And Intercepts
   'Sem.Mods(20)
    Sem.BeginGroup("Missing20.sav")
    Sem.AStructure("ecq1  = () + (1) Rumination + (1) e_ecq1")
    Sem.AStructure("ecq2  = () +     Rumination + (1) e_ecq2")
    Sem.AStructure("ecq3  = () +     Rumination + (1) e_ecq3")
    Sem.AStructure("ecq4  = () +     Rumination + (1) e_ecq4")
    Sem.AStructure("ecq5  = () +     Rumination + (1) e_ecq5")
    Sem.AStructure("ecq6  = () +     Rumination + (1) e_ecq6")
    Sem.AStructure("ecq7  = () +     Rumination + (1) e_ecq7")
    Sem.AStructure("ecq8  = () +     Rumination + (1) e_ecq8")
    Sem.AStructure("ecq9  = () +     Rumination + (1) e_ecq9")
    Sem.AStructure("ecq10 = () +     Rumination + (1) e_ecq10")
    Sem.AStructure("ecq11 = () +     Rumination + (1) e_ecq11")
    Sem.AStructure("ecq12 = () +     Rumination + (1) e_ecq12")
    Sem.AStructure("ecq13 = () +     Rumination + (1) e_ecq13")
    Sem.AStructure("ecq14 = () +     Rumination + (1) e_ecq14")

    Sem.AStructure("poms4d  = () + (1) Sadness + (1) e_poms4d")
    Sem.AStructure("poms8d  = () +     Sadness + (1) e_poms8d")
    Sem.AStructure("poms12d = () +     Sadness + (1) e_poms12d")
    Sem.AStructure("poms14d = () +     Sadness + (1) e_poms14d")
    Sem.AStructure("poms20d = () +     Sadness + (1) e_poms20d")
    Sem.AStructure("poms23d = () +     Sadness + (1) e_poms28d")
    Sem.AStructure("poms33d = () +     Sadness + (1) e_poms33d")

    Sem.AStructure("psqik1 = () + (1) Sleep Quality + (1) e_psqik1")
    Sem.AStructure("leukocyt = () + (1) Immunity + (1) e_Imm1")
    Sem.AStructure("lymphocy = () +     Immunity + (1) e_Imm2")

    Sem.AStructure ("consult   = () + (1) Health care + (1) e_health1")
    Sem.AStructure ("telephone = () +     Health care + (1) e_health2")

    Sem.AStructure("Sleep Quality <-->Rumination")
    Sem.AStructure("Sleep Quality <--> Sadness")
    Sem.AStructure("Sleep Quality <--> Immunity")
    Sem.AStructure("Sleep Quality <--> Health care")

    Sem.AStructure("e_psqik1 (0)")

    Sem.FitModel
  Finally
    Sem.Dispose
  End Try
End Sub
```

If you compare Table 9.1 with Table 7.5, you will observe the following modifications:

1. The Sem.BeginGroup line is modified as it is necessary to use the raw data.
2. The Sem.Mods(20) line is deleted, as modification indices cannot be calculated if data are missing.
3. FIML on incomplete data demands estimation of means and intercepts.

Part of the output is shown in Table 9.2.

Table 9.2 Example 1: Output

```
Minimum was achieved
Function of log likelihood = 2455.278
Number of parameters = 90
```

Maximum Likelihood Estimates

Regression Weights: (Group number 1 - Model 1)

			Estimate	S.E.	C.R.	P Label
ecq1	<---	Rumination	1.000			
ecq2	<---	Rumination	.313	.113	2.780	.005
ecq3	<---	Rumination	.799	.087	9.189	***
ecq4	<---	Rumination	.819	.092	8.938	***
ecq5	<---	Rumination	.436	.100	4.357	***
ecq6	<---	Rumination	.399	.103	3.876	***
ecq7	<---	Rumination	.326	.057	5.748	***
ecq8	<---	Rumination	.623	.082	7.608	***
ecq9	<---	Rumination	.880	.095	9.283	***
ecq10	<---	Rumination	.168	.039	4.357	***
ecq11	<---	Rumination	.651	.088	7.379	***
ecq12	<---	Rumination	.184	.103	1.793	.073
ecq13	<---	Rumination	.363	.111	3.253	.001
ecq14	<---	Rumination	.066	.100	.665	.506
poms4d	<---	Sadness	1.000			
poms8d	<---	Sadness	.925	.076	12.128	***
poms12d	<---	Sadness	.786	.069	11.320	***
poms14d	<---	Sadness	.614	.081	7.614	***
poms20d	<---	Sadness	.779	.067	11.645	***
poms23d	<---	Sadness	.572	.061	9.333	***
poms28d	<---	Sadness	.494	.058	8.531	***
poms33d	<---	Sadness	.635	.073	8.724	***
psqik1	<---	e_psqik1	1.000			
leukocyt	<---	Immunity	1.000			
lymphocy	<---	Immunity	.290	.084	3.455	***
consult	<---	Health care	1.000			
telephone	<---	Health care	1.103	.329	3.356	***

Table 9.2 Cont'd

Intercepts: (Group number 1 - Model 1)

	Estimate	S.E.	C.R.	P Label
ecq1	1.541	.074	20.716	***
ecq2	1.926	.085	22.686	***
ecq3	.918	.063	14.485	***
ecq4	.887	.067	13.225	***
ecq5	1.824	.075	24.222	***
ecq6	1.461	.078	18.838	***
ecq7	.280	.042	6.601	***
ecq8	.655	.061	10.815	***
ecq9	1.255	.069	18.179	***
ecq10	.143	.029	4.938	***
ecq11	1.000	.065	15.300	***
ecq12	1.979	.078	25.400	***
ecq13	1.614	.084	19.207	***
ecq14	2.434	.075	32.273	***
poms4d	.446	.049	9.071	***
poms8d	.469	.048	9.820	***
poms12d	.360	.043	8.371	***
poms14d	.271	.048	5.632	***
poms20d	.308	.042	7.394	***
poms23d	.237	.037	6.390	***
poms28d	.166	.035	4.779	***
poms33d	.277	.044	6.313	***
psqik1	.752	.051	14.681	***
leukocyt	6.634	.122	54.458	***
lymphocy	1.774	.043	41.387	***
consult	1.206	.070	17.245	***
telephone	.905	.076	11.888	***

Covariances: (Group number 1 - Model 1)

			Estimate	S.E.	C.R.	P Label
Rumination	<-->	Sadness	.205	.043	4.730	***
Rumination	<-->	Immunity	.252	.106	2.370	.018
Sadness	<-->	Immunity	-.070	.073	-.963	.336
Health care	<-->	Rumination	.094	.056	1.689	.091
Health care	<-->	Sadness	.130	.044	2.956	.003
Health care	<-->	Immunity	.117	.104	1.128	.260
Sleep Quality	<-->	Rumination	.150	.049	3.078	.002
Sleep Quality	<-->	Sadness	.186	.037	5.080	***
Sleep Quality	<-->	Immunity	.267	.094	2.827	.005
Sleep Quality	<-->	Health care	.170	.055	3.113	.002

(Continued)

Table 9.2   Cont'd

Model Fit Summary

The saturated model was not fitted to the data of at least one
group. For this reason, only the 'function of log likelihood'.
AIC and BCC are reported. The likelihood ratio chi square
statistic and other fit measures are not reported.

CMIN

Model	NPAR	CMIN
Default model	90	2455.278

AIC

Model	AIC	BCC	BIC	CAIC
Default model	2635.278	2658.397		

You will observe that neither χ^2 nor most of the fit indices are computed. This is because calculation of these figures demands calculation of at least one alternative model for comparison with the 'default model,' and such calculations do not automatically take place when you have incomplete data. You therefore have to estimate (at least) one model for comparison.

For calculation of χ^2 you need a basis model that fulfills the following demands:

1. It fits the data better than your 'default model.'
2. Your model is nested under your basis model.
3. In fact the basis model should be accepted as 'true.'

A basis model that fulfills these requirements is the saturated model.

When you use the programming interface, AMOS does not automatically estimate the saturated model—you have to do it yourself.

Now, there are a lot of saturated models (all equivalent) so why not choose the simplest one, the program of which is shown in Table 9.3.

Even if the model specification only demands means to be estimated, AMOS estimates variances and covariances too. However, there is no reason to show the complete output, as the only output you need is the few lines:

```
Minimum was achieved

Function of log likelihood = 1757,609

Number of parameters = 405
```

found at the beginning of the output at the place where you expect to find the χ^2-test.

Table 9.3 Example 1: Program for estimation of a saturated model

```
Public Sub Main()
  Dim Sem As New AmosEngine
  Try
    Sem.TextOutput
    Sem.Smc
    Sem.Standardized
    Sem.ModelMeansAndIntercepts
    Sem.AllImpliedMoments
    Sem.BeginGroup("Missing20.sav")

    Sem.Mean("ecq1")
    Sem.Mean("ecq2")
    Sem.Mean("ecq3")
    Sem.Mean("ecq4")
    Sem.Mean("ecq5")
    Sem.Mean("ecq6")
    Sem.Mean("ecq7")
    Sem.Mean("ecq8")
    Sem.Mean("ecq9")
    Sem.Mean("ecq10")
    Sem.Mean("ecq11")
    Sem.Mean("ecq12")
    Sem.Mean("ecq13")
    Sem.Mean("ecq14")

    Sem.Mean("poms4d")
    Sem.Mean("poms8d")
    Sem.Mean("poms12d")
    Sem.Mean("poms14d")
    Sem.Mean("poms20d")
    Sem.Mean("poms23d")
    Sem.Mean("poms28d")
    Sem.Mean("poms33d")
    Sem.Mean("psqik1")

    Sem.Mean("leukocyt")
    Sem.Mean("lymphocy")

    Sem.Mean ("consult")
    Sem.Mean ("telephone")

    Sem.FitModel
  Finally
    Sem.Dispose
  End Try
End Sub
```

These figures and the corresponding ones from your model in Table 9.2 can be used to calculate a χ^2 value for your model in the following way.

You subtract the function of log likelihood for the saturated model from the one for 'your' model and the number of parameters for 'your' model from that of the saturated model:

	Function of log likelihood	Number of parameters
Your model	2455.278	90
Saturated model	1757.609	405
	697.588	315

The difference between the values of log likelihood is then distributed as χ^2 with degrees of freedom equal to the differences in number of parameters.

If you consult a statistical table, you will find this to be highly significant ($P < 0.000$ as in the analysis based on complete data).

As mentioned several times, it is often better to base the judgment of model fit on fit indices rather than on the χ^2-test because of the latter's dependence on sample size. Unfortunately you must compute your preferred fit indices by hand (using the formulas in Chapter 5). This, however, necessitates estimation of the independence model in addition to the saturated model.

If you use the graphic interface you avoid most of the calculation problems connected with missing data, as all these calculations are then done automatically, and you get the usual output you know so well.

A Few Concluding Remarks

You may have wondered why I have chosen the factor model and not the causal model from Table 7.7 for demonstration of FIML estimation with missing data. The reason is simple: It is not possible to estimate the causal model if you have missing data, because the need for estimating means and intercepts eats up your degrees of freedom. This is not apparent from a mere calculation of variances, covariances, means and the number of parameters to be estimated. The crucial point is that the covariance structure and the means structure must be identified *separately*. In this case the covariance structure is over-identified while the means structure is under-identified—and the extra degrees of freedom in the covariance structure cannot save the identification of the means structure. This is a real limitation of this method if you have only a single sample.

In this case the missing values were chosen by simple random sampling from all the measurements: The data were *Missing Completely At Random* or *MCAR* (Rubin, 1976). This means that the probability that a value is missing is independent of one and every variable measured or missing. Under this condition all the methods for dealing with missing data mentioned so far give consistent estimates, although of course only FIML is efficient in the statistical sense, as it uses all available information in the data.

In all probability such a simple 'selection model' is very rare in practice. It is more realistic to assume that the probability that a measurement is missing is independent of its value *conditional* on the values of the measured variables. Even in this situation—called *Missing At Random* or *MAR* by Rubin (op. cit.)—FIML estimation as implemented in AMOS will give efficient and consistent estimates, while other methods will be inefficient and (in most cases) also lack consistency.

As mentioned earlier, FIML estimation will not be consistent if the MAR condition is not met, but FIML will still be less biased than the other solutions to the missing data problem. This situation is called *Non-Ignorable* or NI by Rubin (op. cit.).

2. Bootstrapping as an Aid to Deal with Non-Normal Data

ML-estimation is based on an assumption of multivariate normality of the manifest variables, and so are the large-sample properties of GLS. If the data fails to meet this assumption, it could have serious consequences:

1. The program could run into convergence problems.
2. The asymptotic χ^2-values get excessively large.
3. The standard errors of parameter estimates are under-estimated.

Even if you do not run into convergence problems, the last two mentioned problems could easily lead you astray in the interpretation of the output.

Now, there are several ways to cope with non-normality:

1. You can transform variables to (near-)normality.
2. You can use an estimation method that makes no distributional assumptions such as ULS or ADF. However, as mentioned earlier, testing in ULS is a bit complicated, and ADF makes large demands on the sample size.
3. Since the consequences are generally more with test statistics than with parameter values, you can use GLS or ML, and then regulate the test statistics using so-called *robust statistics* (see e.g. Chou et al. (1991)). This may, in many cases, be the best way to solve the problem, but it is not available in the present version (16) of AMOS.
4. You can use bootstrapping—the topic of this chapter.

What then is bootstrapping?

Most statistical inference is based on the concept of a *sampling distribution* of a sample statistic, i.e. the distribution of a sample statistic taken across repeated samples of the same size from the same population. Now, we usually take only one sample, and consequently we do not have an actual empirical sampling distribution on which to base our inference. Instead we have to *derive* the sampling distribution from assumptions about the population from which the only sample was taken— e.g. an assumption of multivariate normality.

The idea behind bootstrapping is that you consider your sample to be your population. From this 'population' you the take e.g. 500 samples *with replacement*.

From each sample you then calculate the required sample statistic. This gives you an empirical sampling distribution, and in addition averaging the various sample statistics, you get an estimate of the parameter and an empirical standard error of the estimator.

This in short is the principle of bootstrapping, and it can be used to obtain empirical standard errors of whatever statistic you may want, including various fit indices, squared correlation coefficients, etc.

It is tempting also to use bootstrapping as a remedy against samples that are too small to give meaningful test results based on the asymptotic properties of ML or GLS. However, as the whole process is based on considering the original sample to represent the population from which it was taken, the sample should be large enough to guarantee stable estimates—and of course the sample selection should also be based on simple random sampling.

As you will probably have guessed, bootstrapping demands that the original data file is used as input—a covariance and mean summary of the data is not enough.

Example 2

The quality domain of the FRL scale (see Example 8.3) refers to health, price/quality relation, novelty seeking, preference for organic food, taste and freshness, and thus is a six-factor domain, each factor being measured by three items.

As you may expect everyone to prefer quality for money and good tasting food, it is no surprise that the distributions of answers to the items measuring these two factors are severely skew. The items used to measure these two dimensions are shown in Table 9.4. As usual, you can find the data on the book's website.

I will use the program in Table 9.5 to demonstrate the use of bootstrapping in this situations. For space considerations I will consider only these two factors.

Two new statements are 'Sem.Bootstrap (1000)', which orders AMOS to draw 1000 random samples of size 994 with replacement from the original sample of 994 and 'Sem.ConfidenceBC', which orders AMOS to calculate bias-corrected 95%-confidence intervals. Part of the output is shown in Table 9.6.

Table 9.4   Example 2: Items used in the analysis

Price/quality relation

   v64: I always tries to get the best quality for the best price.

   v13: I compare prices between product variants in order to get the best value for money.

   v07: It is important for me to know that I get quality for all my money.

Taste

   v05: I find taste in food products important.

   v21: When cooking, I first and foremost consider the taste

   v50: It is important to choose food products for their nutritional value rather than for their taste.

Table 9.5   Example 1: Program

```
Public Sub Main()
  Dim Sem As New AmosEngine
  Try
    Sem.TextOutput
    Sem.Bootstrap (1000)
    Sem.ConfidenceBC (95)
    Sem.ResidualMoments
    Sem.NormalityCheck
    Sem.BeginGroup ("France94Quality.sav")
    Sem.GroupName ("France 1994")
    Sem.AStructure ("v64 = (1) quality + (1) e_64")
    Sem.AStructure ("v13 =     quality + (1) e_13")
    Sem.AStructure ("v7  =     quality + (1) e_7")
    Sem.AStructure ("v5  = (1) taste   + (1) e_5")
    Sem.AStructure ("v21 =     taste   + (1) e_21")
    Sem.AStructure ("v50 =     taste   + (1) e_50")
    Sem.FitModel
  Finally
    Sem.Disposev
  End Try
End Sub
```

Table 9.6   Example 2: Partial output from bootstrapping

```
Minimum was achieved
Chi-square = 85.088
Degrees of freedom = 8
Probability level = .000
```

Maximum Likelihood Estimates

Regression Weights: (France 1994 - Model 1)

	Estimate	S.E.	C.R.	P Label
v64 <--- quality	1.000			
v13 <--- quality	.938	.132	7.126	***
v7 <--- quality	.322	.053	6.044	***
v5 <--- taste	1.000			
v21 <--- taste	1.482	.169	8.788	***
v50 <--- taste	.853	.111	7.706	***

(Continued)

Table 9.6 Cont'd

Standardized Regression Weights: (France 1994 - Model 1)

	Estimate
v64 <--- quality	.729
v13 <--- quality	.511
v7 <--- quality	.302
v5 <--- taste	.611
v21 <--- taste	.755
v50 <--- taste	.324

Covariances: (France 1994 - Model 1)

	Estimate	S.E.	C.R.	P Label
taste <--> quality	.290	.044	6.555	***

Correlations: (France 1994 - Model 1)

	Estimate
taste <--> quality	.405

Squared Multiple Correlations: (France 1994 - Model 1)

	Estimate
v50	.105
v21	.570
v5	.374
v7	.091
v13	.261
v64	.532

0 bootstrap samples were unused because of a singular covariance matrix.
0 bootstrap samples were unused because a solution was not found.
1000 usable bootstrap samples were obtained.

Regression Weights: (France 1994 - Model 1)

Parameter	SE	SE-SE	Mean	Bias	SE-Bias
v64 <--- quality	.000	.000	1.000	.000	.000
v13 <--- quality	.147	.003	.931	−.007	.005
v7 <--- quality	.137	.003	.339	.017	.004
v5 <--- taste	.000	.000	1.000	.000	.000
v21 <--- taste	.214	.005	1.500	.018	.007
v50 <--- taste	.144	.003	.861	.008	.005

Table 9.6 Cont'd

Standardized Regression Weights: (France 1994 - Model 1)

Parameter	SE	SE-SE	Mean	Bias	SE-Bias
v64 <--- quality	.088	.002	.733	.004	.003
v13 <--- quality	.051	.001	.501	-.009	.002
v7 <--- quality	.075	.002	.306	.004	.002
v5 <--- taste	.052	.001	.611	.000	.002
v21 <--- taste	.054	.001	.755	-.001	.002
v50 <--- taste	.039	.001	.323	-.001	.001

Covariances: (France 1994 - Model 1)

Parameter	SE	SE-SE	Mean	Bias	SE-Bias
taste <--> quality	.062	.001	.292	.002	.002

Correlations: (France 1994 - Model 1)

Parameter	SE	SE-SE	Mean	Bias	SE-Bias
taste <--> quality	.088	.002	.411	.007	.003

Squared Multiple Correlations: (France 1994 - Model 1)

Parameter	SE	SE-SE	Mean	Bias	SE-Bias
v50	.025	.001	.106	.001	.001
v21	.082	.002	.572	.002	.003
v5	.064	.001	.376	.003	.002
v7	.050	.001	.099	.008	.002
v13	.049	.001	.254	-.007	.002
v64	.128	.003	.545	.013	.004

The first part of the output is the traditional one, with χ^2-square test and parameter estimates. A χ^2 of 85.088 with 8 degrees of freedom is significant according to any traditional criteria (but remember χ^2 is inflated with non-normal data) but, as mentioned before, this test is of limited value with such a large sample. In order to save space I have not reported the variance estimates.

Then comes the bootstrapping part of the output, starting with a report on the bootstrapping process itself. In this case everything went well, but if a considerable share of the bootstrap samples should be useless because of the problems mentioned in the output, then perhaps you should look for another solution to your problem.

The bootstrapping parameter estimates follows. The first column (SE) shows the estimates of the standard errors of the various parameter estimates, while the second (SE-SE) shows the standard errors of the standard errors themselves.

Table 9.7 Comparison of ML and bootstrap estimates of standard errors

Parameter	ML estimate	Bootstrap estimate	Difference	Difference in pct.
v13 <--- quality	0,132	0,147	0,015	11
v7 <--- quality	0,053	0,137	0,084	158
v21 <--- taste	0,169	0,214	0,045	27
v50 <--- taste	0,111	0,144	0,033	30
taste <--> quality	0,044	0,088	0,044	100

Then comes the mean of the parameter estimates calculated across the 1000 samples and the difference (Bias) between the bootstrap mean and the maximum likelihood estimated parameter value. Perhaps you are surprised that the two sets of parameter estimates are so different given the large sample, but this happens quite often. The last column shows the standard error of the bias estimate.

As you can see from the Table 9.7, the bootstrap estimates of standard errors are generally much larger than the ML estimates—and in two cases at least 100% larger.

You will observe that you can obtain bootstrap estimates of standard errors of standardized parameter estimates, coefficients of determination and the various fit indices.

Now, it is one thing to obtain bootstrapped estimates and something else to test the significance of the various parameters as well as of the whole model.

Instead of calculating critical values and P-values, we can order bias-corrected confidence intervals. This part of the output is shown in Table 9.8.

The interval can be used to test the hypothesis that the parameter is 0 against the two-sided alternative that it is not—exactly the same test that the traditional P-values refer to: If a confidence interval contains 0, the hypothesis that the parameter is 0 cannot be rejected at alpha (100–95)%.

The last column can be interpreted as a traditional P-value of the two-sided test; e.g. $P = 0.002$ in the last column of the covariance table, means that a $(1.000—0.002)100\% = 99.8\%$ confidence interval would have 0.000 as its lower limit. Observe that, in this way you can also test hypotheses about standardized estimates, etc.

What remains is a test of the model as a whole, i.e. a bootstrapped χ^2-test.

In fact, Bollen and Stine (1993) have invented an 'empirical χ^2-test' to be used in judging a model when using bootstrapping. The idea is the following:

As the χ^2-test is a test of the (very unlikely!) hypothesis that your model is 100 pct. correct, the Bollen-Stine approach is to transform your input data so that the model fits the (transformed) data exactly and then obtains an empirical distribution of the C-statistic across bootstrap samples taken from this 'population.' This distribution is then taken to be the distribution under the hypothesis of a correct model.

AMOS then calculates the 'empirical P-value' as the share of the bootstrap samples having C-values larger than the χ^2 obtained from the ML estimation.

In order to use this test, you must run another bootstrapping, the program of which is shown in Table 9.9.

Table 9.8 Example 2: Bias-corrected confidence intervals

Regression Weights: (France 1994 - Model 1)

Parameter	Estimate	Lower	Upper	P
v64 <--- quality	1.000	1.000	1.000	...
v13 <--- quality	.938	.671	1.236	.001
v7 <--- quality	.322	.164	.766	.001
v5 <--- taste	1.000	1.000	1.000	...
v21 <--- taste	1.482	1.136	1.971	.002
v50 <--- taste	.853	.579	1.142	.002

Standardized Regression Weights: (France 1994 - Model 1)

Parameter	Estimate	Lower	Upper	P
v64 <--- quality	.729	.559	.921	.002
v13 <--- quality	.511	.417	.602	.001
v7 <--- quality	.302	.179	.479	.002
v5 <--- taste	.611	.511	.718	.002
v21 <--- taste	.755	.658	.874	.001
v50 <--- taste	.324	.248	.404	.002

Covariances: (France 1994 - Model 1)

Parameter	Estimate	Lower	Upper	P
taste <--> quality	.290	.178	.428	.002

Correlations: (France 1994 - Model 1)

Parameter	Estimate	Lower	Upper	P
taste <--> quality	.405	.266	.628	.002

Squared Multiple Correlations: (France 1994 - Model 1)

Parameter	Estimate	Lower	Upper	P
v50	.105	.061	.164	.002
v21	.570	.433	.763	.001
v5	.374	.261	.515	.002
v7	.091	.032	.229	.002
v13	.261	.174	.362	.001
v64	.532	.313	.848	.002

Table 9.9   Example 2: Program for Bollen–Stine testing

```
Public Sub Main()
  Dim Sem As New AmosEngine
  Try
    Sem.TextOutput
    Sem.BootBS
    Sem.Bootstrap (1000)
    Sem.BeginGroup ("France94Quality.sav")
    Sem.GroupName ("France 1994")
    Sem.AStructure ("v64 = (1) quality + (1) e_64")
    Sem.AStructure ("v13 =     quality + (1) e_13")
    Sem.AStructure ("v7  =     quality + (1) e_7")
    Sem.AStructure ("v5  = (1) taste   + (1) e_5")
    Sem.AStructure ("v21 =     taste   + (1) e_21")
    Sem.AStructure ("v50 =     taste   + (1) e_50")
    Sem.FitModel
  Finally
    Sem.Dispose
  End Try
End Sub
```

This bootstrapping procedure is *only* for calculation of the BS statistic, and no standard errors or confidence intervals can be calculated in the same run. The first part of the output is just as in Table 9.6, but when you reach the Bootstrapping part of the output you will see the output shown in Table 9.10. The *P*-value is small, as could be expected with a sample of nearly 1000. Together with the *P*-value, the distribution of the *C*-statistic is shown.

Other Uses of Bootstrapping

Even if Bootstrapping cannot cure all problems, it has uses other than analysis of non-normal data: You can use bootstrapping to compare the merits of different estimation methods and different models and on the book's website you are given the opportunity to use it for testing the significance of indirect and total effects.

A Final Note!

After having read this chapter—and especially after having struggled with the exercises on the website—you will be well aware that a covariance or correlation summary of your data can cover up a lot of problems in the raw data: non-normality non-linearities, outlayers, etc.

Give this a thought next time you read a journal article, where a covariance or correlation matrix is the only kind of data published.

Table 9.10 Example 1: Bollen–Stine output

`Bollen-Stine Bootstrap (Model 1)`

`The model fit better in 1000 bootstrap samples.`

`It fit about equally well in 0 bootstrap samples.`

`It fit worse or failed to fit in 0 bootstrap samples.`

`Testing the null hypothesis that the model is correct, Bollen-Stine`

`bootstrap p = .001`

`Bootstrap Distributions (Model 1)`

`ML discrepancy (implied vs sample) (Model 1)`

```
                                   | — — — — — — — — — — — — — — — —
                        1.333      | * *
                        3.375      | * * * * * * * * * * * *
                        5.417      | * * * * * * * * * * * * * * **
                        7.458      | * * * * * * * * * * * * * * * * * **
                        9.500      | * * * * * * * * * * * * * * * *
                       11.542      | * * * * * * * * * * * * * **
                       13.584      | * * * * * * * * **
 N = 1000              15.625      | * * * * * * * *
 Mean = 9.678          17.667      | * * * *
 S. e. = .152          19.709      | * **
                       21.751      |*
                       23.792      |*
                       25.834      |*
                       27.876      |*
                       29.917      |*
                                   | — — — — — — — — — — — — — — — —
```

☞ In this chapter you have met the following concepts:

Listwise and Pairwise Deletion	Function of log likelihood
Mean Imputation	Bootstrapping
Regression Imputation	Bollen-Stine χ^2-test

Besides, you have been introduced to the AMOS commands:

Sem.Bootstrap()

Sem.ConfidenceBC()   BootBS

Questions and Exercises

1. Judge the virtues and vices of various imputation methods.
2. State the characteristics of the three missing data concepts: missing completely at random,' 'missing at random' and 'non-ignorable,' and comment on the various methods for coping with the problem in each of the three situations.
3. What is bootstrapping and what sort of problems could it help to solve? Comment on its virtues and vices. What demands does it place on the data?

Reference List

Bollen, K. A. and R. A. Stine (1993) 'Bootstrapping goodness-of-fit measures in structural equation modeling,' in K. A. Bollen and J. S. Long (eds), *Testing Structural Equation models*, Newbury Park, CA: Sage.

Chou, C.-P., P. M. Bentler, and A. Satorra, (1991) 'Scaled test statistics and robust standard errors for nonnormal data in covariance structure analysis: a Monte Carlo study,' *British Journal of Mathematical and Statistical Psychology*, 4: 21–37.

Rubin, D. B. (1976) 'Inference and missing data,' *Biometrika*, 63: 581–92.

A

Statistical Prerequisites

This appendix is intended as a statistical refresher, and can be read as an introduction to the book or consulted when necessary during reading of the main text.

The Appendix contains the following sections:

1. Probability and Probability Distributions
2. Describing Your Data
3. Sample and Population (Including Estimation and Testing)
4. Correlation and Regression

1. Probability and Probability Distributions

If A_i for $i = 1, 2, 3, \ldots$ is a series of mutually exclusive and collectively exhaustive *events*, having probabilities $P(A_i)$ of happening, then X is called a *random variable*, if the value of X depends on A.

A *probability function* is a function $f(X)$ that assigns a probability to every possible value of X. If $f(X)$ is a probability function, then

$$\sum_i X_i = 1.00 \tag{1}$$

if X is discrete—i.e. can only take on a countable number of values, and

$$\int_i X_i = 1.00 \tag{2}$$

if X is continuous—i.e. can take on all values (possibly only in one or more intervals).

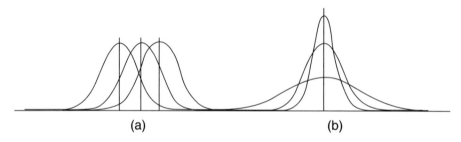

(a)   (b)

Figure A.1   Normal distributions: (a) Distributions with same σ, but different μ; (b) Distributions with same μ but different σ

In this book the most frequent event is that respondent i is included in a random sample from some population, and X_i is the value of some measurement taken on this respondent, e.g. his or her answer to a question in a questionnaire.

The Normal Distribution

The probability function you will most often meet in this book is the *normal distribution*. The normal distribution is a symmetrical, bell-shaped distribution, as can be seen from Figure A.1. The normal distribution is continuous with probability function

$$f\left(x|\mu, \sigma^2\right) = \left(\sigma\sqrt{2\pi}\right)^{-1}e^{-(x-\mu)^2/2\sigma^2} \tag{3}$$

The distribution has two *parameters* μ and σ^2. μ is the so-called *expected value* (the 'mean') of the distribution, and σ^2 is the *variance* (a measure of the 'spread'). I will have more to say on expected value and variance later on.

If e.g. you want to calculate the probability that a normal distributed random variable with $\mu = 20$ and $\sigma^2 = 4$ takes on values less than or equal to 25, you *standardize* the variable to have $\mu = 1$ and $\sigma^2 = 1$, by subtracting μ and dividing by σ:

$$P\left(X \leq 25\,|\mu = 20;\ \sigma^2 = 4\right) = P\left(\frac{X - \mu}{\sigma} \leq \frac{25 - 20}{2}\right) = P(Z \leq 2.5) = 0.994$$

The value 0.994 can be read from a table of the *standard normal distribution*.

The Chi-Square Distribution

The *Chi-Square distribution*—usually denoted by χ^2—is a continuous one-parameter distribution. Its parameter is usually denoted by ν (the Greek letter *nu*), which can take on all positive integer values. The distribution is right-skewed, the skewness declining with increasing values of ν. For $\nu \to \infty$ *Chi-Square* approaches a normal distribution. See Figure A.2.

The main purpose of χ^2 is as a measure of a model's accordance with the some data.

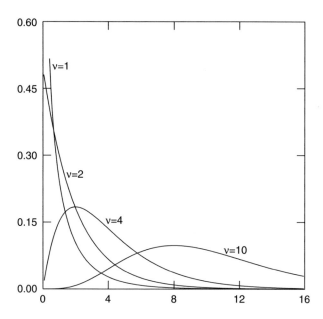

Figure A.2   Chi-square distributions

2.   Describing Your Data

The most obvious way to describe your sample data is to depict the distribution in a histogram, but often you need only to summarize the characteristics of the distribution in a few figures.

The central tendency in a distribution of a variable X is most often summarized in the *mean* of the observations:

$$\overline{X} = \frac{\sum\limits_{i=1}^{n} X_i}{n} \tag{4}$$

where n is the sample size. Likewise the spread of the data is most often measured by the *variance*, the mean of the squared deviations around the mean:

$$s^2 = \frac{\sum\limits_{i=1}^{n} (X_i - \overline{X})^2}{n-1} \tag{5}$$

Defining the variance as the *mean* of the squared deviations around the mean, you may wonder why I divided by $n-1$ and not n in the expression (2). An explanation follows in Section 3.

Now, the variance is measured in units other than the data, which could be a little annoying: Dealing with peoples' heights measured in inches, the spread would be measured in square inches! To solve this little problem we take the square root of the variance in order to obtain the *standard deviation*:

$$s = \sqrt{s^2} = \sqrt{\frac{(X - \overline{X})^2}{n-1}} \tag{6}$$

and so we are back in the original measurement units.

The mean and variance (or standard deviation) say nothing (or little) about the shape of the distribution. We need a measure for describing the skewness. In AMOS skewness is measured by:

$$M_3 = \frac{\sum\limits_{i=1}^{n} (X_i - \overline{X})^3}{ns^2} \tag{7}$$

If $M_3 = 0$, the distribution is symmetric, if $M_3 > 0$, it has a long upper tail, and if $M_3 < 0$, it has a long lower tail.

The last descriptor of univariate distributions is:

$$M_4 = \frac{\sum\limits_{i=1}^{n} (X_i - \overline{X})^4}{ns^4} \tag{8}$$

which describes the 'peakyness' or *kurtosis* of the distribution: If $M_4 = 0$, the distribution is as peak as the normal distribution, if it is larger than 0, it is flatter (has longer tails) than the normal distribution, and if $M_3 < 0$, it is peakier (has shorter tails) than the normal distribution.

3. Sample and Population

Usually your interest is not in the sample itself, but in making inference about the population from which the sample was drawn. Then the sample statistics defined in equations (1)–(8) are considered *estimators* of the equivalent population parameters as shown in Table A.1, where N is the size of the population.

For continuous variables integrals should be substituted for the summation signs. I have chosen to forego the complications of distinguishing between finite and infinite populations—so in the following think about a finite population being large enough to consider it infinite!

Estimation and Degrees of Freedom

It seems reasonable to use

$$\hat{\sigma}^2 = \frac{\sum\limits_{i=1}^{n} (X_i - \overline{X})^2}{n} \tag{9}$$

Table A.1 Sample statistics and population parameters

Sample	*Population*
$\overline{X} = \dfrac{\sum\limits_{i=1}^{n} X_i}{n}$	$\mu = \dfrac{\sum\limits_{j=1}^{N} X_j}{N}$
$s^2 = \dfrac{\sum\limits_{i=1}^{n} (X_i - \overline{X})^2}{n-1}$	$\sigma^2 = \dfrac{\sum\limits_{j=1}^{N} (X_j - \mu)^2}{N}$
$M_3 = \dfrac{\sum\limits_{i=1}^{n} (X_i - \overline{X})^3}{ns^2}$	$\mu_3 = \dfrac{\sum\limits_{j=1}^{N} \left(X_j - \mu\right)^3}{N\sigma^2}$
$M_4 = \dfrac{\sum\limits_{i=1}^{n} (X_i - \overline{X})^4}{ns^4}$	$\mu_4 = \dfrac{\sum\limits_{j=1}^{N} \left(X_j - \mu\right)^4}{N\sigma^4}$

as an estimator of $\hat{\sigma}^2$. In fact it can be shown that $\overline{X}$ and σ^2 are *maximum likelihood estimators* of the corresponding population parameters—i.e. they give the values of the parameters that have the largest probability of producing the sample statistics (assuming the specification of the distribution in the population is correct).

However, it can be shown that (9) has a tendency to underestimate the population variance. This is no surprise, because ideally the unknown μ should be used in the nominator of (9), and the sample will of course cluster more around $\overline{X}$ than around μ. In order to correct for this the denominator is reduced by 1 in equation (5). Of course this is no proof that reducing the denominator by 1 is the right thing to do, but it is!

Looking at the nominator, it consists of a sum of squares of n terms. However, these n terms are not independent: If you know the values of the first $n-1$ terms, you also know the last term because of the restriction:

$$\sum_{i=1}^{n} (X_i - \overline{X}) = 0 \qquad (10)$$

so you could say that in a way s^2 is the 'mean' of *independent* squared deviations around the sample mean.

s^2 is an *unbiased* estimator of σ^2. This means that if you take a 'large' number of samples from the population and calculates s^2 of every sample, then the average of s^2 across the samples—the expected value of the *sampling distribution* of the mean—will equal σ^2.

The denominator $n-1$ in (5) is called the *degrees of freedom*, and the general rule is that for each estimate based on sample information that is substituted for a parameter value, you loose one degree of freedom.

It deserves mentioning that as estimation in SEM-models is generally based on maximum likelihood estimation or other estimation methods with similar large sample properties, all variances and covariances in the output are maximum likelihood estimates using n as denominator, and the entries in the input covariance matrix are also supposed to be maximum likelihood estimates.

The standard deviation of a sampling distribution is called the *standard error* of that particular estimator. In the case of the sample mean, the standard error is:

$$\sigma_{\overline{X}} = \frac{\sigma}{\sqrt{n}} \tag{11a}$$

and is estimated as:

$$s_{\overline{X}} = \frac{s}{\sqrt{n}} \tag{11b}$$

If the sample is sufficiently large—or if the population from which it is drawn is normal—the sampling distribution of the mean is normal. This means that a 95% *confidence interval* for the mean can be constructed as:

$$\mu \approx \overline{X} \pm 1.96s \tag{12}$$

Meaning that the probability is 0.95 that the actual interval contains the (unknown) parameter μ.

Interval estimates for other parameters are constructed in similar ways.

Properties of Estimators

The quality of estimators are judged on several criteria, of which the most important are:

1. An estimator $\hat{\theta}$ is *unbiased*, if $E(\hat{\theta}) = \theta$.
2. An estimator $\hat{\theta}$ is *efficient*, if its sampling distribution has a small variance.
3. An estimator is *consistent*, if it tends to be near the population parameter as the sample becomes larger. If an estimator is biased, consistency assures that the bias becomes smaller as the sample size increases.
4. An estimator is *sufficient*, if it contains all information from the sample that bears on the unknown parameter. For example, $\overline{X}$ is a sufficient estimator of μ: Once you have computed $\overline{X}$, no other sample statistic can add to the information about μ.

It can be shown that $\overline{X}$ is unbiased, consistent and sufficient. Besides $\overline{X}$ is the most efficient of all unbiased estimators of μ.

The Central Limit Theorem

This theorem states that if $X_i (i = 1, 2, 3, \ldots, n)$ is a sequence of identically distributed random observations from a population and $f(X_i)$ has a finite variance, then

$$\hat{\theta} = \sum_i \alpha_i X_i \tag{13}$$

converges towards a normal distribution as $n \to \infty$.

This in fact secures that most of the estimators you will meet in this book are asymptotically normally distributed.

Statistical Testing

Often you want to test a hypothesis about the population from which the sample is taken. The idea is that you make all calculations on the assumption that the hypothesis you want to support is false and if you then end up with an unlikely result, either a miracle has happened or your starting point, that your hypothesis is wrong, must be rejected. Usually the last interpretation is the more realistic of the two.

You go through the following steps:

1. Formulation of *null hypothesis* H_0 and *alternative hypothesis* H_1. H_1 is the hypothesis you want to support, and H_0 is the opposite hypothesis.
2. Determination of *significance level* α. α is the maximal probability for rejecting H_0 if H_0 is true. α is most often (arbitrarily) set at 0.05.
3. Choice of a *test statistic* (e.g. $\overline{X}$), the sampling distribution of which is known if H_0 is true.
4. Calculation of the value of the test statistic.
5. Calculation of the *P*-value, the probability of observing the actual value of the test statistics, or a value that casts even more doubt on H_0, assuming that H_0 is true.
6. Conclusion: If $P < \alpha$, reject H_0 (and accept H_1), otherwise accept H_0.

Example 1

You want to test the hypothesis that the mean length of a certain component in a large production batch is at least 25 inches, and you have drawn a simple random sample of 50 components from the batch.

Let us now go through the 6 steps above:

1. $H_0 : \mu \leq 25$
   $H_1 : \mu > 25$
2. α is (traditionally!) set at 0.05.
3. I choose to base my conclusion on the value of $\overline{X}$, which is normally distributed with largest mean $\mu = 25$ and variance given by (11) if H_0 is true.
4. $\overline{X}$ is calculated at 26.5 inches with a standard error of 0.83
5. $P\left(\overline{X} \geq 26.5 \,|\, \mu = 25\right) = P\left(Z \geq \dfrac{26.5 - 25}{0.83}\right) = P(Z \geq 1.81)$ where Z is standard normal distributed. This probability is read from a table of the standard normal distribution to be 0.035.
6. As the probability of getting a sample mean equal to or larger than the one observed is so small (smaller than α) if H_0 is true, we reject H_0 and conclude that (in all probability) $\mu > 25$.

One- and Two-Sided Tests

This was an example of a one-sided test. You will also meet two-sided alternative hypotheses such as

$$H_0 : \mu = 25$$
$$H_1 : \mu \neq 25$$

In this situation you are interested in both positive and negative deviations.

The trouble with this formulation is that you know beforehand that H_0 is false. It is not very likely that $\mu = 25.000000000000...$ and so on in infinity. If your sample is large enough you will reject H_0. So, What is the rationale behind this sort of test?

You will meet this situation whenever you have a 'sharp' null hypothesis and a 'soft' alternative.

The Chi-Square Test

I shall not go deeply into the actual calculations involved, but only point out that χ^2 is used to test the fit of a model to the data at hand. The model could have many forms, but whatever the model, the null and alternative hypotheses are:

$$H_0: \text{The model fits the data exactly}$$
$$H_0: \text{The model does not fit the data}$$

Observe that when testing for model fit in SEM, the roles of the two hypotheses are interchanged: Now H_0 is the hypothesis you want the data to support, and as no model fits the data exactly H_0 is false *a priori* with the consequences mentioned in the preceding section.

4. Correlation and Regression

Traditional correlation and regression analysis is a natural primer for SEM. As an illustration I will use the first twenty observations on the Variables 'Tech' and 'Risk' from Example 4.1, as shown in Figure A.3.

You can calculate the means and the variances of the two variables, but you also need a measure of the interdependence of the two. To that end you can compute their covariance:

$$s_{XY} = \frac{\sum\limits_{i=1}^{n} (X_i - \overline{X})(Y_i - \overline{Y})}{n - 1} \qquad (14)$$

which is an unbiased estimator of the population covariance:

$$\sigma_{XY} = \frac{\sum\limits_{i=1}^{N} (X - \mu_X)(Y - \mu_Y)}{N} \qquad (15)$$

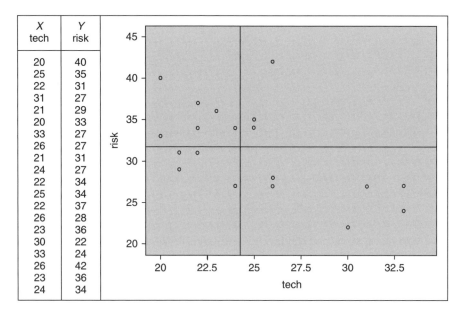

X tech	Y risk
20	40
25	35
22	31
31	27
21	29
20	33
33	27
26	27
21	31
24	27
22	34
25	34
22	37
26	28
23	36
30	22
33	24
26	42
23	36
24	34

Figure A.3 Data for correlation and regression analysis

The covariance is a sort of 'mix' of the two variances (a variable's covariance with itself is its variance).

If $s_{XY} = 0$, the two variables are *linearly* independent, if $s_{XY} > 0$, the two variables are *positively correlated*, i.e. they covariate *linearly* in the way that if one goes up, the other does too and if $s_{XY} < 0$, they covariate linearly in the opposite directions.

A problem with the covariance as a measure of correlation (linear) interdependence is that it has no upper or lower limit as its size depends on the units of measurement—so, how large numerically shall a covariance be before we accept that a (positive or negative) correlation is present?

If we standardize both variables

$$X_i^* = \frac{X_i - \overline{X}}{s_X} \quad \text{and} \quad Y_i^* = \frac{Y_i - \overline{Y}}{s_Y} \tag{16}$$

to have mean $= 0$ and $s^2 = 1$, and then calculates the covariance between the two:

$$r = \frac{\sum \left(X_i^*\right)\left(Y_i^*\right)}{n-1} = \frac{\sum (X_i - \overline{X})(Y_i - \overline{Y})}{(n-1)s_X s_Y} = \frac{\sum (X_i - \overline{X})(Y_i - \overline{Y})}{\sqrt{\sum (X_i - \overline{X})^2 \sum (Y_i - \overline{Y})^2}} \tag{17}$$

we obtain the so-called (*simple*) *correlation coefficient*, which is scale-independent and bounded within the limits $-1 \le r \le 1$. Besides r^2 (*the coefficient of determination*) indicates that proportion of the variance one variable has in common with the other.

In this case we have:

$$r = \frac{-243.9000}{\sqrt{310.5500 \times 532.2000}} = 0.6000 \tag{18}$$

which gives $r^2 = 0.36$. The two variables have 36% of their variance in common. (17) is a biased estimate of the population parameter, which is defined as

$$\rho = \sum_{i=1}^{n} \left(\frac{X - \mu_X}{\sigma_X}\right) \left(\frac{Y - \mu_Y}{\sigma_Y}\right) \Big/ N \tag{19}$$

Means, variances, standard deviations and covariance are calculated as shown in Table A.2.

Table A.2 Calculation of sample statistics

$X = tech$	$Y = risk$	$(X_i - \overline{X})^2$	$(Y_i - \overline{Y})^2$	$(X_i - \overline{X})(Y_i - \overline{Y})$
20	40	23.5225	68.8900	−40.2550
25	35	0.0225	10.8900	0.4950
22	31	8.1225	0.4900	1.9950
31	27	37.8225	22.0900	−28.9050
21	29	14.8225	7.2900	10.3950
20	33	23.5225	1.6900	−6.3050
33	27	66.4225	22.0900	−38.3050
26	27	1.3225	22.0900	−5.4050
21	31	14.8225	0.4900	2.6950
24	27	0.7225	22.0900	3.9950
22	34	8.1225	5.2900	−6.5550
25	34	0.0225	5.2900	0.3450
22	37	8.1225	28.0900	−15.1050
26	28	1.3225	13.6900	−4.2550
23	36	3.4225	18.4900	−7.9550
30	22	26.5225	94.0900	−49.9550
33	24	66.4225	59.2900	−62.7550
26	42	1.3225	106.0900	11.8450
23	36	3.4225	18.4900	−7.9550
24	34	0.7225	5.2900	−1.9550
Σ	497	634	310.5500	532.2000	−243.9000
$\Sigma/20$	24.85	31.70			
$\Sigma/19$			16.3447	28.0105	−12.8368
$\sqrt{\Sigma/19}$			4.04	5.29	
	↑	↑	↑	↑	↑
	$\overline{X}$	Y	s_X^2	s_Y^2	s_{XY}

Simple Regression Analysis

While the covariances and correlation coefficients are measures of covariation, and as such measures of what we could call a 'symmetric' relationship, in (simple) regression analysis one variable (e.g. X) is called the *independent* variable or *predictor* or *regressor* and the other (Y) is called the *dependent* or *criterion* variable, and the purpose is to estimate the parameters in the model:

$$Y_i = \beta_0 + \beta_1 X_i + \varepsilon_i \tag{20}$$

with the purpose of predicting the value of Y from knowledge of the value of X.
   It is assumed that:

1a. The values of X are known and fixed *a priori* (e.g. through an experimental design), or
1b. X is a stochastic variable that is uncorrelated with ε and the distribution of which is independent of the regression coefficients.

In addition we assume that

2. the error terms are un-correlated and all have expected value zero and the same variance.

Under these conditions the parameters of (20) can be estimated using least squares minimizing the variance of ε_i.
   The estimated *regression coefficients* b_0 and b_1 are called *regression weights* in AMOS. If the error terms can be assumed normally distributed, you can calculate confidence intervals for the population parameters and test various hypotheses about them.
   If the variables are standardized before the analysis, the regression coefficients are usually called *beta coefficients* or in AMOS *standardized regression weights*.

Regression Analysis using SPSS

After having opened the data set in SPSS you choose Analyze/Regression/Linear as shown in Figure A.4a, and the window in Figure A.4b pops up. You select the variable *risk*, and by clicking the top little triangle, you move the variable from the left panel to the box marked 'Dependent.' Then you select the variable *tech* and move it to the box marked 'Independent' by clicking the appropriate little triangle. When you click 'OK,' the output in Table A.3 is shown.
   I will only comment on the output in the third table—the two first tables will be commented on in the next section on multiple regression.
   In the table you find the estimates of the parameters making out the line shown in Figure A.5. The equation for the estimated regression line is

$$\hat{Y} = 54.217 - 0.785X \tag{21}$$

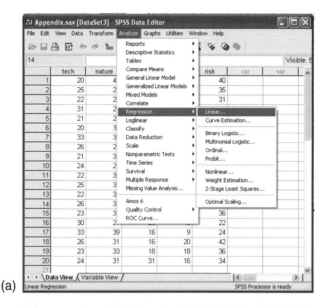

(a)

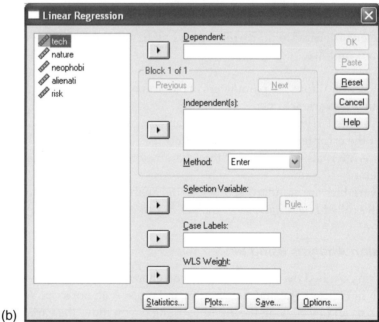

(b)

Figure A.4   Example 1: First steps in regression analysis in SPSS

and the standard deviation of the error term ε is estimated at 4.350. It is found in the first table, where it is called *Standard Error of the Estimate*.

Next to the estimates 54.217 and -0.785 are the standard errors of the sampling distributions for the two estimates. If ε_i (for $i = 1, 2, \ldots, n$) follow the same normal distribution with mean zero, then $t = b_j/std(b_j)$ has a t-distribution with $n - 2$ degrees of freedom (because we have estimated two parameters in the regression

Table A.3 Example 1: Output from SPSS

Model Summary

Model	R	R square	Adjusted R square	Std. Error of the estimate
1	.600(a)	.360	.324	4.350

a Predictors: (Constant), tech

ANOVA(b)

Model		Sum of Squares	df	Mean Square	F	Sig.
1	Regression	191.554	1	191.554	10.122	.005(a)
	Residual	340.646	18	18.925		
	Total	532.200	19			

a Predictors: (Constant), tech
b Dependent Variable: risk

Coefficients(a)

Model		Unstandardized Coefficients		Standardized Coefficients	t	Sig.
		B	Std. Error	Beta		
1	(Constant)	51.217	6.211		8.246	.000
	tech	-.785	.247	-.600	-3.181	.005

a Dependent Variable: risk

line: β_0 and β_1. The degrees of freedom is a parameter in the t-distribution). The t-distribution resembles the normal distribution, but has fatter tails. However, the more degrees of freedom, the more the t-distribution approaches the normal distribution.

Even if ε_i is not normally distributed, the sampling distributions of β_0 and β_1 are asymptotically normally distributed—thanks to the central limit theorem—which makes testing possible if the sample is sufficiently large.

Next to the standardized coefficients (Beta), we find the t-values for the two (un-standardized) regression coefficients and in the last column are the *significance probabilities* or P-values of a test of $H_0: \beta_j = 0$ against $H_0: \beta_j \neq 0$. As is evident, this null hypothesis is rejected for both coefficients at any reasonable level of significance.

Multiple Regression

Introducing another predictor, making

$$Y_i = \beta_0 + \beta_1 X_{1i} + \beta_2 X_{2i} + \varepsilon_i$$ (22)

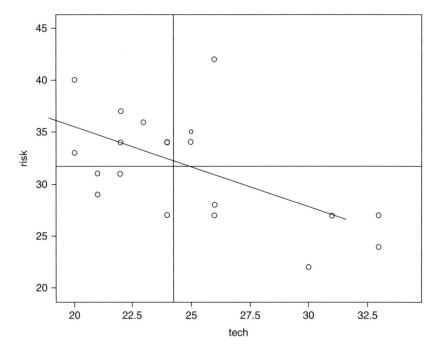

Figure A.5   Example 1: Regression line

does not make any principal difference, but adds to the calculations and opens up for the problems associated with *co-linearity*. Co-linearity is correlation among regressors. If the regressors co-vary it is easy to see that it could be difficult to measure their individual effects on the criterion variable—and consequently the standard error of the regression coefficients are increased.

The correlation coefficient between the actual Y-values and the values $\hat{Y}_i$ predicted by the estimated regression function is called the *multiple correlation coefficient*, and is usually designated R. The square of R is called the *multiple coefficient of determination*, and as you will have guessed it shows how large a proportion of its variance Y share with the regressors taken as a whole, or as it is usually expressed: How large a proportion in the variation in Y that is 'explained' by variation in the regressors.

R^2 is upward biased—especially if the number of regressors is large compared to the number of observations. The *adjusted R^2*, defined as

$$R^2_{adjusted} = 1 - (1 - R^2)\,\frac{n-1}{n-k-1} \tag{23}$$

where k is the number of regressors adjusts R^2 downwards in order to compensate for this.

Perhaps you expect the sum of the simple correlation coefficients squared to equal R squared, i.e.:

$$R^2 = r^2_{X_1Y} + r^2_{X_2Y} \qquad (24)$$

but this is only true in the absence of co-linearity.

Multiple Regression using SPSS

Using 'tech' and 'alienation' as regressors gives the output shown in Table A.4.

In the first table you find the multiple correlation coefficient R, the (multiple) coefficient of determination R^2, the adjusted R^2, and the standard error of estimate, i.e. the standard deviation of ε.

The sum of squares in the second table is defined as follows:

$$\text{Regression sum of squares:} \qquad \sum_i \left(\hat{Y}_i - \overline{Y} \right)^2 \qquad (25a)$$

$$\text{Residual sum of squares:} \qquad \sum_i \left(Y_i - \hat{Y} \right)^2 \qquad (25b)$$

$$\text{Total sum of squares:} \qquad \sum_i \left(Y_i - \overline{Y} \right)^2 \qquad (25c)$$

Table A.4 Example 1 (continued); Output from multiple regression analysis

Model Summary

Model	R	R Square	Adjusted R Square	Std. Error of the Estimate
1	.818(a)	.669	.630	3.219

a Predictors: (Constant), alienati, tech

ANOVA(b)

Model		Sum of Squares	df	Mean Square	F	Sig.
1	Regression	356.002	2	178.001	17.174	.000(a)
	Residual	176.198	17	10.365		
	Total	532.200	19			

a Predictors: (Constant), alienati, tech
b Dependent variable: risk

Coefficients(a)

Model		Unstandardized Coefficients		Standardized Coefficients	t	Sig.
		B	Std. Error	Beta		
1	(Constant)	23.856	8.265		2.886	.010
	tech	-.344	.214	-.263	-1.609	.126
	alienati	1.041	.261	.650	3.983	.001

a Dependent variable: risk

The regression sum of squares is that part of the sum of squares for Y that is 'explained' by the regression function, while residual sum of squares is the 'unexplained' sum of squares measuring the deviations of the observations from the regression line—or in the case of multiple regression the regression plane.

As you may have guessed (and as you can easily verify):

$$R^2 = \frac{\Sigma_i \left(\hat{Y}_i - \overline{Y}\right)^2}{\Sigma_i \left(Y_i - \overline{Y}\right)^2} \tag{26}$$

The F-test is a traditional analysis of variance F-test of the hypothesis

$$H_0: \beta_j = 0 \quad \text{for all values of } j \quad \text{or} \quad H_0 : R^2 = 0 \tag{27}$$

and is then a test of the regression function taken as a whole.

As can be seen from the second table the regression function is highly significant, and from the third table it appears that only alienation is significant. Remember, however: These are two-sided tests. The one-sided P-value for 'tech' is 0.063, so if you have formulated a one-sided hypotheses *before* observing the data, 'tech' is nearly significant at the traditional significance level 0.05.

B

AMOS Graphics

In this appendix I illustrate the use of AMOS' graphic interface in the analysis of the model from Example 7.1 as shown in Figure 7.1b.

This is only meant as a *very* short demonstration of AMOS Graphics. To master this interface and exploit its many possibilities, you will need a good deal of training. One way to obtain that is to re-analyze the examples in this book using the graphic interface.

I will recommend that while reading the following, you go through the various steps on your computer.

For easier reference the model from Figure 7.1b is repeated in Figure B.1.

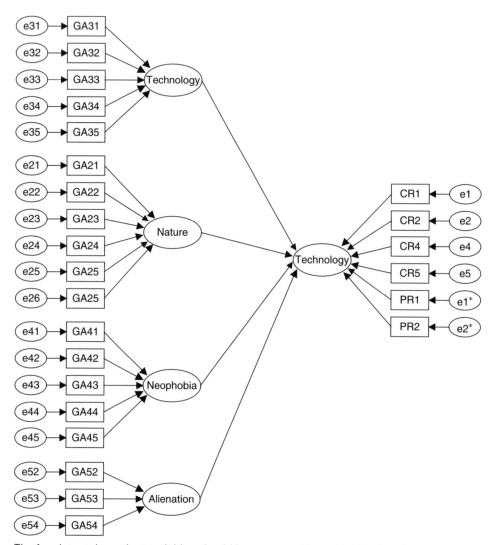

The four latent dependent variables should be connected by six double-headed arrows, but these are not shown in order to make the illustration clearer.

Figure B.1 Model from Figure 7.1b

When you click the AMOS Graphics icon, the window shown in Figure B.2 pops up.

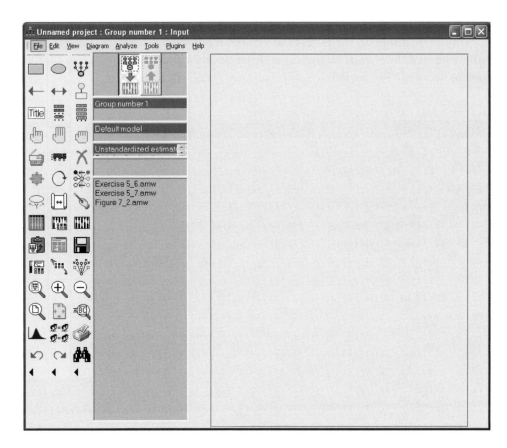

Figure B.2   The opening page of the AMOS graphic interface

To the right you see your working place, and to the left, you have your toolbox. When you point at a tool, a short text pops up telling you the function of the tool in question. The column between your working place and your toolbox shows (from the top): That you view the input diagram and that you are programming your default model.

You start by choosing the 'indicator' tool 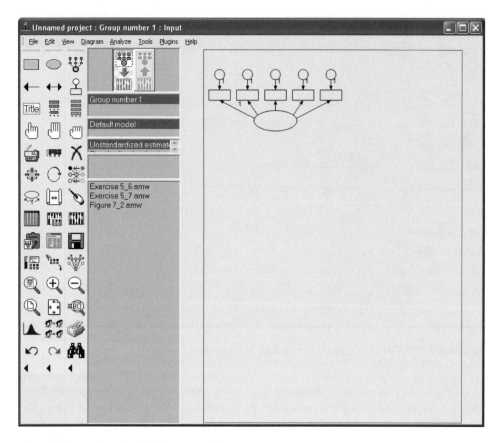, and place the mouse pointer where you want your first latent variable—in this case the variable 'Technology.' Then you click six times. The first click produces an ellipse (the size of which you determine by dragging the mouse) to symbol the latent variable, and each of the following five clicks adds an indicator. After your six clicks, your window should look as shown in Figure B.3.

Figure B.3   Using the 'indicator' tool

You now choose the 'rotate' tool and click in the ellipse. This click will rotate the diagram clockwise by 90°. Then you choose the 'reflect' tool

and click the ellipse once more, and your screen should look as in Figure B.4. Of course, you could instead have clicked the rotate tool three times.

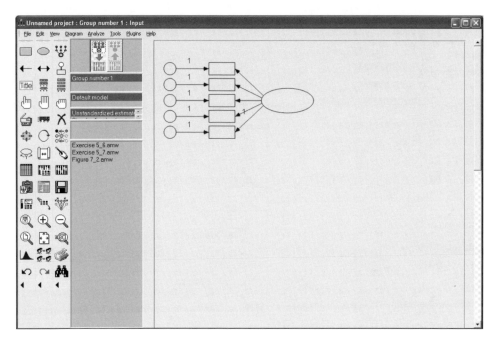

Figure B.4   Using the 'rotate' and the 'reflect' tools

Now you choose the 'select all' tool [hand icon] followed by the 'duplicate' tool [copy icon]. Then each time you click the duplicate tool on the selected object, the object will be duplicated (all copies are overlaid), so now you just move them to the wanted

positions using the 'move' tool [move icon]. After then having reflected the dependent variable, your screen should look like Figure B.5.

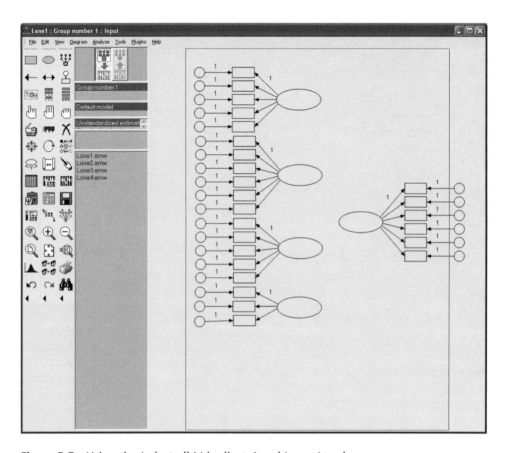

Figure B.5 Using the 'select all,' 'duplicate' and 'move' tools

What remains is to add a disturbance to the endogenous variable, to connect each of the exogenous variables to the endogenous variable by single headed arrows, and to connect all exogenous variables to each other by two-headed arrows.

To add the disturbance term you choose the 'error' tool ⌷ and click in the (latent) endogenous variable. To add one- and two-headed arrows, you choose the 'path' tool ← or the 'covariance' tool ↔ , move the mouse pointer to the starting variable, press the button and hold it down while you move the mouse pointer to the target variable, where you release the button. Your diagram should now look like Figure B.6.

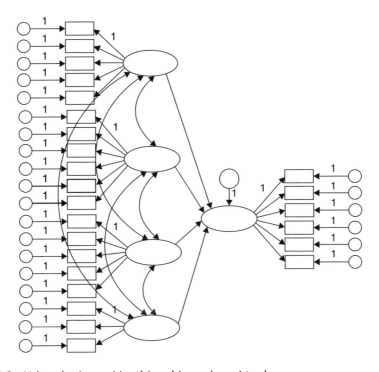

Figure B.6   Using the 'error,' 'path' and 'covariance' tools

As you can see, the double-headed arrows indicating co-linearity make the picture much more 'messy' than the one in Figure B.1. Now, this model is very simple, and you can imagine how it could be almost impossible to get a clear view of a more complicated model. This is one of several reasons why I have preferred to use the programming interface in this book.

What now remains in order to complete the drawing is to name the various variables. You right-click on the upper-most latent variable symbol, and after having chosen 'Object Properties,' the dialog box shown in Figure B.7a pops up. You choose 'text,' after which the dialog box looks as in Figure B.7b. Then you set the font size to 10 and write in the variable name—in this case 'Technology'—and close the dialog box.

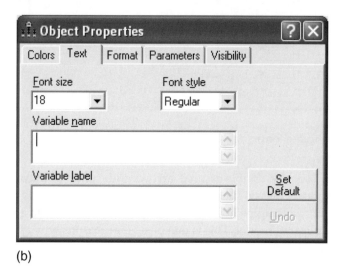

(a)

(b)

Figure B.7   Naming the latent variables

You repeat this procedure for each of the remaining three exogenous variables, the endogenous variable and the errors and disturbance, naming them as in Figure B.1, and your screen should now look as in Figure B.8.

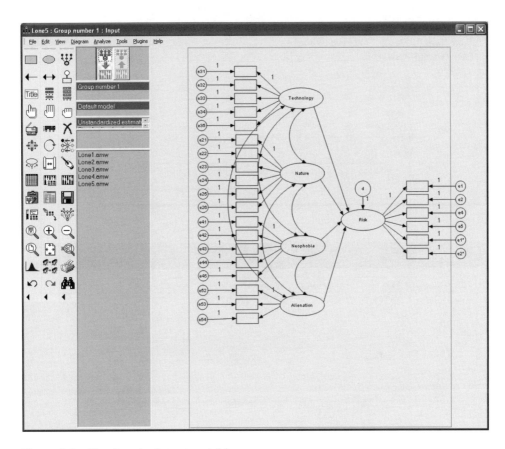

Figure B.8 Naming the latent variables

Of course you could name the manifest variables in the same way, but this would involve a lot of clicking, and there is an easier way. This necessitates that you bring in your data, but, anyway, this has to be done at some point—and why not now?

From the file menu you choose 'Data files' and the window shown in Figure B.9a pops up.

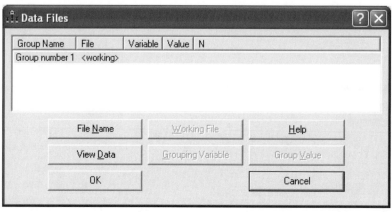

(a)

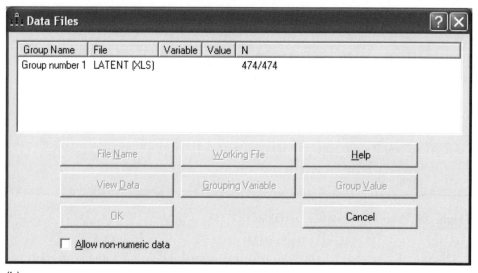

(b)

Figure B.9 Opening your data file

When you click 'File Name', you open up the documents file, where you can look for the data file you want to analyze. When you have found it, you click OK, and the window in B.9a changes to B.9b. You choose the file and click OK to close the window.

Now choose 'View/Variables in dataset,' and the screen should look as in Figure B.10.

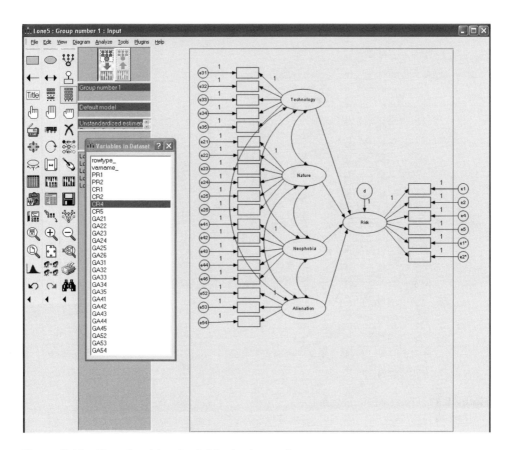

Figure B.10 Choosing 'view/variables in dataset'

Now you can just choose the variables in the list one by one and with the mouse button pressed down move the mouse pointer to the corresponding manifest variable box in the drawing. Your model is now finished, as shown in Figure B.11.

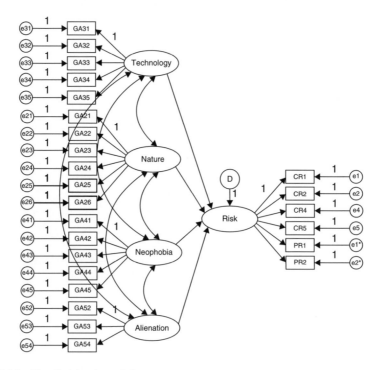

Figure B.11   The finished model

Now you have finished your model, what is left is to estimate its parameters. You choose 'Analyze/Calculate Estimates.' When you now click the right icon at the top of the second column, Figure B.11 changes to Figure B.12.

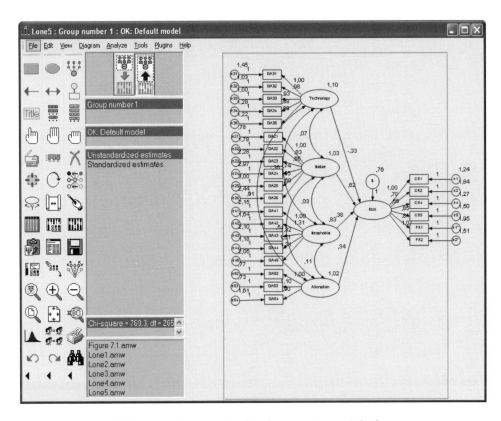

Figure B.12 Graphic output (un-standardized regression weights)

As you can see, you can choose to view either the un-standardized or the standardized regression weights. If you choose 'View/Text Output,' you will get the output shown in Table 7.2.

Index